I-SAAN N₁

AMUNDSEN AIR SHIP

"Shenandoah" at her mooring mast Tacoma, Wash. Oct.19ᵗʰ 1924

ZEPPELIN No.3   870-1

Olympia Stadium, Detroit, MI, January 31, 1975. *Robert Alford*

Market Square Arena, Indianapolis, IN, April 17, 1977. *Robert Alford*

Market Square Arena, Indianapolis, IN, April 17, 1977. *Robert Alford*

Richfield Coliseum, Cleveland, OH, April 27, 1977. *Robert Alford*

"They're part of the vocabulary of rock 'n' roll. They're the vowels of the alphabet of rock 'n' roll. Most people miss the subtlety. They miss the craft. All Led Zeppelin is a roots-based rock 'n' roll band—English folk music, rockabilly, country . . . there's all sorts of things in that music. They're another example of how much inspiration there is in the things that have come before us; if you just open your mind, you make something completely new and unique in that."

—*Chris Robinson, Black Crowes*

"Phenomenal! It's such great, melodic, hard, heavy rock 'n' roll. It doesn't have a trace of corny in it at all."

—*Kid Rock*

"The first time I heard Led Zeppelin, I had to pull over. What an amazing, amazing band. I mean, obviously, one of a kind and a complete mystique, an enigma and probably one of the heaviest bands of all time, amazing songwriters. I mean, four of the greatest musician that ever graced the rock 'n' roll stage as far as I'm concerned."

—*Richie Sambora, Bon Jovi*

"There's only a handful of acts that basically created a genre of music. You can say that about Bill Monroe, Bob Wills, probably Count Basie and Charlie Parker and Dizzy Gillespie and a handful of other people—and Led Zeppelin. . . . They got there first and they were the sum of their parts. "

—Steve Earle

"They're the bridge between heavy metal and pomp rock. I can't call their music songs; it just exists in its own relentless groove. It has its own space, I think, which is great. They created what didn't exist before. That's always a sign of a band's prominence."

—Ray Davies, the Kinks

"They are one of my favorite rock 'n' roll bands. The power, the songwriting, the innovation, how they took the blues and electrified it and turned it into its own thing—to absolutely thunder. Jimmy Page is one of the best guitar players ever, Bonham the same with the drums, John Paul Jones and Robert Plant—the combination is just one of those one-in-a-million things."

—Lenny Kravitz

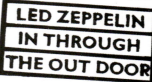

LED ZEPPELIN
IN THROUGH
THE OUT DOOR

robert plant

LED·ZEPPELIN

robert plant
tour 83

LED·ZEPPELIN

JIMMY PAGE

"SUMMERFEST" AT THE STADIUM
PRESENTS
AN EVENING WITH
LED·
ZEPPELIN
SAT. AUGUST 6, 1977
BUFFALO NEW YORK

LED
ZEPPELIN

JON BREAM

WITH

ROBERT ALFORD
CHARLES AURINGER
WILLIAM S. BURROUGHS
GARTH CARTWRIGHT
GEORGE CASE
BARRY CLEVELAND
JIM DEROGATIS
ANDREW EARLES
CHUCK EDDY
DAVID FRICKE
DANNY GOLDBERG
GARY GRAFF
BARNEY HOSKYNS
GREG KOT
EDDIE KRAMER
TERRY MANNING
ROBERT MATHEU
WILLIAM MCKEEN
CHARLES SHAAR MURRAY
CHRIS RIEMENSCHNEIDER
MELISSA RUGGIERI
GENE STOUT
JAAN UHELSZKI

WHOLE LOTTA

THE ILLUSTRATED HISTORY OF THE HEAVIEST BAND OF ALL TIME

LED ZEPPELIN

DEDICATION

For all the friends, family, readers, and complete strangers who
have gone to concerts with me . . . .

J.B.

First published in 2008 by Voyageur Press, an imprint of MBI Publishing Company,
400 First Avenue North, Suite 300, Minneapolis, MN 55401 USA

Voyageur Press titles are also available at discounts in bulk quantity for industrial or sales-
promotional use. For details write to Special Sales Manager at MBI Publishing Company,
400 First Avenue North, Suite 300, Minneapolis, MN 55401 USA.

To find out more about our books, join us online at www.voyageurpress.com.

Library of Congress Cataloging-in-Publication Data

Bream, Jon.
  Whole lotta Led Zeppelin : the illustrated history of the heaviest band of all time / Jon Bream.
       p. cm.
  Includes bibliographical references, discography, and index.
   ISBN 978-0-7603-3507-9 (hb w/ jkt)
  1. Led Zeppelin (Musical group) 2. Rock musicians–England–Biography. I. Title.
  ML421.L4B74 2008
   782.42166092'2–dc22
   [B]
                                    2008023139

Editors: Michael Dregni and Dennis Pernu
Designer: John Barnett/4 Eyes Design

Printed in China

Permissions
"A Taste of Decadence" and "The *Starship*" copyright © 2002 by Richard Cole and Richard Trubo
reprinted from *Stairway To Heaven: Led Zeppelin Uncensored* by permission of HarperCollins
Publishers and Simon and Schuster UK.

"The Return of Led Zeppelin" by David Fricke reprinted from *Rolling Stone*, December 13, 2007.
Copyright © Rolling Stone LLC. All rights reserved. Reprinted by permission.

U.S Tour, 1977. *Adrian Boot/urbanimage.tv*

contents

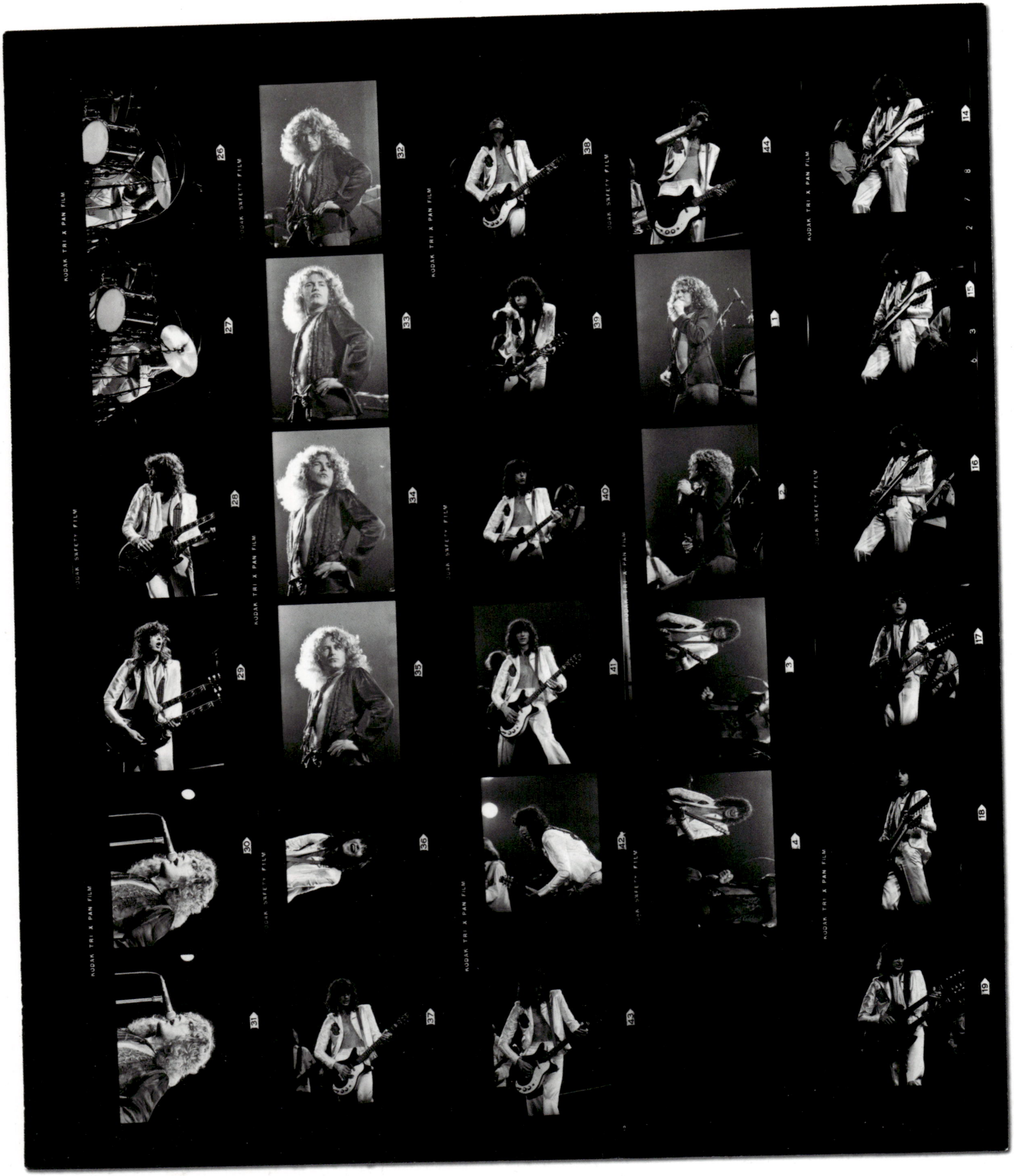

Preface
Front Row Seat

At concerts, I've sat next to Cameron Diaz, behind Sammy Hagar, and with Jerry Garcia. In more than thirty years as a music critic, I've sat close enough to the stage to get (intentionally) doused by Prince's "Purple Rain" squirt-gun guitar and far enough from the action that, even with high-power binoculars, I couldn't tell if Jimmy Buffett was barefoot or wearing flip-flops. Only once have I been in the front row at an arena concert: Led Zeppelin, January 18, 1975, at Met Center in suburban Minneapolis, Minnesota.

At the end of "Stairway To Heaven," the stage exploded into a blinding burst of white light and LED ZEPPELIN was spelled out in five-foot-high blinking lights at the back of the stage. (Sorry, Gene Simmons, Zep did it first.) Experiencing the power, the brightness, and rock radio's most beloved song in the front row was absolutely overwhelming. I'd never felt the volume, intensity, and force of rock 'n' roll quite like that—not even when I "performed" in costume with Alice Cooper for two nights in 1979 (the lights were startlingly hot on stage and the energy from the audience positively buoying, but that was choreographed theater, not spontaneous rock 'n' roll).

Truth be told (critics get paid to be honest), that 1975 Zeppelin concert, despite my once-in-a-lifetime seats, wasn't one for the ages. The first gig on Zeppelin's tenth U.S. tour, the show was marred by opening-night kinks. Robert Plant perceptively pronounced the performance "rusty." His voice was not in mid-tour form, and Jimmy Page was hampered by a broken finger on his fretting hand. Moreover, after promising a three-hour show, the band came up forty-five minutes short. Can you imagine a Zeppelin show at which they didn't play "Dazed And Confused"?

The next time Led Zeppelin came to Minneapolis, this critic incurred the wrath of Mr. Plant. Over the years, I've been called out at concerts by stars many times—Prince (at least three times, but that's another book), Billy Joel, the Eagles' Glenn Frey, Lyle Lovett, and k. d. lang. But the voice of Zeppelin was the first to do it.

In 1977, Led Zeppelin did something that no superstars had done before—or since: play two consecutive nights in the Twin Cities in different arenas. On April 12 at Met Center, the quartet took the stage seventy-five minutes late. Back in those days, tardy starts weren't uncommon, but they were usually because the performers were powdering their noses. Zep's excuse on this night was their flight from Chicago, via private jet, of course, was delayed by rain. Between the late arrival and the frequent firecrackers ignited by tired-of-waiting fans, Zeppelin seemed distracted. Page was uninspired and workman-like. Plant was not as frenetic as usual. Being an earnest young critic, I described the latter's performance as "more strikingly macho than sexy" and observed that he "lacked feeling and concentration" on a sloppy version of "Stairway To Heaven."

After the concert Zeppelin's crew packed up its equipment and set up across town at the St. Paul Civic Center for the April 13 show. Plant apparently read my review in the *Minneapolis Star*, that city's afternoon paper. He didn't mention me by name at the second show, as I listened intently halfway back on the main floor, but he had a few choice bleeps that referenced comments in my review. And you know what? He and Zeppelin truly kicked butt that night.

Reviews are supposed to provide perspective for readers, not motivation for artists. More than thirty years later, after a one-shot Zeppelin reunion show in London in December 2007 that has caused millions of fans to pine with off-the-charts anticipation for a reunion tour, it is time to provide some perspective on Led Zeppelin. We've asked some of rock's best-known stars and critics from the United States and the United Kingdom—some of whom witnessed Zep firsthand, others who were too young—to revisit and reexamine the wildest, loudest, and heaviest rock band of all time. Welcome to your front row seat for a Whole Lotta Led Zeppelin.

Jon Bream
Minneapolis, MN
February 2008

Met Center, Bloomington, MN, April 12, 1977. Tom Sweeney, Minneapolis Star Tribune

Lift Off
1968–1969

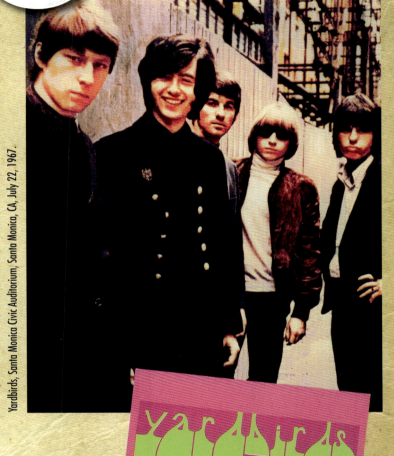

Led Zeppelin is, was, and always will be Jimmy Page's band. Unlike the Stones, the Beatles, and the Who, this British band didn't bring an outside producer into the recording studio. Page was the producer—and the chief songwriter, the architect, the mixing supervisor, the leader. But his group didn't start as Led Zeppelin.

In May 1966, Page joined his pal Jeff Beck in the Yardbirds. Despite "For Your Love" and other Yardbirds hits, the newcomer didn't realize the shape of things to come. The vaunted Page/Beck double-guitar attack was short-lived because, in October 1966, Beck bowed out two shows into a U.S. tour with Dick Clark's Caravan of Stars, leaving Page as the main man. When he went into the studio the following year to make what would be his only Yardbirds album (*Little Games*), the guitarist butted heads with singles-oriented producer Mickie Most, who was riding high with hits by Lulu, Herman's Hermits, and Donovan. Meanwhile, the Yardbirds' aggressive new manager, Peter Grant, kept the band on the road—Japan, France, and especially the United States. That proved too much touring for singer Keith Relf and drummer Jim McCarty, who quit in the summer of '68. Page, feeling obligated to honor commitments for an autumn swing through Scandinavia, began looking for replacements.

Terry Reid, eighteen, was his first choice. "He was the only vocalist I knew, but he'd just signed up with Mickie Most so he was out of the question," Page told *CREEM* magazine in 1974. "[Reid] did suggest Robert Plant—said he lived in Birmingham and that we should try and track him down. So we went to see him at a college gig, and I had a chat with him and said I was trying to get something together and would he be interested to come down and have a chat? He came down and stayed for a couple of nights, and it just went on from there."

Yardbirds, Santa Monica Civic Auditorium, Santa Monica, CA, July 22, 1967.

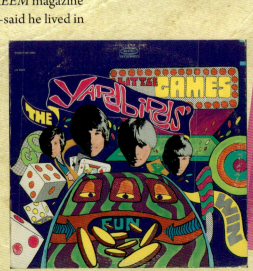

Yardbirds, *Little Games*, released July 24, 1967.

Yardbirds, Kerrisdale Arena, Vancouver, BC, July 31, 1967. Artist: Bob Masse.

Those couple of nights included bonding over Page's record collection—from Howlin' Wolf and Buddy Guy to Elvis Presley and Iron Butterfly. The object of their mutual affection was, oddly enough, American folk singer Joan Baez's interpretation of the traditional "Babe I'm Going to Leave You."

John Bonham, a loud and manic drummer, was an old buddy of Plant's, having played with the singer in the Band of Joy. After lots of arm-twisting, he was recruited away from Tim Rose's band. Page decided to replace bassist Chris Dreja, an original Yardbird, with multi-instrumentalist John Paul Jones, who had contacted Page after reading an article about a new band in *Disc* magazine. (Jones had led the cello section for the Yardbirds' tune "Little Games" a year earlier.) The guitarist gathered the quartet for a test drive in a tiny room below a London record store. They broke the ice with "The Train Kept A-Rollin'," and the New Yardbirds, as an August 5, 1968, press release declared, were born.

"I think what it is, is that the four members of Led Zeppelin were so different as personalities in their everyday lives and what made them tick, we were just totally different, but somehow we were brought by divine providence together to play," Page told Detroit writer Gary Graff in 2003. "Even in the first rehearsal we did. We rehearsed one number in this rehearsal room. There was this sort of stunned silence, anticipation. It was like heaven knows what it was. None of us had actually played with our musical equals; all of a sudden there was the four of us joined together, and it was just really eerie. It was so good that it was eerie. And that aspect of it was with us from that first day to the last."

"We all did it for different reasons," Jones told the *San Diego Union Tribune* in 2003. "I wanted to get out of studio work. We had to persuade Bonzo to leave Tim Rose because he had doubts about us. Bonzo wasn't sure we could pay him more than 40 pounds [about $120 U.S.] a week so we really had to work on him. Robert saw it as a natural progression. Jimmy had the idea to start a band while he was in the Yardbirds. As soon as we started playing together, we said: 'This is good, so who cares how long it lasts?' We didn't plan any further. We didn't plan for world domination."

The two weeks of New Yardbirds gigs in Denmark, Norway, and Sweden turned out to be the rehearsals for the debut album, *Led Zeppelin*. "It came together really

Blues legend Howlin' Wolf, a Zep influence over whom Page and Plant bonded early on. *Chess Records*

"I'd have to say my main blues influence was Howlin' Wolf, and his stuff wasn't just straight groove, playing on the beat, either. I loved his voice and the sheer intensity of the music as well as the timing of it. I've often thought that in the way the Stones tried to be the sons of Chuck Berry, we tried to be the sons of Howlin' Wolf."

—*Jimmy Page on the band's first rehearsal, quoted in Cameron Crowe's "Led Zeppelin: Light And Shade"*

The heaviest band of all time's namesake (right).

Yardbirds Goodbye

The Yardbirds make their farewell London appearance at the Marquee Club tonight (Friday) and their final University performance is set for Liverpool tomorrow (Saturday)—after which the group disbands. Leader Jimmy Page has now decided to name his new group Led Zeppelin, and this will make its stage debut in late October.

The new group has already cut a single and LP for early December release, and it was announced this week that Led Zeppelin has been signed by Harold Davison.

Newspaper clipping announcing the Yardbirds' last gigs and the debut of Led Zeppelin, autumn 1968.

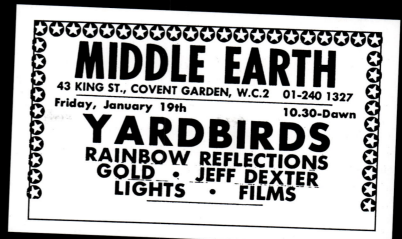

✪ MIDDLE EARTH ✪
43 KING ST., COVENT GARDEN, W.C.2 01-240 1327
Friday, January 19th   10.30-Dawn
YARDBIRDS
RAINBOW REFLECTIONS
GOLD · JEFF DEXTER
LIGHTS · FILMS

Yardbirds, Middle Earth Club, London, January 19, 1968.

✪ MIDDLE EARTH ✪
43 KING ST., COVENT GARDEN, W.C.2 01-240 1327
                                    10.30 - Dawn
Friday, January 26th
FAIRPORT CONVENTION
ROBERT PLANT'S BAND OF JOY
PEGASUS · THE FLUTE GIRL
JEFF DEXTER
LIGHTS · FILMS · EVENTS
                      Guests 20/6d.
Members 10/6d.

Band of Joy, Middle Earth Club, London, January 26, 1968.

"The room was about 18x30, very small. We just played one number 'Train Kept A-Rollin,' and it was there immediately. An indescribable feeling."

—Jimmy Page on the band's first rehearsal, quoted in Cameron Crowe's "Led Zeppelin: Light And Shade"

"They may be world-famous, but a couple of shrieking monkeys are not going to use a privileged family name without permission."

—Countess Eva von Zeppelin

November 9, 1968
MIDDLE EARTH
presents at the
ROUNDHOUSE
CHALK FARM   229 1438
Saturday, November 9th
                        10.30-Dawn
YARDBIRDS
now known as
LED ZEPPELIN
JOHN LEE HOOKER
DEVIANTS · JOHN JAMES · TYRES
JEFF DEXTER · LIGHTS
Members 16/.   Guests 26/.

Early U.K. club gig, Roundhouse, London, November 9, 1968.

DECEMBER 26 THRU 30
LEE MICHEALS and CHICAGO TRANSIT AUTHORITY
NEW YEARS SPECIAL
JOHNNY RIVERS Plus CHICAGO TRANSIT AUTHORITY
JANUARY 2 THRU 5
LED ZEPPELIN AND ALICE COOPER
FEATURING: JIMMY PAGE formly of the yard birds
JAN 9 THRU 19
TIM HARDIN and music from "LIL BROWN"
WHISKY a GO GO   sunset strip 652-4202
                  NO AGE LIMIT.

First U.S. tour, Whiskey a Go Go, Los Angeles, January 2 and 4–5, 1969.

The New Yardbirds, Marquee Club, London, October 18, 1968. The concert was the first in the U.K. by the lineup that was to become Led Zeppelin. *Graham Wiltshire/Hulton Archive/Getty Images*

quick," Page told *CREEM* in 1974 of the first LP. "It was cut very shortly after the band was formed. For material, we obviously went right down to our blues roots. I still had plenty of Yardbirds riffs left over. By the time Jeff [Beck] did go, it was up to me to come up with a lot of new stuff. It was this thing where [Eric] Clapton set a heavy precedent in the Yardbirds, which Beck had to follow and then it was even harder for me, in a way, because the second lead guitarist had suddenly become the first. And I was under pressure to come up with my own riffs. On the first LP, I was still heavily influenced by the earlier days. I think it tells a bit, too. The album was made in three weeks."

Knowing his way around the music business, Page took an uncommon approach with his new project: "I wanted artistic control in a vise grip, because I knew exactly what I wanted to do with these fellows," he told *Guitar World*. "In fact, I financed and completely recorded the first album before going to Atlantic [Records]. It wasn't your typical story where you get an advance to make an album—we arrived at Atlantic with tapes in hand. The other advantage to having such a clear vision of what I wanted the band to be was that it kept recording costs to a minimum. We recorded the whole first album in a matter of thirty hours. I know because I paid the bill."

Atlantic Records, home to Aretha Franklin, Ray Charles, and the Rascals, was Page's handpicked choice. He was as particular about the record label as he was about the sound in the studio. "I made it very clear to them that I wanted to be on Atlantic rather than their rock label, Atco, which had bands like Sonny & Cher and Cream," Page said. "I didn't want to be lumped in with those people; I wanted to be associated with something more classic."

The momentous first performance as Led Zeppelin was October 25, 1968, at Surrey University in England. The new moniker came courtesy of either Keith Moon or John Entwistle, partners in the Who's rhythm section. In 1966, Page, Beck, Moon, Entwistle, and keyboardist Nicky Hopkins had discussed forming a band. Moon or Entwistle—both claimed credit—then famously uttered something about the band going down "like a lead zeppelin,"

a reference to the German airship designed by Count Ferdinand von Zeppelin in the early 1900s, a forerunner to today's blimps.

Ever-aggressive manager Grant found an opportunity for his new band when the Jeff Beck Group canceled a U.S. tour opening for Vanilla Fudge. On Christmas Eve, Zeppelin, with a road crew of one, flew to Los Angeles for a trio of shows at the Whiskey a Go Go.

(continued on page 35)

"I was at their first New York appearance at the Fillmore East when I was like sixteen, seventeen years old and it changed my life. They were opening for Iron Butterfly and a friend of mine—I think he was the lead singer of my band at the time—he told me about this new band, they're gonna be great. I got a hold of the record and it blew me away. Then when I went to see them live, it was just like, 'Whoa . . .' I said to myself, 'This is gonna be the next big band,' and we know the history after that."

—*Ace Frehley, KISS*

THIS SPREAD: Gladsaxe Teen Club, Gladsaxe, Denmark, September, 1968. *Jorgen Angel/Redferns*

"Well, looking back on the first Zeppelin album in particular, if I'd been more relaxed and less intimidated, it would've been that much better for me. I would've sung the same songs with the same phrasing, but my performances weren't that great. The records were super—they're all good, there ain't a bad record—but looking back, you get very analytical, and that relates to the mood that you're in or the conditions that you work under, and I was very intimidated back then. I didn't know if I really belonged back then—that first record especially feels like that for my contribution. But, as a collection of songs, and the way they're played, it's all great."

—Robert Plant, *High Times, 1991*

First photo shoot for Atlantic Records, London, England, 1968.
Dick Barnatt/Redferns

(continued from page 30)

Robert Plant told *Rolling Stone* writer Cameron Crowe, "It was the first place I ever landed in America: the first time I ever saw a cop with a gun, the first time I ever saw a twenty-foot-long car. There were a lot of fun-loving people to crash into. People were genuinely welcoming us to the country, and we started out on a path of positive enjoyment. Throwing eggs from floor to floor and really silly water battles and all the good fun that a nineteen-year-old boy should have. It was just the first steps of learning how to be crazy."

Released on January 12, 1969, *Led Zeppelin* was panned in the highly influential *Rolling Stone*, causing a grudge the band would hold for a long, long time. Nonetheless, radio supported the album, and fans showed up at the gigs, even though the band, according to its singer, "made no money on that first tour."

Plant told Crowe: "Atlantic had done a good job with the white label copies of the first album, getting them out to the FM stations a couple of days before we got to town. The reaction was very good. We weren't even billed the majority of the time. I remember the marquee that read VANILLA FUDGE, TAJ MAHAL PLUS SUPPORTING ACT. I didn't care; I'd been playing for years, and I'd never seen my name up there so it meant nothing to me. But the reception that we got was something else again, and that was especially surprising because in some of those towns the albums had not yet reached the stores. Even so, after about the third number, you could feel that the buzz coming back to us from the audience was different than what they'd given the other bands. Jimmy and I were both chronically ill and only played one gig out of three [at the Whiskey] we were supposed to have played. And I saw the GTOs [girl group featuring Pamela Miller] and I saw everything buzzing around me. I saw the Plaster-Casters, and I saw rows and rows and rows of possibilities, you know? And I said, 'Man, there's no end.'

"So that was it; that was the first tour. By the time we got to the East Coast, it was really hot. It was really surprising; it just devastated me. The antics, the tricks, and just the whole world that I'd slipped into, after having to struggle back in the Midlands of England just to play. And suddenly we were in places like Steve Paul's Scene, where the mini-Mafia would be kicking the tables over and chicks would be sleazing up to you and everything like that I mean, why stop ever?" ◗

Backstage pass, U.S. tour, 1969.

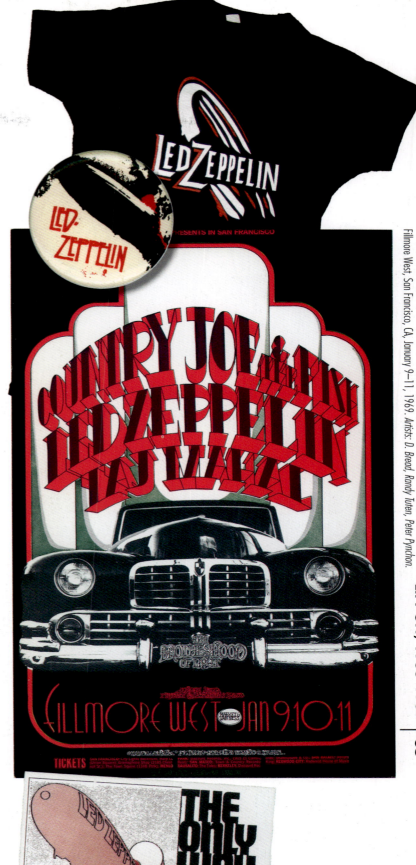

Fillmore West, San Francisco, CA, January 9–11, 1969. Artists: D. Bread, Randy Tuten, Peter Pynchon.

Few musicians have ever matched Jimmy Page in their embodiment of the quixotic qualities that make for a pioneering guitar hero, visionary producer, and legendary rock star. The founder and leader of Led Zeppelin, Page was also the member who took the band's breakup the hardest. Across the decades since, he has struggled to regain even a semblance of the creativity that once flowed from him. Yet for some ten years with Zeppelin, Page was a model of beauty and darkness, a guitarist who reveled in leading the biggest, loudest rock band on earth while reportedly dabbling in the occult, drug addiction, and every decadent pleasure going.

James Patrick Page was born in Heston, West London, on January 9, 1944. His parents were middle-class professionals who encouraged their son's interest in the arts. Aged twelve, Page, inspired by the Elvis Presley song "Baby Let's Play House," picked up a guitar and tried to emulate Scotty Moore's sizzling rockabilly guitar solo. Page took a handful of guitar lessons, then concentrated on teaching himself, listening to rock 'n' roll, blues, and folk guitarists. Aged fourteen, he featured on British TV as part of a skiffle group, playing the folk-blues music that swept the nation up in a craze.

Page was a diligent school pupil with a strong interest in science and briefly considered a career as a laboratory assistant. He went on to art school to study painting—and play guitar. He lasted a mere year and a half at college; his desire to make music had won out.

Joining British rock 'n' roll band the Crusaders, Page toured with them for two years before falling seriously ill with glandular fever. Disillusioned with the hard life of a traveling musician, Page enrolled at Sutton Art College. He maintained his interest in music by regularly attending concerts in London, often jamming with such leading figures of the nascent British blues movement as Cyril Davis and Alexis Korner. Through London's Marquee Club, he encountered two other blues-fixated, guitar-playing teenagers—Jeff Beck and Eric Clapton.

Page's guitar-playing skills were noted, and he quickly found regular work as a session musician. The fruits of his first session, "Diamonds" by Jet Harris and Tony Meehan, went to No. 1 in 1963 in the United Kingdom. Suddenly, England's hot producers—including Shel Talmy and Mickie Most—were turning to Page. In the next three years, his résumé of hit singles rivaled a Motown bass player's:

the Kinks' "You Really Got Me," Marianne Faithful's "As Tears Go By," the Nashville Teens' "Tobacco Road," Them's "Here Comes The Night," Tom Jones' "It's Not Unusual," the Who's "Can't Explain" (Page playing rhythm to Pete Townshend's lead), Crispian St. Peters' "Pied Piper," Brenda Lee's "Is It True," and Donovan's "Sunshine Superman," among others. (Note to trivia buffs: his guitar was heard on the demo for the Rolling Stones' "Heart Of Stone" but not the final recording.) Page also contributed licks to recordings by Screaming Lord Sutch, Marianne Faithful, Nico, Jackie DeShannon (who Page was briefly in a relationship with), and Joe Cocker, among others. He was also employed as house producer for Immediate Records by Rolling Stones manager Andrew Loog Oldham. At Immediate, he recorded several blues numbers with Eric Clapton of the Yardbirds.

"My session work was invaluable," Page told *Guitar World*. "At one point I was playing at least three sessions a day, six days a week! And I rarely ever knew in advance what I was going to be playing. But I learned things even on my worst sessions—and believe me, I played on some horrendous things. I finally called it quits after I started getting calls to do Muzak. I decided I couldn't live that life anymore; it was getting too silly. But being a session musician was good fun in the beginning—the studio discipline was great. They'd just count the song off, and you couldn't make any mistakes."

In 1965, Page cut his own first single, "She Just Satisfies." He wasn't satisfied, however: "There's nothing to be said for that record except it was very tongue-in-cheek at the time," he told *CREEM* magazine in 1974. "I played all the instruments on it except for the drums and sang on it too, which is quite, uh, unique. It's better forgotten."

Page had turned down an offer to replace Clapton in the Yardbirds in 1965, instead recommending his longtime friend, Jeff Beck. But when offered the role of bassist a year later, Page took it. He shifted to guitar when the band's rhythm guitarist, Chris Dreja, moved to bass. Thus, Page and Beck played guitars side by side until Beck's departure. In May 1966, Page and Beck teamed up (with bassist John Paul Jones and drummer Keith Moon of the Who) on the instrumental "Beck's Bolero," a B-side for Beck's first solo single. Page also played on the final Yardbirds' album, 1967's *Little Games*, but the LP's pop-rock sounds met only limited success. Yet the band's live performances won them a loyal following as Page led the band in creating a psychedelic blues-rock sound.

JIMMY PAGE

Jimmy Page, Atlantic Records press photo, 1972.

fontana

45

STEREO

A

TF 533
878 374-7

(P) 1965 Phonogram
Ltd. (London)

The copyright
in this sound
recording is owned
by Phonogram
Ltd. (London)

**JIMMY PAGE
SHE JUST SATISFIES**
(Jimmy Page/Barry Mason)
Biem/Stemra
Copyright Control

Jimmy Page's first single, "She Just Satisfies" b/w "Keep Moving," 1965.

When Yardbirds founding members Keith Relf and Jim McCarty announced they were leaving the struggling band in 1968, Page and bassist Dreja were left with the name and a contracted tour of Scandinavia. Page attempted to recruit Terry Reid—then one of the most highly rated singers on the British rock scene. Reid passed, but he recommended the largely unknown Robert Plant. Plant brought with him drummer John Bonham. When Dreja announced he was leaving music to concentrate on photography, Page put a call in to his old session buddy John Paul Jones.

The new band played the July 1968 Scandinavian dates as the New Yardbirds. Scrambling for a new name, Page recalled a joke made by Who rhythm section John Entwistle and Keith Moon about a joint jam session succeeding "like a lead zeppelin." Now, manager Peter Grant changed the spelling from "lead" to "led" to avoid mispronunciation, and Led Zeppelin went about recording their debut album in a mammoth thirty-six-hour session in January 1969.

Page produced all of Led Zeppelin's albums, channeling black American blues riffs through fuzz boxes, wah-wah pedals, and overdriven amplifiers to create epic rock guitar riffs. Conscious that he wanted the band to emphasize "light and shade," Page also picked out British folk melodies on acoustic guitar. A riff bandit, Page literally lifted several tunes outright from folk and blues artists, something that would later prove costly to the band when sued by the original composers. Led Zeppelin's immediate international success allowed Page to develop heavy rock guitar, experiment with feedback, weird theremin sounds, and bowing his guitar. At the same time, he also developed the studio as a creative space: drums detonated like canons; sound effects were layered, looped, and dubbed; the texture of the music was worked like a painter mixing oils and colors.

Fame and fortune also allowed Page to indulge in his wildest fantasies. He was famous for his taste in groupies (one, Los Angeles' Lori Maddox, was said to be only fourteen when they met and thus had to be hidden from authorities), interest in black magic (he set up a shop and printing press specializing in the occult), the many mansions he owned (including the Scottish mansion that once belonged to notorious sorcerer Aleister Crowley), and an alleged hunger for hard drugs.

Technically, Page was the least accomplished of Led Zeppelin's members, yet his guitar playing remains hugely inspirational. Of his many memorable guitar solos, none is more famous than that on 1973's "Stairway To Heaven" where he employed in concert a double-neck Gibson EDS-1275 that was

to become his trademark. "Stairway To Heaven" demonstrated Page's ability to shift from folksy finger picking to lethal hard rock. Page has often been voted Best Guitarist in rock music polls, and "Stairway To Heaven" is among the world's most popular songs.

Following Led Zeppelin's dissolution in 1980, Page recorded little of note. He contributed the soundtrack to the dire *Death Wish 2* and was publicly lambasted by fellow Satanist (and cult film director) Kenneth Anger for failing to deliver a suitable soundtrack to his *Lucifer Rising* film. In the mid-1980s, Page formed the Firm with vocalist Paul Rodgers for two albums of sub-Zeppelin heavy rock. A 1988 solo album, *Outrider*, attracted little notice. During the 1980s, police raided Page's Windsor mansion, and he was prosecuted for possessing hard drugs. In 1993, he teamed up with David Coverdale, vocalist with Zep-imitators Whitesnake, for the Coverdale–Page album, again, this effort sounding like a poor imitation of Led Zeppelin's heyday.

In 1994, Page and Robert Plant began working together again as Page–Plant; bassist John Paul Jones was not invited to the reunion. The duo issued *No Quarter*, a well-received album of acoustic reinterpretations of Zeppelin material. Their 1998 studio album *Walking Into Clarksdale* was produced by Steve Albini, but failed to attract critical or commercial interest and the duo separated. In 1999, Page teamed up with American retro-rockers the Black Crowes to tour the Zeppelin songbook. A solid live album resulted but the pairing ended in acrimony. Page played guitar as Puff Daddy rapped over "Kashmir" for the *Godzilla* soundtrack and reached back to his roots to jam with Jerry Lee Lewis on "Rock And Roll" for the Killer's album of duets, *Last Man Standing*.

Through his Brazilian wife, Jemina, Page has become involved with charitable efforts to help Brazil's street children. For his efforts he was made an honorary citizen of Rio de Janeiro in 2006 and was named an officer of the Order of the British Empire (OBE) by the queen.

Following Led Zeppelin's successful London reunion concert in December 2007, Page announced he would like to see the band undertake a world tour. ✈

"He's the Wagner of the Telecaster. He's the Mahler of the Les Paul. He's brilliant."
— Robert Plant on Jimmy Page, interviewed on MTV

Robert Plant: Middle-Class Blues Boy
by Garth Cartwright

Where Mick Jagger's pouting, camp stage presence set the standard for 1960s rock vocalists, Robert Plant's bare chest, golden hair, and orgasmic shriek established a new threshold across the 1970s. And it's an image that remains iconic today. Iconic, yes, and open to parody: Plant himself is openly critical of the heavy metal dunces that continue to imitate—badly—what Led Zeppelin pioneered. Refusing to engage in self-parody—unlike Jagger, who appears trapped by the persona he created almost fifty years ago—Plant, an intelligent man and extremely versatile vocalist, has moved on comprehensively from the image he projected as singer in the world's heaviest band, Led Zeppelin.

Robert Anthony Plant was born on August 20, 1948, in West Bromwich, in England's West Midlands. His father worked as an engineer and played in a brass band. Robert was a bookish child who early on decided he wanted to be Elvis Presley. He grew up inspired by African American blues and soul music; he recalls his parents cutting the plug off his Dansette record player after he played "I Like It Like That" by New Orleans R&B singer Chris Kenner seventeen times in a row.

The teenage Plant initially followed his parents wishes that he study to be an accountant, but after two weeks of working as an accredited clerk he threw the training aside and announced his decision to follow a career in music. His parents were aghast, but ultimately felt they had to let their son work the blues out of his system. He sang for the band Listen, which was signed by CBS Records, and Plant made his recording debut with Listen on a cover of the Rascals' "You Better Run." After Listen disbanded, Plant cut two solo singles for CBS, which marketed him as pop balladeer akin to Tom Jones.

In 1966, at age twenty, he married and took a job on a road-paving crew to support his pregnant wife.

Plant labored away during the day while singing in a variety of local bands at night. As vocalist in the Crawling King Snakes, he met drummer John Bonham; both would later play in the Band of Joy. Although none of these bands achieved anything beyond provincial fame, Plant's powerful tenor vocal did establish his reputation as a blues-rock shouter of note. He sang occasionally with British blues mainstay Alexis Korner and, in 1968, joined the band Hobbstweedle, which took its name from J. R. R. Tolkien's *The Lord Of The Rings*—perhaps an early sign of Plant's fixation with fantasy.

When Jimmy Page approached vocalist Terry Reid to sing in the New Yardbirds, Reid passed on the offer but suggested Page check out Plant. Page thus attended a concert by Plant with Hobbstweedle at a teacher training college in the city of Birmingham. Page and Plant found they shared similar musical passions and set about forming Led Zeppelin, Plant championing Bonham as the band's drummer.

The instant success of Led Zeppelin definitely owed a good degree to Plant: his tall, lithe figure, flowing blonde hair, wailing vocals, and lyrics infused with sexual allusion and Tolkeinesque imagery created a vivid, compelling presence that marked the band out from so many others also playing "heavy blues." Plant would co-write the majority of Led Zeppelin songs with Page, and the duo became the band's focal points, both tossing manes of hair and pulling poses that would be imitated by generations to come. Led Zeppelin's reputation as road warriors with a penchant for extreme hedonism went before them, and Plant was the ultimate groupie conquest. Indeed, the singer's sexual magnetism earned him the nickname "Percy," and legend has Plant declaring "I am a golden god!" from the balcony of the Continental Hyatt House in Los Angeles in 1975.

Yet Plant was brought back to earth later that year when he and his wife, Maureen, were seriously injured in a car crash in Rhodes, Greece. This meant Plant had to sing his vocals for *Presence*, the band's seventh album, from a wheelchair and forced Led Zeppelin to cancel the year's remaining tour dates. Worse was to come.

In 1977, while on tour in the United States, Plant's son Karac died, forcing the cancellation of the tour. By now Led Zeppelin's sound was changing, becoming less oriented toward heavy blues, more focused on melody and keyboards. When Bonham died in 1980, Plant had no qualms about calling it quits. He embarked on a solo career in 1982 with the well-received *Pictures At Eleven* and has since regularly toured and released albums. He was vocally critical of the new heavy rock bands that imitated Zeppelin and in 1988 challenged Rick Rubin's sampling of Zeppelin for his Def Jam productions by sampling Zep himself on his own *Now And Zen* album.

Plant's solo career flagged in the 1990s, leading him to reunite with Page in 1994 as Page–Plant. This attracted much media attention and found the duo touring the world playing Zeppelin numbers. Yet the poor sales that met their 1998 album *Walking Into Clarksdale* pushed Plant's return to performing solo. His recent albums include West African elements—Plant has performed at Mali's Festival in the Desert—and refusing to conform to nostalgia and rock music clichés.

"Maybe it would be a relief if I just behaved myself and stuck to the corporate repetition," mused Plant on his refusing simply to do Led Zeppelin over and over. "I've got to be known as a chap that likes variety, for my own sake, never mind anyone else's. This is crucial to me. I couldn't go on and reinvent the spirit of the huge monster that was because I couldn't feel comfortable. I don't know the guy who sang in Led Zeppelin. I see some very funny pictures of him, then I see rock's vile offspring trotting behind in lurex pants and leather gloves with the fingers cut off."

That said, Plant did agree to reform Led Zeppelin for a one-off charity gig in memory of Atlantic Records founder Ahmet Ertegun in December 2007. The concert, held in London's O2 Arena, was a huge success. Previous Zeppelin reunions at awards events had been embarrassing shambles—Plant refused even to join Page, Jones, and Bonham Jr. when the band was given the Grammy Lifetime Achievement Award in 2005. Yet the 2007 reunion concert led to suggestions that a worldwide tour would now be in the cards. Plant was, at the same time, enjoying the greatest success of his solo career with *Raising Sand*, an album cut with bluegrass superstar Alison Krauss. The album's huge commercial impact in the United States resulted in the duo winning Best Pop Collaboration for "Gone Gone Gone" at the February 2008 Grammy Awards. Said Plant of the project:

"Since I was a kid, I've had an absolute obsession with particular kinds of American music. Mississippi Delta blues of the thirties, Chicago blues of the fifties, West Coast music of the mid-sixties—but I'd never really touched on dark Americana. I was invited to do a show at the Rock and Roll Hall of Fame to celebrate the life of Leadbelly. Throughout my life, from the very early stages in the folk clubs in Worcestershire, everybody was singing Leadbelly songs. I thought it would be a good idea to try a duet so I contacted Alison. We had nothing to lose and everything to gain. We rehearsed in a hall for the Armenian residents of Cleveland, Ohio, and it was really good singing together. I thought I'd probably been around too long but she taught me to sing delicate harmonies. I really had to think and learn about musical intervals. I'm absolutely ecstatic because there's nothing worse than being stereotyped. Alison brought such texture to my world. It was fascinating and very good fun."

Plant, about to turn sixty, remains a singer on a quest to make fresh, earthy music.

Robert Plant, press photo.

LED ZEPPELIN   **Robert Plant**

"His vocal range was unbelievable. I thought, 'Wait a minute. There's something wrong here. He's not known.' I couldn't figure it out. I thought, 'He must be a strange guy or something.' Then he came over to my place and I could see that he was a really good guy. I still don't know why he hadn't made it yet."

—Jimmy Page on Robert Plant, quoted in Cameron Crowe's "Led Zeppelin: Light And Shade"

John Paul Jones: Music In His Blood
by Garth Cartwright

The musician we know as John Paul Jones was born John Baldwin on January 3, 1946, in Sidcup, Kent, just outside of London. He divided his formative years between the Kent countryside and the bombed-out streets of post–World War II London. Inspired by his musician father, Joe Baldwin, the youth strove to achieve greater things via music. This striving has driven him throughout his life, and even today he retains a remarkable enthusiasm for making music. Ironically, for a man so interested in working with many different musicians, Jones is Led Zeppelin's "invisible man." Where Page, Plant, and Bonham were among the world's most recognizable rock stars, Jones fostered a quiet aura, one that allowed him to avoid the excesses of stardom and retain a privacy his bandmates would later come to envy. "I liked the fact that the fans didn't recognize me," Jones noted during a 2007 interview, "it meant I could pull up outside one of our concerts in a VW van and I was just another hippie."

The young John Baldwin started learning piano at age six. His father was a pianist and arranger for dance bands, especially the Ambrose Orchestra. Mrs. Baldwin was also a musician and toured with Joe. This led to John both experiencing life on the road at an early age and being put in Christ College boarding school in Blackheath, in southeast London, where he majored in music. From an early age, John had his ears wide open; he describes his initial musical heroes as bluesman Big Bill Broonzy, jazz bassist and composer Charlie Mingus, and the classical pianist and composer Sergei Rachmaninoff. Aged fourteen, John became choirmaster and organist at a local church and purchased his first bass guitar. His first paycheck came from a gig with his father, and over time he played at weddings, military bases, and a yacht club. He joined his first band, the Deltas, at fifteen. He then began playing jazz-rock with Jett Blacks, a London collective that would include guitarist John McLaughlin, who was soon to be a jazz fusion superstar and mainstay of Miles Davis' early 1970s band.

In 1962, John Baldwin began working as a session man; his expertise on bass and keyboards and his skills as an arranger found him in demand as the British pop industry exploded. In early 1963, he landed a rock gig with Jet Harris and Tony Meehan, who had just recorded a No. 1 single, "Diamonds," with Jimmy Page on guitar. He changed his name when Andrew Loog Oldham, manager and producer of the Rolling Stones, suggested it would suit his rising star. The new name—John Paul Jones—was borrowed from an American revolutionary whom Baldwin discovered in a 1959 movie.

Among the sessions Jones played on were hit recordings by Donovan, such as "Sunshine Superman," Dusty Springfield, Lulu, Cliff Richard, Rod Stewart, Wayne Fontana and the Mindbenders' "Groovy Kind Of Love," and Tom Jones' "Delilah." He also added the string arrangement on "She's A Rainbow" by the Rolling Stones. As a versatile bassist, he backed the likes of the Supremes and Tom Jones in concert, and his arrangements with the Andrew Loog Oldham Orchestra are now revered as easy-listening classics. At the same time, Jones tried cutting a solo single, "Baja," in 1964, but it went nowhere. Returning to session work, he played bass on Jeff Beck's "Beck's Bolero" and cello on the Yardbirds' *Little Games*—recordings that also featured Jimmy Page, who had taken over leadership of the disintegrating pop-rock band.

When the duo again found themselves working together—this time on Donovan's 1968 *The Hurdy Gurdy Man* album—Jones mentioned to Page that session work was exhausting him and he would be interested in joining a band that Page was talking of forming. Nothing came of this at first, but when Page found himself trying to form a band from the ashes of the Yardbirds he looked to Jones after Yardbirds bassist Chris Dreja decided to retire from playing music to concentrate on photography.

Jones was the only member of Led Zeppelin with classical training. This—along with his ability to play fluid, rhythmic bass, excellent keyboards, and his years as an arranger—would prove to be hugely beneficial to the band, helping mark out their more complex and melodic songs. In concert he would demonstrate his keyboard abilities on "No Quarter"—which he extended for up to thirty minutes at a time—blending elements of Miles Davis' *Sketches Of Spain*, Rachmaninoff's piano concertos, and the hymn "Amazing Grace." Jones' ability as a multi-instrumentalist added many textures to Zeppelin recordings: he also played mandolin, lute, and clarinet, and he would use bass pedals to shift and alter the sound of instruments.

Having spent so much of his young life in the studio as both session musician and arranger, Jones was invaluable in helping Led Zeppelin develop their sound beyond the blues and folk riffs employed on the early albums. A calm, intelligent man, he was the least affected by the excesses that accompanied the band on the road and, in 1973, actually voiced a desire to leave the band so as to spend more time at home with his young family. Zeppelin manager Peter Grant managed to talk him out of leaving, but the band's increasing reluctance to tour surely had something to do with Jones' desire not to spend so much time on the road.

It was Jones who found Bonham's body on September 25, 1980: partnered in rhythm, the two men worked to build the huge sound that Page and Plant performed over. Led Zeppelin dissolved following Bonham's death, yet this ending sparked a creative freedom for Jones that he has reveled in.

Jones immediately returned to his former occupation as session musician and arranger, now also establishing himself as a master producer. Across the past quarter century, he has either played with, arranged for, or produced R.E.M., Foo Fighters, Robyn Hitchcock, John Martyn, the Butthole Surfers, Diamanda Galas, the Mission, the Datsuns, Ben Harper, and most recently, all-female old-time band Uncle Earl. He has recorded two solo albums—both well received and very individual in their use of space and sound—and contributed to several film scores. Today Jones continues to engage with music he finds challenging and fresh. And, yes, he still writes music for church choirs.

Reflecting on his life as a musician, he recently told *Rolling Stone*, "I like to be free in what I do. I hardly ever play the same bass line twice. Even in songs where it's mapped out, like 'Good Times Bad Times,' I swap it around a little bit. We all enjoy the freedom to do that. In order to have that freedom, you have to know each other so well."

Jones is that rare rock star, unconstrained by image or public expectation and seemingly able to work with different musical forms from across the planet. Whether rocking stadiums as a member of Led Zeppelin or picking a mandolin alongside Uncle Earl, Jones remains a musicians' musician.

John Paul Jones, 1971. *Heilemann Camera Press, London*

"I don't mind being in the background. I wouldn't like to be out front playing like Jimmy. To be any sort of artist, you have to be a born exhibitionist. . . . I believe you should do what you have to do, and if I'm bass, rather than try to lead on bass and push myself, I prefer to put down a good solid bass line."
— John Paul Jones, quoted in Ritchie Yorke's The Led Zeppelin Biography

John Bonham: The Big Bang
by Garth Cartwright

Anecdotes about rock drummers are legion, but none come more touched with myth and psychosis than those surrounding Led Zeppelin's rhythm master, John Bonham. Born in the nondescript Midlands town of Redditch, England, on May 31, 1948, John Henry Bonham demonstrated percussive abilities from an early age, beating on pots and pans in his parents' kitchen. As legend has it, he built his first drum kit out of leftover containers when he was just five. By the age of ten, Bonham had his first real snare drum, a gift from his mother; his parents bought him a full drum kit, a Premier Percussion set, when he was fifteen. Bonham, like many teenagers of the time, was enchanted with rock 'n' roll and the blues while also appreciating the way legendary jazz drummers Gene Krupa and Buddy Rich led their big bands.

Bonham attended Wiltern Public School, leaving before graduating, with the school's headmaster announcing the wayward pupil was unfit even to work as a garbage collector. Initially working for his father's construction company, he joined his first band, Terry Web and the Spiders, in 1964. He subsequently worked with a multitude of bands, mostly based out of the industrial city of Birmingham in the British Midlands. Across this period Bonham developed a reputation as an extremely powerful—and loud—drummer. By the mid-1960s, he formed A Way of Life with bassist Dave Pegg (later a member of folk-rock band Fairport Convention), yet this partnership lasted only a matter of months before Bonham left to join a local blues band, the Crawling King Snakes. The King Snakes' lead singer was a teenage Robert Plant, and the two quickly became good friends, even when Bonham briefly rejoined A Way of Life. He then struck out with Plant as a member of the Band of Joy, an unsigned group playing West Coast psychedelic rock. The Band of Joy toured the United Kingdom in support of American folk singer Tim Rose in early 1968; when Rose returned in late 1968, he again hired Bonham as his drummer. During these years, he won the nickname "Bonzo," borrowed from a cartoon bulldog.

When Jimmy Page began assembling what would become Led Zeppelin, he considered several established drummers—including Procol Harum's B. J. Wilson and session master Aynsley Dunbar—before listening to Plant's insistence that his old mate Bonham was the drummer they needed. Page and the group's manager Peter Grant attended a Tim Rose gig in Hampstead, north London; impressed by Bonham's playing, they offered him the gig. Initially, though, Bonham was reluctant to sign up for a group that appeared to be yet another attempt to breathe life into the Yardbirds—especially when the initial wage offered was less than that going for the drum gig with more established bands. This led Page and Grant to bombard Bonham's favorite pub in Walsall, Three Men in a Boat, with telegrams. At the time, both Chris Farlowe and Joe Cocker were courting Bonham, but he

eventually signed up with Page due to his friendship with Plant and a professed liking for the music—although what exactly this "music" was is unsure as he had dismissed the Yardbirds as "redundant." With Bonham on board, Led Zeppelin was now complete.

Zeppelin was many things but rarely subtle, and Bonham powered the sound. His prowess as a drummer came from his sheer brute force. Bonham's drumming never involved delivering the propulsive R&B rhythms Charlie Watts gave the Rolling Stones or the brilliantly scattershot percussion Keith Moon employed to add dynamics to the Who. Indeed, Bonham owed little even to the hugely powerful drumming of Ginger Baker, who, in Cream, provided the natural role model for Bonham: Baker was steeped in jazz and interested in shading the space in between Eric Clapton's guitar and Jack Bruce's bass. Bonham may have admired and learned from jazz drummers, but what he brought to Led Zeppelin was an ability to build a huge, sledgehammer beat, his rhythms being so forceful they literally punched the Zeppelin sound forward. No drummer ever created such a monstrous sound, and in Bonham's force field of rhythm there ranks the basis of the sound now called heavy metal. This epic drumming, locked with Page's overloaded fuzz guitar, Plant's primal shriek, and Jones' rolling bass lines created an immensely powerful rock sound.

Both as a musician and an individual, Bonham possessed a strong, fiery personality. Where most drummers are largely overlooked in favor of singers and guitarists, Zeppelin's fans recognized Bonham as an essential cog in the band's machinery. Listen to "Whole Lotta Love" and note how alongside Page's gigantic guitar riff and Plant's orgasmic vocals, Bonham's titanic drum patterns slam the song home. So celebrated was Bonham's role in the band he was given the longest onstage instrumental solo with "Moby Dick," a rhythmic epic that could last up to forty-five minutes as the drummer discarded his sticks and attacked the drums with his bare hands.

Bonham's appetites weren't simply for the biggest drum sound and the longest solo; he also participated in the indulgences and debauchery available to a young rock star at the end of the 1960s. Many of the wilder stories surrounding Led Zeppelin's on-the-road misadventures revolve around Bonham.

When not touring Bonham lived a far more sedate life in rural England. Married to Pat Phillips—an English woman he had met after playing a dance in 1964—and father of children Jason and Zoe, he lived in a country mansion and indulged his passion for collecting vintage hot rod motorcycles and cars. As a musician Bonham developed his drumming, adding an international array of percussion instruments to his kit (including orchestral timpani and a huge symphonic gong), which brought out more subtle shades to his playing. From 1973's *Houses Of The Holy* on, Led Zeppelin albums boasted a cleaner production sound that emphasized the textures of Bonham's drumming. Indeed, Bonham's drums would not only influence a generation of heavy rock drummers but would be heavily sampled in the 1980s by rap and house music producers who wanted his huge rhythmic thud to detonate the new dance music they were creating.

Bonham almost never gave interviews, displaying a paranoid loathing of the media. When his friend, Scottish comedian Billy Connelly, tried to interview him for his sole TV appearance, Bonham would only shrug or mutter "Yes." Led Zeppelin became increasingly inactive as a touring outfit in the late 1970s, and Bonham, while enjoying his life as an English country squire, remained restless, his life was allegedly increasingly dominated by alcohol and hard drugs.

Perhaps Bonham realized that touring, especially in the United States, brought out the worst in him: when Page called rehearsals for a forthcoming 1980 U.S. tour, Bonham appeared apprehensive, suggesting to Plant that the singer drum and he'd sing. On September 24, 1980, Bonham attended the first rehearsal. He drank vodka heavily from breakfast on, consuming throughout the day more than three dozen shots and becoming too drunk to drum. The band retired to Page's mansion in Clewer, Windsor, where Bonham kept drinking until he passed out. This was to be one he would never wake from. The coroner concluded Bonham had died from choking on his own vomit while asleep "due to consumption of alcohol." His excessive drinking had caused him to suffer a pulmonary edema—swelling of the blood vessels—due to an excess of fluid. It was, noted the coroner, "death by accidental suicide."

Recognizing Bonham was the motor that drove Led Zeppelin, his band mates announced the dissolution of the supergroup three months after Bonham's death.

Bonham's son Jason—given his first drum kit when he was just five by his father—went on to lead the 1980s heavy rock band Bonham. Led Zeppelin had called on Jason to occupy the drum seat at their rare reformations—his performance at the band's hugely successful London O2 Arena in December 2007 suggests a son capable of filling his father's mighty drum stool. Indeed, Zeppelin bassist John Paul Jones—the man who knows John Bonham's drumming better than anyone else alive—commented on Jason's performance after the concert: "He's as fearless as his dad, that's for sure. But he did an amazing job. When you consider that he had to answer to every drummer in the world after that show . . . with that sort of pressure, to bring all that off was astonishing. 'Kashmir' was absolutely wonderful, the way he led in and out of the choruses and bridges."

Leave it to Foo Fighters' leader Dave Grohl to sum up most musicians and fans' feelings for Bonham's drum legacy: "I don't know anyone who thinks there's a better rock drummer than John Bonham: it's undeniable!"

LED ZEPPELIN   John Bonham

"I've never tried consciously to be one of the best drummers and I don't want to be. A lot of kids come up to me and say, 'There's a lot better drummers than you,' or something. But I enjoy playing to the best of my ability and that's why I'm here doing it. I don't claim to be more exciting than Buddy Rich. But I don't play what I don't like. I'm a simple, straight-ahead drummer and I don't try to pretend to be anything better than I am."

— *John Bonham, quoted in Stephen Davis'*
Hammer Of The Gods

Just as Brian Epstein, manager of the Beatles, was seen as the "fifth Beatle," Peter Grant, manager of Led Zeppelin, was very much the "fifth Zeppelin." Grant, born on April 5, 1935, was in every sense a larger than life character, a man who revolutionized rock management. Via Led Zeppelin, he invented the template for the supergroup.

While there is no doubting the mercurial musical and personal qualities of Led Zeppelin's four members, a good deal of their initial success must be accredited to Grant's forward-thinking management: he ensured the band be seen as a unique outfit, outside of the pop-rock gamut, and focused on developing Zeppelin as a corporation. They were soon recognized as both the loudest and the highest-grossing band in rock history. Not bad for a former professional wrestler and factory worker.

Peter Grant was born in the south London suburb of South Norwood. A towering youth, Grant always appeared much older than his actual age. He chose to leave school at age thirteen, initially working in a sheet-metal factory. Standing six feet five inches tall, he may have appeared suited for manual labor, but he quickly decided this wasn't to his taste. He instead started working for Reuters News Agency—then based in central London's legendary Fleet Street—delivering photographs. This gave him an entrance to the entertainment industry, and he went on to work in a variety of jobs—stagehand, hotel entertainment manager, bouncer, and doorman—until a friend suggested he would do well as a professional wrestler. Grant, who possessed something of a theatrical bent, leapt at the idea and was soon appearing on British television wrestling as Count Massimo and Count Bruno Alassio of Milan. His huge presence led to him being offered bit roles in a number of early 1960s films, including *The Guns of Navarone*, *A Night To Remember*, and *Cleopatra*. He also appeared in a variety of British TV programs, including *The Benny Hill Show*.

When the notorious British rock manager Don Arden hired Grant to act as tour manager for a rock 'n' roll revival show touring the United Kingdom in 1963, Grant began to sense the possibilities—and money—involved in music management. Arden became famous—or notorious—for his thuggish management practices involving the likes of the Small Faces, ELO, and Ozzy Osbourne. He was also the father of Sharon Osbourne, and the ruthless steel she displays in business dealings was inherited from her father. Grant also learned this from Arden. Becoming a talent scout for Arden, Grant met up with Newcastle rockers the Animals, who went on to become a huge international draw with their Mickie Most–produced hit "House Of The Rising Sun." Grant got the job as Animals tour manager, and it was on a U.S. Animals tour that he realized how much money a successful rock band generated and—at the time—how little of it filtered back to the musicians.

Splitting with Arden over his dubious accounting practices with the Animals—the two men would later fight in public when they came across each other—Grant set up RAK Records with Mickie Most. The label went on to have hit after hit well into the 1970s.

Most regularly employed John Paul Jones as his studio arranger and had on occasion hired Jimmy Page to play on pop sessions. It was also Most who suggested in late 1966 to the Yardbirds' manager that Grant would be an asset to the then struggling band. Grant came on board and began traveling with the Yardbirds, ensuring that promoters paid the band and earnings were not wasted. Realizing the Yardbirds' glory days were over, he remained impressed by Page's drive and imagination. Some commentators claim it was Grant's awareness of the popularity of Jeff Beck's post-Yardbirds heavy blues-rock in the United States—and Beck's reluctance to tour—that led him to suggest Page assemble the New Yardbirds.

Realizing Led Zeppelin's potential, Grant negotiated a five-album contract with Atlantic Records. Atlantic was then the most respected and influential label in the music business. Grant won from Atlantic a $200,000 advance, then a new artist record. Aware that America's burgeoning FM rock market valued albums over singles, Grant insisted Zeppelin be promoted as an "album band," thus accounting for the few singles ever released. Aware as well of the mystique of live appearances over the traditional pop marketing formats of TV shows, Grant also insisted the band play live to wow audiences with their power. These strategies certainly worked. Zeppelin albums quickly topped charts on both sides of the Atlantic while the band developed into the world's highest-drawing live rock band. Grant, knowledgeable of how little bands were often pocketing from the concert gate, began taking control of the booking and promotion of Zeppelin concerts; thus, the vast profits to be made when selling out stadiums stayed with the band rather than the promoters and booking agents.

Grant was a huge presence in every sense. His colossal girth, bushy beard, bald head, and massive arms meant he dominated any room he entered. And when acting in what he saw were the band's interests, he wasn't afraid of appearing threatening. His heavy-handed tactics led to much criticism. But the four band members, cocooned in luxury and vast wealth, looked on him as a father figure who could do no wrong.

Grant's understanding of the music industry saw him setting up the band's own publishing company, Superhype Music, when they first formed; after their Atlantic deal was fulfilled, they started the Swan Song label to handle their recordings. Grant then signed Bad Company to Swan Song and managed them as well; they achieved instant success. Grant later claimed Colonel Tom Parker contacted him in 1977 about setting up what would have been the debut European tour for

Atlantic Records' Jerry Wexler (top right) presents Peter Grant and the band with their RIAA-certified gold records for *Led Zeppelin* on July 31, 1969, in Eugene, OR. The LP achieved the honor for 500,000 units sold on July 22, six months after its release.

Elvis Presley. In the scenes filmed backstage of *The Song Remains The Same*, the viewer gets a sense of just how intimidating Grant could be.

Grant would storm into London record shops and smash Led Zep bootlegs; he would also throw anyone out of a concert he suspected of having outlawed recording equipment. Yet Grant's thuggish approach undermined the band when, in 1977, a confrontation with some staff at a concert in Oakland, California, would lead to a brawl and the subsequent arrest of Grant and John Bonham (and two other Zep employees) on assault charges. Perhaps realizing how out of control their fame had gone, Plant and Page kept the band off the road for much of the next few years.

After Led Zeppelin and the closure of Swan Song in 1983, Grant largely retired from the music industry to an estate in Eastbound, south England. He occasionally ventured out in public and became an in-demand speaker for music industry seminars. He lost weight and took to living a much more moderate life. While driving home with his son on November 21, 1995, he suffered a massive heart attack and died at age sixty. 🦇

Peter Grant: "I'm Peter Grant, manager of Led Zeppelin."

Bob Dylan: "I don't come to you with my problems, do I?"

the LPs:
Led Zeppelin
By Greg Kot

The historically inclined might've recognized the image on the cover of the first Led Zeppelin album. It's a facsimile of a photograph of the *Hindenburg* airship as it caught fire over New Jersey in 1937, a disaster that claimed the lives of thirty-five passengers.

But the grainy black-and-white artwork also looked like something else: an exploding phallus. The point was made: Lock up your daughters! Hide your blues purists! Outrage, bombast, and things blowing up inside!

The forty-five minutes of music was recorded and mixed in a mere thirty hours, and it sounds like it: it is easily the most ragged and manic of Zeppelin albums, and all the more thrilling because of it. *Led Zeppelin* captures a road-tested band in the recording studio for the first time together. Jimmy Page and John Paul Jones both had worked countless sessions in London during the sixties, while John Bonham and Robert Plant were relative country boys in the world of headphones and EQ readings. Together, they forged a sound that made most of their contemporaries sound restrained.

Page—as the band's resident visionary—cast himself as producer, and the sound he heard in his head, and eventually captured on tape, had Bonham's drums at the center. *Led Zeppelin* would be indispensable if only to herald the arrival of one of rock's greatest drummers.

At the outset of the opening track, "Good Times Bad Times," Bonham builds tension with the tick-tick-tick of the high-hat, and taps out a muted, syncopated beat on the cowbell. Then the snare drums crash, but it's the kick-drum that grooves hardest. Bonham dances on the foot pedal and the music swings with anvil force. Godzilla has arrived.

Page rips off the first titan riff in a Zep career full of them: two emphatic notes, then a flurry. His solo is imprecise but adventurous; like a downhill skier going much too fast for the icy conditions, it races on the brink of disaster. Though not as flashy as the Who's John Entwistle, Jones drops a few casually deft bass runs into the mix. He provides breathing room between the mayhem created by Page and Bonham. It wouldn't be the last time Jones would play exactly the right thing at the right moment, a master of subtlety in a band not often celebrated for it.

And then there is Plant. He struts, brags, bitches, and strikes poses that might make a gangsta rapper blush. The lyrics matter not a lick; it's about sound rather than poetry, with Plant proclaiming his innate right to taste, feel, and inhale until he can't stand anymore.

This attitude applies to the band's voracious musical appetite, as well. As if to rebut those who would dismiss them as a ham-fisted metal band, Led Zeppelin turned its debut into a sprawling mission statement, a blueprint for all future Zeppelin albums in the way it recasts Chicago blues, British folk, Eastern ragas, and progressive rock. It even presages punk. Yes, punk.

How else to describe "Communication Breakdown"? Two minutes and twenty-seven seconds of compressed fury, with Page, Jones, and Bonham barreling along on four chords—the missing link between Eddie Cochran's "Nervous Breakdown" and Black Flag's "TV Party." Best moment: Plant's cry of "Suck it!" ushering in (yet another) frayed, frenzied Page solo.

The song is immediately preceded by its polar opposite. Page's delicate Bert Jansch–like finger-picking glides over tabla percussion on the instrumental "Black Mountain Side." The juxtaposition is intentional—Page's way of telling the world his band could do anything.

At this early point in the quartet's history, its songwriting had not caught up to its ambition. Three cover songs are included, and one of the originals, "How Many More Times," references everything from "Beck's Bolero" to Albert King's "The Hunter." But the band's arrangements more than compensate. On Willie Dixon's "You Shook Me," a series of solos (Jones' double-tracked organ and electric piano, Plant's harmonica, Page's guitar) plays out over a slow shuffle. The intensity builds, until a climactic guitar-vocal call-and-response between Page and Plant. Yes, Plant can wail, but Page's spectral guitar is extraordinary. Rather than aping blues-rock tropes, he subverts them with distortion and studio effects. If the intent was to distance himself from England's mob of blues-based guitar slingers, he succeeds completely.

The quartet's interpretation of the folk song "Babe I'm Gonna Leave You" is even more radical. In its back and forth between acoustic contemplation and electric combustion, "Babe" points the way to "Stairway To Heaven" three albums later. Plant takes liberties with the lyric until the story line, such as it is, is barely comprehensible. Suffice it to say, Plant needs to ramble, except when he doesn't. Yet the song still sounds positively stunning, a cinema of young-man blues drama.

"Dazed And Confused" is another triumph in arrangement and production. Jones' bass crawls in and lays down the hoodoo blues with Page's weeping-and-wailing to-and-fro guitar figure. Plant loses his heart to a devil woman and screams like a man being sucked into the bowels of hell. The song's midsection is an extended four-way conversation that just keeps getting creepier and creepier until Bonham leads a prison break on triple-time drums that still sends chills every time I hear it.

If there's a weakness on Led Zeppelin, it's that the band doesn't have much to say (lyrically, at least). "Babe, babe, babe"—and all that implies—is the sum of Plant's concerns. He would prove to be far more incisive on subsequent releases. No, Led Zeppelin glories in sheer sound, the alchemy of four gifted musicians making a noise big enough to melt the *Hindenburg*. This is Page's triumph: the way he records Bonham, the breadth of the material, the sequencing of the tracks. A half-century later, it still swings like the biggest you-know-what in England.

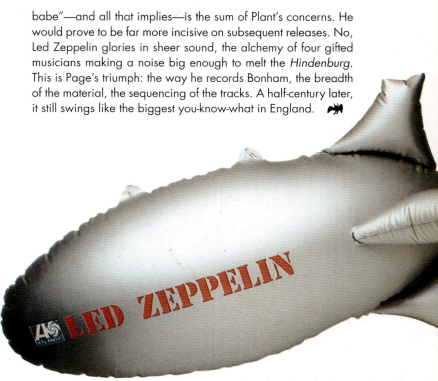

Promotional inflatable zeppelin given to record stores by Atlantic to promote *Led Zeppelin*.

Lord How They Hypnotize

Ann & Nancy Wilson's First Zeppelin Show

By Gene Stout

Ann and Nancy Wilson's first Led Zeppelin concert on May 11, 1969, was an eye-opening, mind-blowing experience.

Driving into Seattle from the suburbs was scary enough for two high school girls who rarely ventured far from home. But nothing prepared them for the British band's raucous afternoon show with Three Dog Night at the Green Lake Aqua Theatre, a 5,600-seat outdoor venue known for its summer Aqua Follies—and not for cultural awakenings.

The two future leaders of Heart were already Zeppelin fans, but they had no idea how titillating a live performance would be.

"They were sexy, out-front men who were talking really openly about sex," Ann recalls. "And it was a scary thing for us because we were very naïve girls. I don't remember much about their singing or playing. My perception was that, 'Wow, this is all about fucking.'

"When we heard 'The Lemon Song,' our eyes got really big." Nancy, several years younger than Ann, couldn't believe what she was seeing "in broad daylight."

"The whole cultural revolution was in full swing at the time and our minds were very open musically. Because everything under the stars was on the radio," she says. "So we were ready for anything—but not Led Zeppelin. They were a whole different breed. They were dangerous. And sexual. They didn't fit into our schoolgirl notions of what sexuality was supposed to be, in the love-and-marriage sort of way.

"We almost thought we were watching something X-rated that we shouldn't be watching. We thought, 'Oh, God, should we really be here?' It was really illicit."

Nancy's memories of the music were just as vivid.

"Page had his violin bow and theremin and everything else going on, and they just extended songs and jammed. And they were sweaty and gorgeous. And they were standing there in front of God and everybody!

"We were shocked and stunned—and changed forever." 🦅

Atlantic Records print advertising for "Good Times, Bad Times" b/w "Communications Breakdown" [*sic*], March 1969.

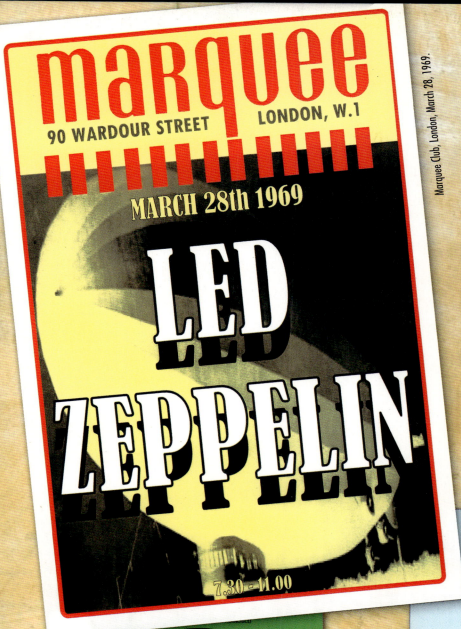

Kinetic Playground, Chicago, IL, May 23–24, 1969.

Fillmore West, San Francisco, CA, April 24 and 27, 1969; Winterland Ballroom, San Francisco, CA, April 25–26, 1969. Artists: Randy Tuten, Peter Pynchon.

Boston Tea Party, Boston, MA, January 23–25, 1969. Artist: Bob Driscoll.

Santa Clara Pop Festival, Santa Clara, CA, May 23, 1969. Manager Peter Grant hired a Lear jet for the day, allowing the band to appear in both Northern California and Chicago. *Artist: Linda Segal.*

"I'd go back to the playback room and listen. It had so much weight, so much power, it was devastating. I had a long way to go with my voice then, but the enthusiasm and sparking of working with Jimmy's guitar . . . it was so raunchy. All these things, bit by bit, started fitting into a trademark for us."

—*Robert Plant,* quoted in Cameron Crowe's "Led Zeppelin: Light And Shade"

"That first album was the first time that headphones meant anything to me. What I heard coming back to me over the cans while I was singing was better than the finest chick in all the land. . . . I had a long ways to go with my voice then, but at the same time the enthusiasm and spark of working with Jimmy's guitar shows through quite well. . . . We were learning what got us off most and what got people off most, and what we knew got more people back to the hotel after the gig."

—*Robert Plant, CREEM, 1974*

Barbarian at the gate, 1969. Robert Plant waits in yet another airport.
Charles Bonnay/Time & Life Pictures/Getty Images

The Rock Pile, Toronto, ON, February 2, 1969.

"'How Many More Times' has the kitchen sink on it, doesn't it? It was made up of little pieces I developed when I was with the Yardbirds, as were other numbers such as 'Dazed And Confused.' It was played live in the studio with cues and nods. . . . I initiated most of the changes and riffs, but if something was derived from the blues, I tried to split the credit between band members. And that was fair, especially if any of the fellows had input on the arrangement. But, of course, you never get any thanks afterwards—and that comment, by the way, is not directed towards John Bonham. . . . I think I did some good things with the [violin] bow on that track, but I really got much better with it later on. For example, I think there is some really serious bow playing on the live album."

—Jimmy Page, Guitar World *magazine, 1993*

On the road. Jimmy Page places his order at a Howard Johnson's hotel restaurant.
Charles Bonnay/Time & Life Pictures/Getty Images

Rose Palace, Pasadena, CA, May 2–3, 1969.

TOUR DATES

9.7.68	Gladsaxe Teen Club, Gladsaxe, Denmark
9.7.68	Brondby Pop Club, Brondby, Denmark
9.8.68	Reventlowparken, Lolland, Denmark
9.8.68	Fjordvilla, Roskilde, Denmark
9.12.68	Stora Scenen, Stockholm, Sweden
9.13.68	Inside Club, Stockholm, Sweden
9.14.68	Angby Park, Knivsta, Sweden
9.15.68	Liseburg Amusement Park, Göteberg, Sweden
9.17.68	Club Bongo, Malmö, Sweden
9.18.68	Göteberg, Sweden
9.20–21.68	Koncerthaus, Stockholm, Sweden
9.22.68	Bergen, Norway
9.23.68	Oslo, Norway
9.24.68	Oslo, Norway
10.4.68	Mayfair Ballroom, Newcastle, England
10.18.68	Marquee Club, London, England
10.19.68	Liverpool University, Liverpool, England
10.25.68	Great Hall, Surrey University, Guildford, England (debut as Led Zeppelin)
10.26.68	Bristol Boxing Club, Bristol, England
11.9.68	Roundhouse, London, England
11.16.68	College of Technology, Manchester, England
11.23.68	Sheffield University, Sheffield, England
11.29.68	Crawdaddy Club, Richmond, England
12.10.68	Marquee Club, London, England
12.13.68	Bridge Place Country Club, Canterbury, England
12.16.68	Bath Pavilion, Bath, England
12.19.68	Civic Hall, Exeter, England
12.20.68	Wood Green Fishmongers Hall, London, England
12.26.68	Denver Auditorium Arena, Denver, CO
12.27.68	Seattle Center Arena, Seattle, WA
12.28.68	Pacific Coliseum, Vancouver, BC
12.29.68	Civic Auditorium, Portland, OR
12.30.68	Gymnasium, Gonzaga University, Spokane, WA
1.2, 4–5.69	Whiskey a Go Go, Los Angeles, CA
1.9–12.69	Fillmore West, San Francisco, CA
1.13.69	Fox Theater, San Diego, CA
1.15.69	Memorial Auditorium, University of Iowa, Iowa City, IA
1.17–19.69	Grande Ballroom, Detroit, MI
1.20.69	Wheaton Youth Center, Wheaton, IL
1.21.69	Hunt Armory, Pittsburgh, PA
1.23–26.69	Boston Tea Party, Boston, MA
1.29.69	Electric Factory, Philadelphia, PA
1.31–2.1.69	Fillmore East, New York, NY
2.2.69	The Rock Pile, Toronto, ON
2.7–8.69	Kinetic Playground, Chicago, IL
2.10.69	Memphis State University, Memphis, TN

2.14–15.69	Thee Image Club, Miami, FL
2.24.69	Lafayette Club, Wolverhampton, England
3.1.69	Van Dike Club, Plymouth, England
3.3.69	Playhouse Theatre, London, England
3.5.69	Top Rank Suite Club, Cardiff, Wales
3.7.69	Bluesville 69 Club/Hornsey Wood Tavern, London, England
3.10.69	Cooks Ferry Inn, London, England
3.13.69	De Montfort Hall, Leicester, England
3.14.69	Konserthuset, Uppsala University, Uppsala, Sweden
3.14.69	Konserthus, Stockholm, Sweden
3.15.69	Teen Club, Gladsaxe, Denmark
3.15.69	Brondby Pop-Club, Brondby, Denmark
3.16.69	Tivolis Koncertsal, Copenhagen, Denmark
3.22.69	Mothers Club, Birmingham, England
3.24.69	Cooks Ferry Inn, London, England
3.28.69	Marquee Club, London, England
3.29.69	Bromley College of Technology, Bromley, England
3.30.69	Farx Club, Southall, England
4.1.69	Klooks Kleek, Hampstead, England
4.2.69	Top Rank Suite Club, Cardiff, Wales
4.5.69	Dagenham Roundhouse, London, England
4.6.69	The Boat Club, Nottingham, England
4.8.69	Bluesville 69 Club/The Cherry Tree, Welwyn Garden City, England
4.9.69	Toby Jug, Tolworth, England
4.13.69	Kimbells, Southsea, England
4.14.69	The Place, Stoke On Trent, England
4.18.69	NYU Jazz Festival, New York, NY
4.24.69	Fillmore West, San Francisco, CA
4.25–26.69	Winterland Ballroom, San Francisco, CA
4.27.69	Fillmore West, San Francisco, CA
5.1.69	UC–Irvine Crawford Hall, Irvine, CA
5.2–3.69	Rose Palace, Pasadena, CA
5.4–5.69	Civic Center, Santa Monica, CA
5.9.69	Edmonton Garden, Edmonton, AB
5.10.69	PNE Agrodome, Vancouver, BC
5.11.69	Green Lake Aqua Theatre, Seattle, WA
5.13.69	Civic Auditorium, Honolulu, HI
5.16.69	Grande Ballroom, Detroit, MI
5.17.69	Convocation Center, Ohio University, Athens, OH
5.18.69	Guthrie Theater, Minneapolis, MN
5.23.69	Kinetic Playground, Chicago, IL
5.23.69	Santa Clara Pop Festival, Santa Clara Fairgrounds, San Jose, CA
5.24.69	Kinetic Playground, Chicago, IL
5.25.69	Merriweather Post Pavilion, Columbia, MD
5.27–29.69	Boston Tea Party, Boston, MA
5.30–31.69	Fillmore East, New York, NY

TOUR DATES

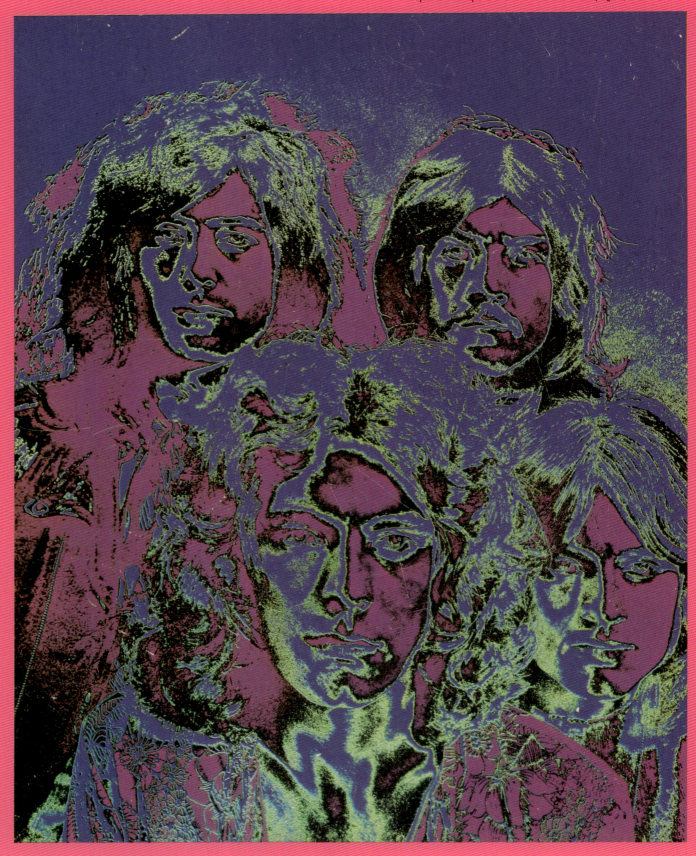

Psychedelic band portrait from the LP-sized hardcover program, U.S. tour, 1969.

Ramblin' On
1969-1970

Summer of '69 was pivotal for Led Zeppelin, especially in England. Because Jimmy Page and company steadfastly refused to release singles to radio, they had to find another way to get their music heard on the BBC, the nation's main radio channel.

"In those days there was a thing called needle time, when the BBC was only allowed to play four or so hours of gramophone records per day," John Paul Jones told Detroit writer Gary Graff in 1997, when Zeppelin's *The BBC Sessions* were officially released on CD. "And so, if you didn't get played on the Top 40 radio, which was two-and-a-half-minute singles—which we didn't do—the only other outlet was to do these shows where we were allowed to expand and play like five-, six-, seven-minute songs. So, yeah, it was quite a big deal, and it was a way to get the music to the audience that couldn't make the gigs, perhaps."

Zeppelin appeared three times in eleven days on the BBC, playing numbers from their debut disc and previewing tunes, including "Whole Lotta Love," from *Led Zeppelin II*. They covered Robert Johnson's "Traveling Riverside Blues," a lyric from which was appropriated later by Robert Plant for *Led Zeppelin II*'s "The Lemon Song." During these radio appearances, the roguish boys behaved themselves. "It was a bit of a strange atmosphere, and we were sort of a young, unruly, enthusiastic cocky band taking over the place. But our behavior was proper, anyway," Jones told Graff. "Page and I were studio musicians before that, so we knew how to behave in a studio. The lunacy came in being on the road later, I suppose. We kind of learned it from other people, to be honest: 'Here's what rock 'n' roll bands did on the road.' I never knew that before. We were perfect gentlemen and professional. You don't go trashing studios—that's ridiculous."

Before you could say "what is and never should be," Zeppelin flew to the States for more and more performances. Over the course of six months, between concerts, the band managed to squeeze in recording sessions in Los Angeles, New

The band poses for a publicity photograph around the time of the release of *Led Zeppelin II*.

Chrysalis

in association with Peter Grant
presents

LED ZEPPELIN

In concert with their friends

LIVERPOOL SCENE
AND
BLODWYN PIG

BIRMINGHAM, Town Hall, Friday, 13th June, at 7.30 p.m.

MANCHESTER, Free Trade Hall, Sunday, 15th June, at 7 p.m.

NEWCASTLE, City Hall, Friday, 20th June, at 7.30 p.m.

BRISTOL, Colston Hall, Saturday, 21st June, at 7.30 p.m.
(BLODWYN PIG NOT APPEARING)

PORTSMOUTH, Guildhall, Thursday, 26th June, at 7.30 p.m.

Handbill, U.K. tour, 1969.

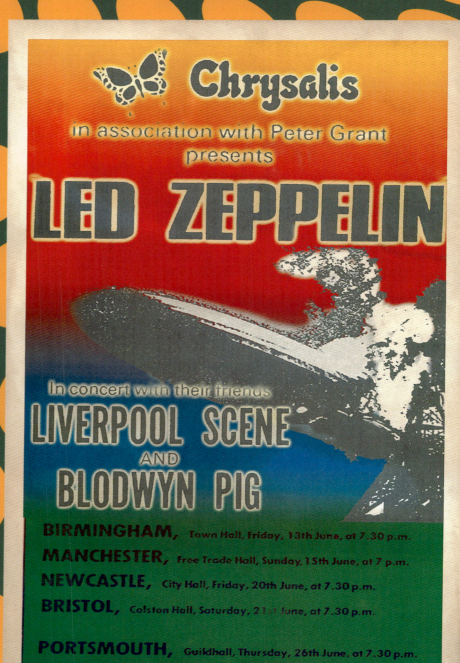

Chrysalis

in association with Peter Grant
presents

LED ZEPPELIN

In concert with their friends

LIVERPOOL SCENE
AND
BLODWYN PIG

BIRMINGHAM, Town Hall, Friday, 13th June, at 7.30 p.m.

MANCHESTER, Free Trade Hall, Sunday, 15th June, at 7 p.m.

NEWCASTLE, City Hall, Friday, 20th June, at 7.30 p.m.

BRISTOL, Colston Hall, Saturday, 21st June, at 7.30 p.m.

PORTSMOUTH, Guildhall, Thursday, 26th June, at 7.30 p.m.

U.K. tour poster, 1969.

LED
ZEPPELIN

Program, U.K. tour, 1969.

York, and London. Most of the songs were written in hotel rooms and dressing rooms, with Plant becoming Page's co-writer.

"I'd never really written a song until Zep got together, so the crafting of lyric and melody was developing all the time," Plant told British journalist Nigel Williamson. "The writing process is quite personal and intimate, but working with Jimmy was very stimulating. He was my senior in every respect, but the melding was good, and by about the eighth song we wrote together, I began to realize that I had something with this guy that was very special. I was no longer just chancing it so I was feeling better and better all the time. *Led Zeppelin II* was very virile. That was the album that was going to dictate whether or not we had the staying power and the capacity to stimulate. It had changed color completely from the first album. It had become much more creative and imaginative."

Released on October 22, 1969, *Led Zeppelin II* debuted at No. 15 in the United States and soon displaced the Beatles' *Abbey Road* at No. 1 on *Billboard's* album chart. The LP was buoyed by an edited version of "Whole Lotta Love" as a single in the United States, where it peaked at No. 4 in December. (Zeppelin steadfastly refused to offer singles in the United Kingdom.) By now, the band had become huge in the States, commanding guarantees of $100,000 per concert. The group was so big that ever-shrewd manager Peter Grant turned down an offer to perform at the soon-to-be legendary Woodstock festival in upstate New York in August 1969 because he didn't want to compete for attention with the likes of the Who, Jimi Hendrix, Jefferson Airplane, and Sly & the Family Stone.

Although Zeppelin was big in the States, it was a slow time for English Zep fans. Between December 1969 and April 1970, the quartet performed 153 concerts in the States compared with a mere twenty-eight in the United Kingdom. On January 9, 1970, the band decided to play a high-profile concert at Royal Albert Hall and film it for a documentary. (The footage, which included Bonham's four-year-old son, Jason, fooling around on the drums, was not released until 2003's *Led Zeppelin DVD* featuring concerts from 1970 to 1979.) Manager Grant kept the band on the road, including a return to Scandinavia. A gig in Copenhagen on February 28 created a problem that had nothing to do with the band's notorious roguish ways

(continued on page 64)

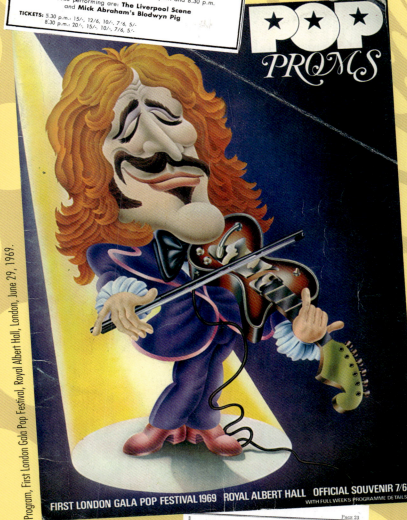

If you live around London
Your only chance to see
THE AMAZING

LED ZEPPELIN
(Jimmy Page, Robert Plant, John Paul Jones
John Bonham)
is at the Royal Albert Hall on
SUNDAY, 29th JUNE, 1969, at 5.30 p.m. and 8.30 p.m.
Also performing are: The Liverpool Scene
and Mick Abraham's Blodwyn Pig
TICKETS: 5.30 p.m.: 15/-, 12/6, 10/-, 7/6, 5/-
8.30 p.m.: 20/-, 15/-, 10/-, 7/6, 5/-.

FIRST LONDON GALA POP FESTIVAL 1969   ROYAL ALBERT HALL   **OFFICIAL SOUVENIR 7/6**
WITH FULL WEEKS PROGRAMME DETAILS

Program, First London Gala Pop Festival, Royal Albert Hall, London, June 29, 1969.

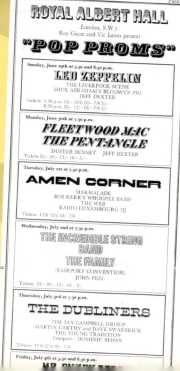

Page 23
ROYAL ALBERT HALL
London, S.W.7.
Roy Guest and Vic Lewis present
"POP PROMS"

Sunday, June 29th at 5.30 and 8.30 p.m.
LED ZEPPELIN
THE LIVERPOOL SCENE
MICK ABRAHAM'S BLODWYN PIG   JEFF DEXTER
Tickets: 5.30 p.m. 15/- 12/6 10/- 7/6 5/-
8.30 p.m. 20/- 15/- 10/- 7/6 5/-

Monday, June 30th at 7.30 p.m.
**FLEETWOOD MAC
THE PENTANGLE**
DUSTER BENNET   JEFF DEXTER
Tickets 25/- 20/- 15/- 10/- 3/-

Tuesday, July 1st at 7.30 p.m.
AMEN CORNER
MARMALADE
BOB KERR'S WHOOPEE BAND
THE WEB
RADIO LUXEMBOURG DJ
Tickets: 17/6 12/6 10/- 7/6

Wednesday, July 2nd at 7.30 p.m.
**THE INCREDIBLE STRING
BAND
THE FAMILY**
(FAIRPORT CONVENTION)
JOHN PEEL
Tickets: 25/- 20/- 15/- 10/- 5/-

Thursday, July 3rd at 7.30 p.m.
THE DUBLINERS
THE IAN CAMPBELL GROUP
MARTIN CARTHY and DAVE SWARBRICK
THE YOUNG TRADITION
Compere — DOMINIC BEHAN
Tickets: 17/6 12/6 10/- 7/6

Friday, July 4th at 5.30 and 8.30 p.m.

"I remember the day in 1969 or 1970, the first time they came through Montreal. My brother John went to see them at the Forum, and I remember the next morning he came down and talked about the show. I totally remember that. I remember his excitement and picking that up off of him. I was probably nine or ten, picking up that vibe from him of going to see a show and being totally blown away, your whole mind just being destroyed by something that was so powerful. I could recognize that something special had happened the night before."

—Michael Timmins, Cowboy Junkies

"Zeppelin was also about the group's many, many followers. For a generation of kids, teenage angst was easily aided by a good set of headphones and a decent copy of *Led Zeppelin II*. Now that generation has their own kids, and the recordings sound even better"

—Cameron Crowe, "Led Zeppelin: Light And Shade"

Bath Festival Of Blues '69

PROGRAMME TWO SHILLINGS

Program, Bath Festival, Shepton Mallet, England, June 28, 1969.

"I discovered, some time during the last few years, that my musical diet was light on carbohydrates, and that the rock riff is nutritionally essential—especially in cars and on book tours, when you need something quick and cheap to get you through a long day. Nirvana, [Radiohead's] *The Bends* and The Chemical Brothers restimulated my appetite, but only Led Zeppelin could satisfy it; in fact, if I ever had to hum a blues-metal riff to a puzzled alien, I'd choose Zeppelin's 'Heartbreaker,' from *Led Zeppelin II*. I'm not sure that me going 'DANG DANG DANG DA-DA-DANG, DA-DA-DA-DA-DA DANG DANG DA-DA-DANG' would enlighten him especially, but I'd feel that I'd done as good a job as the circumstances allowed. Even written down like that (albeit with upper-case assistance), it seems to me that the glorious, imbecilic loudness of the track is conveyed effectively and unambiguously. Read it again. See? It rocks"

—Nick Hornby, Songbook, *2002*

How Soft Your Fields So Green

By Jon Bream

In her 1987 memoir, *I'm With The Band: Confessions Of A Groupie*, über-groupie Pamela Des Barres shared her diary entry from July 31, 1969, written when she was twenty-year-old sexpot Pamela Miller: "Jimmy Page is coming to town today. I don't know whether I want to be with him or not, who knows what diseases I'd get? Such a sweet and lovely precious looking cherub, why is it that he's perverted?"

Miss Pamela, as she was known, was there for the, uh, music, too. "Led Zeppelin live in 1969 was an event unparalleled in musical history," she wrote. "They played longer and harder than any group ever had, totally changing the concept of rock concerts. They flailed around like dervishes, making so much sound that the air was heavy with metal. Two hours after the lights went out, as the band sauntered offstage, the audience was delirious, raving, parched mass, crawling through the rock and roll desert thirsting for an encore. Twenty long minutes later, mighty Zeppelin returned to satiate their famished followers."

Pamela graduated from famished follower to Page's girlfriend, traveling with the band, sitting between Page and Plant as they watched Elvis Presley perform in Las Vegas. She had the honor of being the only woman allowed on Zeppelin's stage because, she details, tour manager Richard Cole would introduce her as Mrs. Page. She wrote about whips in Page's suitcase and quoted him as saying, "Don't worry Miss P., I'll never use those on you, I'll never hurt you like that."

Then there was the time Pamela recounts tripping on mescaline with a sober Page, who was "making sure I was having a good time. He liked to be in control, and didn't take many drugs or drink much alcohol. I think he believed his beauty was too important to tamper with. He was always in the mirror, primping on his splendid image, and putting perfect waves in his long black hair with a little crimping machine. He used Pantene products, and whenever I smelled them, for years afterward, I remembered being buried in his hair." ☥

(continued from page 61)

off stage. A woman named Eva von Zeppelin, who claimed to be a relative of the famous Ferdinand von Zeppelin, had confronted the rockers in October 1969, telling them they could not appropriate her surname without permission. Upon their return to Denmark, she threatened them once again. Realizing that sometimes a word has two meanings, Led Zeppelin gave in, releasing the statement, "We shall call ourselves The Nobs when we go to Copenhagen."

A bigger controversy was brewing over Led Zeppelin's lyrics. Plant had a propensity to purloin phrases from folk and blues songs. The website www.turnmeondeadman.net analyzes Plant's Zeppelin lyrics and compares them to blues and folk songs. Even the singer admitted Zep's debt to the blues to U.S. journalist Cameron Crowe, who wrote the liner notes for 1993's *Led Zeppelin: The Complete Studio Recordings*: "Since I've been playing guitar myself, I've realized more than ever that the whole thing, the whole band really, came straight from the blues. Everything."

In 1985, blues songwriting giant Willie Dixon, who penned hits for Howlin' Wolf and Muddy Waters, sued Led Zeppelin, charging that sections of "Whole Lotta Love" on *Led Zeppelin II* were lifted from his "You Need Love."

On that track, Plant wrote: "You need coolin', baby, I'm not foolin'/I'm gonna send ya back to schoolin'/Way down inside, honey, you need it/I'm gonna give you my love/I'm gonna give you my love."

Compare that to what Dixon wrote: "I ain't foolin' you need schoolin'/Baby you know you need coolin'/Baby, way down inside, woman you need love."

The parties settled out of court and Dixon received subsequent songwriting credit and royalties on *Zeppelin II*.

Bluesman Willie Dixon was a deep Led Zeppelin influence. His "You Need Love" became a basis for "Whole Lotta Love," and later releases of the Zeppelin tune added Dixon's name to the credits.

In a 1993 interview with *Guitar World* magazine, Page discussed relying on other sources for musical inspiration:

"Well, as far as my end of it goes, I always tried to bring something fresh to anything that I used. I always made sure to come up with some variation. In fact, I think in most cases, you would never know what the original source could be. Maybe not in every case—but in most cases. So most of the comparisons rest on the lyrics. And Robert was supposed to change the lyrics, and he didn't always do that—which is what brought on most of the grief. They couldn't get us on the guitar parts of the music, but they nailed us on the lyrics. We did, however, take some liberties, I must say [laughs]. But never mind; we did try to do the right thing, it blew up in our faces. . . . When we were up at Headley Grange recording *Physical Graffiti* [in 1975], Ian Stewart came by and we started to jam. The jam turned into "Boogie With Stu," which was obviously a variation on "Ooh My Head" by the late Ritchie Valens, which itself was actually a variation of Little Richard's "Ooh My Soul." What we tried to do was give Ritchie's mother credit because we heard she never received any royalties from any of her [late] son's hits, and Robert did lean on that lyric a bit. So what happens? They tried to sue us for all of the song! We had to say bugger off. We could not believe it. So anyway, if there is any plagiarism, just blame Robert [laughs].

But seriously, blues men borrowed from each other constantly, and it is the same with jazz. It is even happened to us. As a musician, I am only the product of my influences. The fact that I listened to so many various styles of music has a lot to do with the way I play. Which I think set me apart from so many other guitarists of that time—the fact that I was listening to folk, classical, and Indian music in addition to the blues and rock."

Or as Paul Simon put it one evening on *The Tonight Show* while explaining three famous pieces of music that inspired Simon & Garfunkel's mammoth 1970 hit "Bridge Over Troubled Water": "If you borrow from one source, they call you a plagiarist; but if you borrow from three sources, they call you prolific." ◖

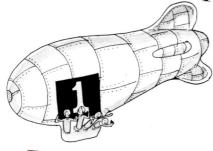

ASCAP ad celebrating "Whole Lotta Love."

"Whole Lotta Love" b/w "Living Loving Maid (She's Just A Woman)," released November 7, 1969.

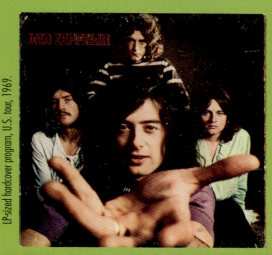

LP-sized hardcover program, U.S. tour, 1969.

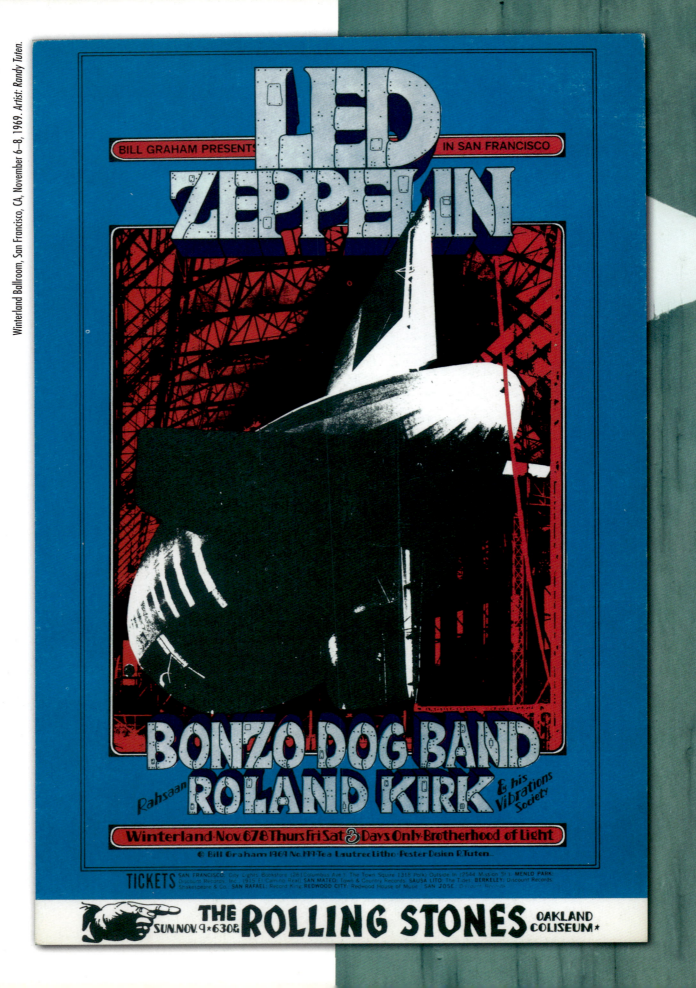

GEORGE WEIN PRESENTS
THE 16TH ANNUAL

NEWPORT JAZZ FESTIVAL

JULY 3 THRU 6, 1969
AT FESTIVAL FIELD
NEWPORT, R.I.

THURSDAY JULY 3 AT 6 P.M.
FOR THE JAZZ AFICIONADO
GEORGE BENSON QUARTET
KENNY BURRELL QUARTET
BILL EVANS/JEREMY STEIG
YOUNG-HOLT UNLIMITED
FREDDIE HUBBARD QUINTET
SUNNY MURRAY QUINTET
ANITA O'DAY
SUN RA SOLAR ARKESTRA
PHIL WOODS AND THE
   EUROPEAN RHYTHM MACHINE

FRIDAY JULY 4 AT 2 P.M.
GIANT JAM SESSION : JIMMY SMITH, HOST
including Art Blakey, Benny Green,
Hampton Hawes, Paul Jefferies, Jo Jones,
Albert Mangelsdorff, Howard McGhee,
Ray Nance, Ake Persson, Slam Stewart,
Sonny Stitt, Buddy Tate,
Jimmy Crawford, and others.

FRIDAY JULY 4 AT 8 P.M.
AN EVENING OF JAZZ-ROCK
JEFF BECK
BLOOD, SWEAT AND TEARS
ROLAND KIRK QUARTET
STEVE MARCUS
TEN YEARS AFTER
JETHRO TULL

SATURDAY JULY 5 AT 2 P.M.
GARY BURTON QUARTET
MILES DAVIS QUINTET
JOHN MAYALL
MOTHERS OF INVENTION
NEWPORT ALL STARS with
   Red Norvo, Tal Farlow, Ruby Braff,
   George Wein, Don Lamond, and
   Larry Ridley

SATURDAY JULY 5 AT 8 P.M.
ART BLAKEY QUINTET
DAVE BRUBECK TRIO
   WITH GERRY MULLIGAN
STEPHANE GRAPELLI
THE SAVAGE ROSE
SLY AND THE FAMILY STONE
O.C. SMITH
WORLD'S GREATEST JAZZ BAND
   With Maxine Sullivan

SUNDAY JULY 6 AT 11 AM
"THE LIGHT IN THE WILDERNESS"
AN ORATORIO BY DAVE BRUBECK
Erich Kunzel, Conductor
Dave Brubeck Trio
Robert Hale, Baritone
David Matthews, Organ
Chorus Pro Musica,
Alfred Nash Patterson, Director

SUNDAY JULY 6 AT 2 P.M.
AN AFTERNOON WITH JAMES BROWN

SUNDAY JULY 6 AT 8 P.M.
SCHLITZ MIXED BAG
WILLIE BOBO SEXTET
HERBIE HANCOCK SEXTET
B.B. KING
BUDDY RICH ORCHESTRA
WINTER
LED ZEPPELIN

The Newport Jazz Festival expresses its appreciation to
Jos. Schlitz Brewing Co. for its generous assistance with
Sunday Evening Concert.

Evening and Sunday Afternoon Tickets
$3.50, $4.50, $5.50, $6.50
Box Seats $10.00
Friday and Saturday Afternoon
Tickets, General Admission $4.00

Do Not Send Cash or Stamps
Mail orders will be filled in order of receipt
Address mail orders to:
Newport Jazz Festival, Newport, R.I. 02840
Tel. (401) 846-5900

FESTIVALS PRODUCED BY FESTIVAL PRODUCTIONS, INC.
MORGAN STATE JAZZ FESTIVAL, June 21, 22, Morgan State College, Baltimore, Md.
HAMPTON JAZZ FESTIVAL, June 26-28, Hampton Institute, Hampton, Va.
MIAMI JAZZ FESTIVAL, June 27-29, Marine Stadium, Miami, Fla.
NEWPORT JAZZ FESTIVAL, July 3-6, Festival Field, Newport, R.I.
LAUREL POP FESTIVAL, July 11, 12, Laurel Race Course, Laurel, Md.
PHILADELPHIA POP FESTIVAL, July 11, 12, Spectrum, Philadelphia, Pa.
LONGHORN JAZZ FESTIVAL, July 18-20, Dallas, Austin, Houston, Texas
NEWPORT FOLK FESTIVAL, July 16-20, Festival Field, Newport, R.I.
RUTGERS JAZZ FESTIVAL, July 26, 27, Rutgers U., New Brunswick, N.J.
LAUREL JAZZ FESTIVAL, Aug. 1-3, Laurel Race Course, Laurel, Md.

The Texas International
POP FESTIVAL

SATURDAY	SUNDAY	MONDAY
August 30	August 31	September 1
Canned Heat	Chicago Transit	Crosby, Stills,
Chicago Transit	Authority	Nash & Young
Authority	James Cotton	Delaney &
James Cotton Blues	Delaney &	Ronnie & Friends
Band	Ronnie & Friends	B.B. King
Janis Joplin	Incredible String	Nass
B.B. King	Band	Sly and the
Herbie Mann	B.B. King	Family Stone
Rotary Connection	Led Zeppelin	Spirit
Sam & Dave	Herbie Mann	Sweetwater
	Sam & Dave	Ten Years After
		Tony Joe White

FREE CAMPING NEARBY
light show by Electric Collage
stage and sound by Harley

LABOR DAY WEEKEND
AUG. 30-31, SEPT. 1

3 BIG DAYS
Daily 4 P.M.

DALLAS INTERNATIONAL MOTOR SPEEDWAY

INTERSTATE 35 E   only 12 miles north of Dallas

The Texas International
POP FESTIVAL

produced by the people that brought you the July Fourth
Atlanta Pop Festival and Showco of Dallas

TICKETS: $6 per day advance, $7 at the gate; advance
booklet $18. Mail orders to "POP TICKETS", P.O. Box
2051, Dallas, Texas 75201. Please enclose certified check
or money order with self-addressed, stamped envelope.

Please send ___
☐ Saturday ☐ Tickets at $ ___ for:
☐ Sunday ☐ Monday
☐ Advance Booklet $18

Name ___
Address ___
City ___ State ___ Zip ___

THE PAVILION
3 ALL NITE
AT FLUSHING MEADOW PARK

An Outdoor Ballroom With Dancing And Food
"PERFECT FOR ROCK, SPACIOUS AND AIRY..."
   Robert Christgau,
   N.Y. Times

FRI-SAT

LED ZEPPELIN
FRI LARRY CORYELL
SAT BUDDY GUY
FRI-SAT RAVEN

DANCE, WALK AROUND, BRING A BLANKET & SIT.
Tickets available in advance at RECORD HUNTER, 5th Ave. & 42 St.
and on the night of the show at the Box Office. (From 5 PM each night)

For information call 699-9202
DIRECTIONS: By car—Grand Central Pkwy. or Van Wyck Expwy. to
Shea Stadium exit. By subway—Flushing IRT to Willets Point (Shea
Stadium) station.

Artist: Frank Bettencourt.

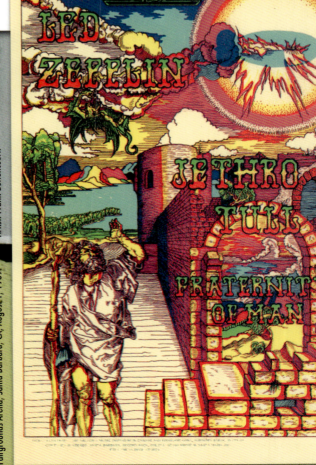

JIM SALZER PRESENTS IN SANTA BARBARA AT THE FAIRGROUNDS ARENA

AUGUST 1

LED ZEPPELIN
JETHRO TULL
FRATERNITY OF MAN

"We played with them once. We were just kind of an up-and-coming band. Terry Knight, our manager, had hooked up with the New York mafia at Premier Talent, Frank Barselona and those guys. They were handling Led Zeppelin, so they said, 'Let's put Grand Funk on with Led Zeppelin and try to move them up.' We were supposed to do ten dates, and the first one was at Olympia [Stadium] in Detroit. We came out and started doing our show and got about halfway through and the audience was going crazy. By the time we got to 'Inside Looking Out,' they were tearing out the bleachers. There was this confrontation going on at the side of the stage between Peter Grant and Terry Knight. Peter wanted us off the stage right now. He's 6-foot-3, 300 pounds, and here's little Terry, 5-foot-10, telling him, 'No, they're not gonna go off the stage.' Supposedly Peter picked Terry up right under the throat, by the shirt collar, staring him right in the face: 'Get that fucking band off the stage right now!' Of course, Terry wasn't gonna do it, so they pulled the plug. They cut the power. Terry went on stage and made some sort of announcement after they got the PA back on that Led Zeppelin didn't want Grand Funk back on—which just infuriated them more. Two nights later we played at the Cleveland Public Hall, and that was the last show we ever did with them, the end of our tour with Led Zeppelin."

—Don Brewer, Grand Funk Railroad

Dusseldorf, Germany, March 11, 1970. *Michael Ochs Archives/Getty Images*

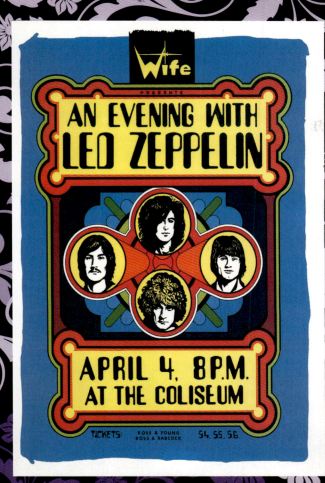

All This Wonder Of Earthly Plunder
by Jon Bream

The legend of Led Zeppelin started with its very first tour of the United States. They were the wildest, horniest, and most debauched band in the history of rock 'n' roll—at least until Mötley Crüe came along.

The classic episode is a fishy tale at the Edgewater Inn in Seattle in May 1969. The Edgewater, which still exists as the Edgewater Hotel—featuring a British suite in which the Beatles stayed—overlooks picturesque Elliott Bay. You could literally fish out the window of your hotel room, and legend has it that Zeppelin caught a sea creature—a British tabloid said it was an octopus, John Paul Jones once said it was a dead shark, and a third version has it as a red snapper—and proceeded to insert the ocean catch into the private orifices of a young woman. Apparently, the dubious deed was captured on film by a member of Vanilla Fudge, who was Zep's supporting act. Although you won't find this footage on YouTube, the infamous incident was immortalized by Frank Zappa and the Mothers in a tune called "The Mud Shark" on the live album, *Fillmore East: June 1971*.

Then there was the Zep concert in Toronto at which Robert Plant introduced his bandmate by saying, "On lead guitar—and as many chicks as he can find—Jimmy Page." Of course, the raunchiness wasn't limited to Page. Drummer John Bonham took part in his fair share of bacchanalia, such as the time he drove his motorcycle around the lobby of Hollywood's Hyatt House (a.k.a. the Riot House) or ran on stage during the Jeff Beck Group's set at the Flushing Meadows Festival in New York and took off all his clothes.

Ellen Sander, who was covering rock music for *Life* magazine, traveled with Zeppelin in 1969 to do a cover story on the burgeoning band, but on her final night on the road two band members "attacked me, shrieking and grabbing at my clothes, totally over the edge. I fought them off until Peter Grant rescued me but not before they managed to tear my dress down the back." To the dismay of the band, she and her editors canceled the story, but she finally reported on the rowdiness in her 1973 book, *Trips: Rock Life In The Sixties*.

Zeppelin's raunchy reputation became so notorious that, as journalist-turned-filmmaker Cameron Crowe tells the story, when Grant introduced himself to Bob Dylan at a Los Angeles party as "Peter Grant, manager of Led Zeppelin," Dylan responded, "I don't come to you with my problems, do I?" Commented Crowe, who witnessed the exchange: "It was the only time I'd ever seen Grant at a loss for words." 🦅

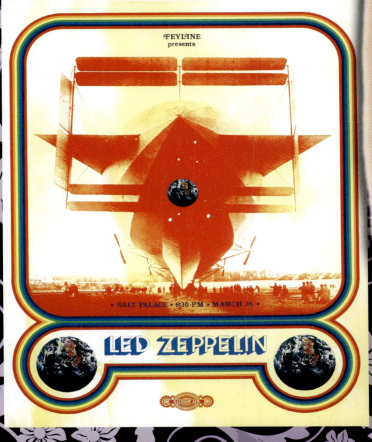

Salt Palace, Salt Lake City, UT, March 26, 1970. *Artist: Kenvin Lyman.*

Arizona Coliseum, Phoenix, AZ, April 18, 1970. *Artist: Kenvin Lyman.*

"Jimmy's a wonderful player. He's very tasty with his style and heavy-rock licks. I had the pleasure of meeting Jimmy way back in the '60s: I was in the studio working an awful lot, with about five different artists a week, and Jimmy called me when he got out to California and said, 'Hey, man, I want to come hang out with you.' I said, 'Great, man, I'd love it.' We had a chance to hang out in the studio for about a week. I tried to get him to record with us in the studio but he said, 'No, no, no.' He just wanted to listen to me. We had a great time, and he told me how much he admired the records I played on back in the Ricky Nelson days, the Elvis stuff, and even the Merle Haggard country things. We sat around with acoustic guitars and just played whenever we could fit a jam in between recording sessions.."

—*James Burton*

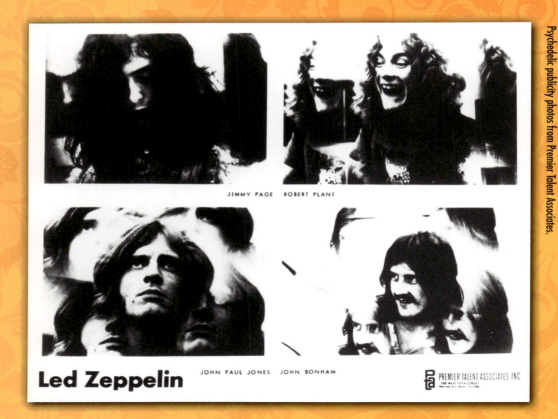

Psychedelic publicity photos from Premier Talent Associates.

A TASTE OF DECADENCE

By Richard Cole with Richard Trubo

Richard Cole was Led Zeppelin's tour manager for twelve years—and as responsible for many of the antics and misadventures as the bandmembers. This is an excerpt from his history-cum-memoir, **Stairway To Heaven: Led Zeppelin Uncensored.**

By the second American tour, we always had plenty of girls hanging around the stage doors and the hotels. Plant and Page seemed to be their main interests, but many of the young ladies weren't particular. While the band began to rely on me to arrange whatever late-night entertainment they desired, the girls made it easy.

Even by this early period in Zeppelin's history, I could already see recreational patterns developing that would persist throughout the band's lifetime. There were the girls, of course, whom we began to party with, sometimes to excess. And there were endless bottles of alcohol, too. Both, of course, were welcome diversions from the stresses of traveling and the record-company pressures that hit us hard during that second U.S. tour. But we soon began to overdo it. The alcohol and later the drugs, too, eventually caught up with the band and began taking their toll. And as early as 1969, there were already signs of an eventual downhill slide.

When it came to girls, Jimmy would say, "The younger, the better." More than the others, Jimmy seemed to lust after the girls whose faces were childlike and innocent and whose bodies had barely taken shape. But he wasn't the only one who enjoyed the young ones. Maybe it was a sign of our immaturity, but after all, we were only twenty or twenty-one ourselves, so a fourteen- or fifteen-year-old wasn't total madness—or at least it didn't seem so at the time. And as for the married members of the band, most were able to at least temporarily overlook the fact that they had wives waiting for them back in England; if there were ever any guilt pangs, I never saw them.

"My dream," Jimmy once told me, "is to find a young, Joni Mitchell lookalike . . . thin, angular features, long blond hair, a voice that could sing you to sleep."

I kept my eyes open, but never really filled the prescription to his satisfaction. In fact, I don't think he ever would have been content with anyone but the real thing.

"Richard, I'll tell you what I fantasize about," Jimmy said. "I'd like to have Joni Mitchell sitting on the end of my bed, playing the guitar and singing for me." He didn't elaborate on the fantasy any further, but I presumed that he would have liked a little more from Joni than guitar strumming.

I would often saunter down to the hotel lobbies where the young ladies would congregate and invite some of them up to our rooms. Even though Led Zeppelin and dozens of other rock bands were often accused of exploiting these girls, I thought it was a bum rap. We rarely went looking for them; they made themselves available to us. We never forced them into doing anything they didn't want to. They were looking for some fun—and so were we. There was no emotional involvement on either side. As a blonde in Boston told me, "I just want a good time. If any of you guys want to have some fun, I'm available." She was wearing her high school cheerleader outfit.

Some of the girls were hangers-on from the Yardbirds' days. They had been fans of Jimmy's and hadn't broken their addiction to him. They also appeared to have created their own groupie hierarchy, determined to stay on the first team rather than slip down to benchwarmers. A few became madly jealous if they sensed a decline in attention from Jimmy. And their exchanges with each other often got bitter ("Jimmy always treated me like a lady, which is more than I can say for you!"). Occasionally, their hostile words would deteriorate into hair-pulling, eye-gouging free-for-alls.

The girls and the booze usually went together. But sometimes the liquor was enough. In a few cities in those days, we did two shows a night, usually at 10 P.M. and midnight, and during the hour break between the two performances, we'd uncork some champagne, sometimes several bottles of it. "The booze helps calm my nerves," Bonzo would tell me. "I just feel better when I've had a drink or two." In actuality, he would have ten to twelve drinks.

One night in Kansas City, after the second show at a club just south of the Missouri River, I drove the band back to our hotel, the Muehlbach, one of the finest old inns in the city. We went into the hotel bar, and after a few more drinks—Scotch, champagne, gin and tonic—John Paul, Robert, and Jimmy took the elevator to their rooms. Bonzo and I decided there was still more drinking to do. So we kept the bartender company.

Eventually, we became so intoxicated that I doubted we would ever find our way to our rooms. But we tried, weaving through the hotel lobby like a couple of drunks—which we were becoming. Bonzo couldn't stay on his feet any longer and collapsed into an oversized chair and refused to budge.

"Go up without me, Cole," he said, his speech slurring one word after another. "I'll be fine here. I'll be just fine."

I wasn't in any shape to argue. I just wanted to get some sleep. Once inside my room, I took a couple of Mandrax to help me doze off and crawled into bed, expecting to snooze peacefully until morning. But Bonzo had other plans. At about 3 A.M., the phone in my room jarred me awake.

"Richard!"

"Who is this?" I mumbled.

"Hey, Richard. You gotta get me outta here!"

I recognized Bonzo's voice, but was still trying to orient myself. "It's me, Richard. Come down and get me."

"Where are you, you cunt?"

"Where do you think? I'm in jail, that's where I am. Come and bail me out."

Bonham then apparently handed the phone to a cop, who proceeded to explain that Bonzo had been taken to jail for being drunk in a public place—namely, the Muehlbach lobby. He gave me the address of the jail, which was about two miles down the road.

I was furious, but my anger was related more to being awakened than to a concern over Bonham's well-being. Cursing under my breath, I got dressed and stuffed $5,000 in cash into my pocket. Ten minutes later, I was in the police station.

"I'm here to get John Bonham," I told the sergeant at the desk. "I'm his manager." I figured calling myself his manager sounded more impressive than tour manager. "What's it going to cost to bail him out?"

"Cost!" The sergeant snickered. "That son of a bitch isn't going anywhere. He's gonna sleep it off. Come and pick him up in the morning when he's sober."

So at nine the following morning, I returned. Bonham had a sheepish look on his face as they led him to the waiting area of the police station. His face was bruised with one contusion below his left eye and another on the cheek next to it.

"I think the cops roughed me up a little," he whispered. "I really don't remember."

None of us learned much from experiences like that. There were many more drinking episodes during that tour. Particularly when Peter wasn't with us, I was the only one to try to keep Zeppelin in line. And I was usually just as possessed with alcohol—if not more so—than the rest of the band.

In May [1969]—not long before Bonham's twenty-first birthday—Zeppelin performed two shows at the Rose Palace in Pasadena. Barry Imhoff, the promoter of the event, knew what our life-style was becoming by then. So he chose a birthday gift that John couldn't have appreciated any more—a four-foot-tall bottle of champagne!

Between the first and second shows that night, Bonzo single-handedly guzzled nearly a third of the bottle. When it was time for him to maneuver back into the drummer's stool for the second show, he dragged the oversized bottle onto the stage with him. For a sober observer, it was probably a sad sight: There, like a weightlifter pressing a barbell, he raised the bottle over his head between songs and flooded his mouth and throat with alcohol. He was so drunk that he fell off his stool twice. By the time the performance ended, the bottle was empty.

Imhoff still had one more gift for us: Four live octopuses. "What are we supposed to do with octopuses?" I asked.

"They make great bathtub companions," he claimed. "They're much more fun than a rubber duck."

Back at the hotel, we had invited a couple of girls up to our rooms, and I figured they might be able to make better use of the octopuses than I could. "You girls look like you need a little cleaning up," I told them. "Take off your clothes and climb into the bathtub." They agreed, and after they had jumped into the tub, Jimmy

and I carried in the octopuses and tossed them into the water. "We figure you need something to keep you company," Jimmy giggled.

The girls remained remarkably calm, considering there were these creatures swimming around them. As we watched them play, the octopuses somehow instinctively knew just where to congregate and just where to place their tentacles. One of the girls, a little brunette who Jimmy couldn't take his eyes off, gasped and then sighed as one of the octopuses explored her genitals.

"Oh, my God," she squealed. "I've gotta get one of these. It's like having an eight-armed vibrator!"

"Maybe we oughta market these things," I told Jimmy. "It would probably have even more universal appeal than music."

We were in the Los Angeles area for almost a week, and at the Chateau Marmont we ran room service ragged with our appetite for booze. "Los Angeles is something special," Bonzo used to say. "It's different. It's decadent."

Back in England, Zeppelin lived quite normal lives with storybook-like families or girlfriends. But the road—particularly Los Angeles—was becoming a place of excess. Of course, we probably spent many more hours in the States sitting in airports, watching television or talking about music. There were many hours spent in recording studios and even more time onstage. But it's some of the wild, reckless episodes that still stick most vividly in my mind. Seemingly overnight, we found ourselves in a position to do almost anything we wanted, and in L.A. there seemed to be a tidal wave of free-spirited girls who were always cooperative and compliant. For a group of working-class boys from London, it was like finding the Promised Land.

I was in John Bonham's bungalow at the Marmont late one night, and each of us had a girl in tow. Although we certainly weren't Casanovas, we still could have added several notches to the Marmont's cluttered bedposts. By this point, we had devoured a few bottles of booze, and Bonzo and I were each occupying one of the beds in the room, with our clothes in a single pile on the floor.

While I was intertwined pretzel-like with my girl—a bird from Santa Monica named Robin—Bonzo decided to walk into the kitchen to catch his breath and grab a drink of water. While there, he spotted two large industrial-sized cans of baked beans. The chef in him apparently took over.

Bonzo opened the cans, and then, while cradling one in each arm, he pranced into the bedroom.

"Dinnertime!" he announced. "Come and get it!"

As Robin and I looked up in horror, Bonham stood over us, held the cans over our heads, and then tilted them simultaneously on their sides, pouring their cold contents onto our naked bodies.

"You fucker," I screamed, rolling to the opposite end of the bed in a futile attempt to escape the line of fire.

Within seconds, Robin and I were swimming in a gooey, sloppy puddle of beans that covered us from our eyebrows to our ankles. It was a scene out of *Tom Jones*.

Before Robin and I could come up for air, Peter Grant had walked into the bungalow and surveyed the scene. On occasion,

Peter would show anger or disgust over incidents like this. But not that night.

"Peter," yelled Bonzo, "grab a spoon and dig in!" Peter chuckled and then was overcome with a mischievous urge of his own. "Cole, you fucking slob, don't you have any class?" he roared. "Let me add a little sophistication to your life."

Peter grabbed a full bottle of champagne on the nearby dresser, shook and then uncorked it, and proceeded to spray Robin and me with its contents.

Bonham would become almost teary-eyed when we finally had to check out of the Marmont. On our last night there, he had been drinking pretty heavily and decided that he wanted to play doctor. He borrowed a white coat and a room service cart from a hotel valet and lifted a girl named Candy onto the cart. Candy was a pretty, blond teenager from Miami who we had met during the first tour. She showed up unannounced at the Marmont, salivating for some Zeppelin high jinks. We didn't disappoint her.

Bonham undressed her on the cart, cackling as he removed each piece of clothing. Once she was nude, he proclaimed, "It's time for some surgery, my dear."

He scampered into the bathroom and returned with a shaving brush, shaving cream, and razor. "This won't hurt a bit, sweetheart," he told Candy, who lay there submissively as he applied shaving cream to her pubic hair.

For the next ten minutes, the band and I took turns shaving her vagina: Robert with vitality and broad strokes . . . Jimmy with the passion of Rodin or Michelangelo. All the while, Candy giggled her way through the procedure.

When it was over, as we admired our artistic efforts, Robert suddenly interrupted the festivities with a shrill, agonizing wail. "Oh, fuck!" he screamed. "Bonham, how could you? How could you?"

Robert picked up the shaving brush and waved it in the air. "This is mine. This is my fucking brush."

Everyone in the room burst into laughter. John Paul patted Robert on the back. "Enjoy your next shave," he said.

Not all the girls we ran into during that second tour were as pretty as Candy. And, of course, we were in a position to be quite selective. For the unattractive birds—the ones who were painfully hard on the eyes—well, as Bonham said, "If you let any of those dogs up to the room, you're fired!"

The Plaster Casters were some of the most persistent girls, stubbornly overstaying their invitation despite our repeated pleas that they simply vanish. They were determined to make casts of the band members' erect penises, perhaps someday displaying them in the Rock and Roll Hall of Fame. One day at the Marmont, Cynthia P. Caster explained to us how they created the casts that had made them so famous. "First we get the musician excited, any way we can," she said. "Then my assistant does the actual casting while I keep the hard-on going. She's quite talented. You guys should try it. This is really an art form."

Maybe so. But Robert once joked, "There's no way I could keep my dick hard around those fat chicks."

I had known the Plaster Casters from my days with the Yardbirds. And they were still as hefty and as homely as ever. I think that Zeppelin would have chosen celibacy if the Casters were the only alternative. I know I would have.

One afternoon at the Marmont, we were sunning ourselves by the pool. The Casters were there, too, and they really began to torment us. They wanted to make some plaster casts; we wouldn't even entertain the idea. They wanted to make small talk; we wanted them to shut up.

Finally, Bonzo had had enough. "The only way you bitches are going to clam up is to fill your mouths with water!"

He got up from his chaise lounge, walked toward Cynthia, and pushed her toward the edge of the pool. When she was just a step away, he shoved her with the full force of his body. Cynthia became airborne and plunged into the water with the force of a pregnant whale. The resulting tsunami drenched half of the surrounding patio.

Instead of sinking to the bottom of the pool like dead weight, however, Cynthia's multiple layers of clothing—including a black velvet dress with obnoxiously gaudy frills—came to her rescue. The air trapped within her clothes kept her bobbing at the surface, providing enough support so she was able to keep her head above water, although not without a struggle and a lot of splashing.

"Get me out of here, you assholes," she gurgled, barely loud enough to be heard over our laughter.

I leaped into the pool and towed her to the ladder, where she made a rather unladylike exit from the water.

Despite such zaniness, we never lost sight of why we were really in America. "We're here to make music—that's number one," Bonzo would proclaim, often half drunk. Alcohol continued to cause some embarrassing situations, at one time or another affecting every member of the band.

Because of booze, we often became a nightmare to be with on an airplane, particularly when the crew made no efforts to limit the alcohol they served us. During that second tour [1969], on a commercial flight from Athens, Ohio, to Minneapolis, Robert had devoured a few drinks and was feeling much too giddy for the confining quarters of an airplane. So he got up from his seat and began prancing up and down the aisle, looking like a cross between the Pied Piper and a Spanish matador. He was letting loose, allowing himself some temporary liberation from the demands of our touring schedule. He peered in one direction, then another, fluttered his arms and began singing an uncommon refrain:

"Toilets! Toilets! Toilets for Robert!"

He was so loud that the entire planeload of seventy passengers could hear him, and they stared dumbfounded at this bizarre man bounding through the plane like a raving lunatic.

"Where are the toilets? Robert needs a toilet! Toilets!"

Many of the passengers were noticeably disturbed, wondering just what might happen next. I wondered, too, but was more

"You wanna know whether I ever did any of those weird and wonderful things?

interested in waiting for my next drink than in helping Robert to the bathroom. Fortunately, a flight attendant took Robert by the hand and led him toward the bathroom. After he banged on the door and finally barged his way in, his "concert" came to an abrupt end.

At one point during the tour, as incidents like that began to multiply, I recognized that perhaps we all needed some R&R. I suggested that we unwind for a few days in Honolulu, where we already had a show scheduled. The vote in favor was unanimous.

There were two elegant mansions on Diamond Head, with breathtaking views of the Pacific and Waikiki Beach, that many rock bands rented from time to time. Peter was able to get us into one of them, a multimillion-dollar Spanish villa that might have made William Randolph Hearst jealous. During our four days there, we got burned to a crisp in the tropical sun and were treated to sailing expeditions and a luau. I remember relaxing on the beach, listening to Bob Dylan's "Lay Lady Lay," which had just climbed to the top of the charts. Perhaps inspired by Dylan, we spent part of our Hawaiian visit leied with flowers and laid with female bodies.

In a sense, we found ourselves in a no-win situation. When our schedule kept us running nonstop, we yearned for a halt in the action, but during that Hawaiian stay, when there was finally time to relax, we soon found ourselves bored out of our minds. "It's hard to figure," Bonzo observed one day, popping the cap on a bottle of beer. "Either we're running so fast that we're ready to collapse, or we have so little to do that we're going crazy."

Even so, no one was better at creating something to do than Bonzo—and there was no better target for his practical jokes than Plant. Bonham played an occasional prank on John Paul, like the time he flooded Jonesy's room in Hawaii by sneaking a garden hose through the sliding glass door. But John Paul was so easygoing that even when he awoke to find his room turned into a wading pool, he just took it in stride. Those kinds of low-key responses made him a much less attractive guinea pig for the tomfoolery that the rest of us savored. It was much more fun to harass someone like Robert, who would often have hysterical reactions to the pranks aimed in his direction.

From Hawaii, we flew into Detroit for a performance at the Grande Ballroom, a former mattress-manufacturing plant that had been transformed into the city's premiere rock club. Our plane landed in the predawn hours, and it was barely daybreak when we checked into the Congress Hotel on the morning of the concert. We had flown through the night and had been drinking heavily while in the air. We were dead tired, irritable, and just wanted to check into our rooms and get some sleep.

But as we dragged ourselves and our luggage through the hotel lobby, something else besides the need for sleep captured our attention. "There's blood all over the fuckin' carpet," John Paul exclaimed, tiptoeing his way around the still damp patches of blood.

"Ahh, come on, Jonesy," I said. "America's a tough place, but don't be ridiculous."

Then I took a closer look. He wasn't being ridiculous at all.

Less than half an hour before we arrived, there had been an attempted robbery at the hotel. The bellhop had confronted the robber with a loaded pistol, and the lobby had turned into something resembling the showdown in *High Noon*.

"That motherfucker tried to come in and rob us," the bellhop told us, his voice still quivering and his hand still trembling. "I shot the bastard, and he died right here at my feet. They just took the body away."

Robert looked down at the carpet—we swore we could see some steam rising from the fresh bloodstains. "I think I'm going to throw up," Robert moaned. "I really do."

"Get hold of yourself, Robert," I said. "These things happen."

Then Robert exploded. "Jesus Christ, why are we staying in this hotel anyway, Richard? We're working like maniacs, and you put us in a hotel that's like a battlefield."

"Do you think everything that happens is my fault?" I shouted. "I didn't shoot the bastard!"

"Sometimes I wonder!" he muttered.

That night at the Grande Ballroom, things didn't improve much. As the band performed, they had to cope with blown fuses and power outages. Each time they had to stop playing—once right in the middle of "I Can't Quit You Baby," then just as they were launching into "Black Mountain Side"—the overflow crowd grew progressively agitated. Before long, rowdiness bordered on mutiny. Perhaps only the mellowing aroma of marijuana, wafting through the hall and settling upon the audience, kept them from rioting.

"What a fucked-up night!" Bonzo complained as we drove back to the hotel after the performance. "Tell Detroit we're not coming back."

I wondered for the first time whether this chaos was worth it. 🦅

"Watching a big color TV exploding on pavement from a great height was a favorite Zeppelin pastime. The previous year [1972] at an old battle-ground, the Edgewater Inn in Seattle, Led Zeppelin had thrown all their televisions into the sea below. As Peter Grant was paying the bill, the hotel manager wistfully remarked that he had always wanted to chuck a TV out the window himself. 'Have one on us,' roared Grant, and peeled off another $500 bill. The manager went right upstairs and heaved a big Motorola off the balcony."

—Stephen Davis, *Hammer Of The Gods*

Well, I might have done, but I can't remember it." —*Robert Plant, interviewed on MTV*

the LPs:
Led Zeppelin II
By Barry Cleveland

Hearing "Whole Lotta Love" on the radio as a thirteen-year-old was a revelation. I'd begun playing guitar the previous year, and having already extracted every measure of six-string bliss from the grooves of *Led Zeppelin* during the previous nine months, I waited eagerly beside my radio for the new song to rotate back around, each time hoping to get yet another listen to the heavy riffing, the seductive guitar solo, and most of all, the nearly unfathomable freeform middle section. I was living on an island in Florida at the time, and the day that *Led Zeppelin II* finally arrived at the mainland music store I braved the lengthy bus trip there and back, impatiently clutching and examining the LP on the ride home. I can't recall how many hours I spent trying to cop Jimmy Page's licks and tones throughout the following days and weeks—but I do know that by the time I saw Page perform "Whole Lotta Love" as the first encore of Zeppelin's live set a few months later, I had already sworn an irrevocable oath of fealty to the electric guitar.

Of course, I was hardly alone in my adoration. Advance orders of *Led Zeppelin II* had exceeded a half-million units in the United States alone by the time it was released on October 22, 1969. The album quickly went to No. 1 on both sides of the Atlantic, remaining on the U.S. charts for twenty-nine weeks and on the U.K. charts for 138 weeks. To date, *Led Zeppelin II* has sold well in excess of 12 million copies.

The cover of Led Zeppelin's debut featured a photograph of the *Hindenburg* exploding, and another historic photo graces the cover of *Led Zeppelin II*. Graphic designer David Juniper took a World War I–era photo of German Jasta Division pilots that included the notorious Red Baron, sepia-toned it brown, then replaced the pilots' heads with those of the bandmembers, manager Peter Grant, tour manager Richard Cole, actress Glynis Johns (spoofing Glyn Johns, who engineered *Led Zeppelin*), and bluesman Blind Willie Johnson. Beards and sunglasses were added to two others, and the Baron removed entirely. (Note: Juniper mentions nothing of Grant or Cole in his account, includes Neil Armstrong, and says the woman was a girlfriend or muse of Andy Warhol's.) The colorful album title and billowing clouds were airbrushed in behind the photo, and the entire thing was placed on a brown background with white space left to suggest the silhouette of a Zeppelin. The gatefold inner sleeve presents a giant gold Zeppelin mounted on a gleaming temple-like structure inspired by a documentary film about German architecture in the 1920s.

Unlike the band's debut album, which Page has said was recorded and mixed in thirty hours, *Led Zeppelin II* took eight months to complete, as it was recorded piecemeal in studios located in England, the United States, and Canada, whenever Page & Company could break away from their nearly nonstop touring. In some cases that meant cobbling songs together, such as sandwiching the drum solo on "Moby Dick" between the previously recorded intro and outro sections, and grafting the unaccompanied guitar solo section on "Whole Lotta Love" onto tracks that were recorded at a different studio.

The second album was also a landmark in terms of Page's guitar sound. He had deployed a '58 Fender Telecaster (given to him by Jeff Beck) and a heavily modified Supro 1690T Coronado amplifier on the first album. But by the time he began recording *Led Zeppelin II*, Page had acquired his trademark '58 Gibson Les Paul Standard and a Marshall SLP-1969 Super Lead amp, a pairing that he used to craft tones that would define his sound for the next decade and be emulated by generations of guitarists. Additional tonal colors were created using a Sola Sound Tone Bender fuzzbox modified by Roger Mayer and a Vox Cry Baby wah-wah pedal.

One thing that didn't change significantly from the first album to the second, however, was the basic formula of the band's music. Although the songs were somewhat rawer and heavier than those on the debut, they were still derived primarily from the same sources: the early rock 'n' roll and blues tunes that Page and Plant were intimately familiar with and routinely performed in concert. Led Zeppelin has taken a lot of heat—both critical and legal—for plagiarizing other artists, and some of the most egregious examples occur on *Led Zeppelin II*, "Whole Lotta Love" not only appropriated what amounts to entire verses from Willie Dixon's "You Need Love" and bits from various other sources, it actually mimicked the vocal arrangement from the Small Faces' "You Need Loving"—ironically itself a take on the same Dixon song. Similarly, "Bring It On Home" is a blatant rip-off of Dixon's song of the same name as performed by Sonny Boy Williamson, and "The Lemon Song" is a thinly veiled reworking of Howlin' Wolf's "Killing Floor," with the "squeeze my lemon" bits lifted from Robert Johnson's "Traveling Riverside Blues." Bits of poached lyrics from numerous other sources

appear throughout the album, but the above examples are the most significant infractions.

That's not to say that the music is entirely derivative. For example, while it has been suggested that Page appropriated the riff for "Whole Lotta Love" from Muddy Waters' version of "You Need Love" along with the lyrics, if so he must have been listening really closely to hear it flash by. Little three-note figures played in roughly the same rhythm occur here and there, but none of them come close to the epic riff that forms the backbone of the Zeppelin song. And the same goes for most of Page's other riffs. While in some cases they are obviously derived from previous works—for example, the "Moby Dick" riff is rooted in Bobby Parker's "Watch Your Step"—Page endows them with a vibe that is unmistakably his own (not to mention that reworking old riffs into "new" songs is an essential aspect of the evolution of blues). Additionally, songs such as "What Is And What Should Never Be" and "Thank You" are essentially original creations.

Listening to *Led Zeppelin II* today, I'm still struck by the power and creative mojo captured within its grooves—or, in the case of the CD, its pits. From the immortal riffs and fiery solos on "Whole Lotta Love" and "Heartbreaker," to the gorgeous sustained tones and layered lap-steel and acoustic parts on "Ramble On," to the triple-tracked electric harmonies on "The Lemon Song," the so-called Brown Bomber offers a cornucopia of guitar delights in addition to being a brilliant recording and a damn fine collection of rock songs. ✈

Announcement for Led Zeppelin II.

Eddie Kramer and *Led Zeppelin II*
by Barry Cleveland

Eddie Kramer's name is inextricably linked to many 1960s and '70s classic rock albums. The South African-born engineer and producer began recording bands while a teen, and got his first gig at a major studio in 1964. From there he rolled tape for everyone from the Beatles to Blue Cheer, engineering landmark recordings for the Rolling Stones, Traffic, John Mayall, Small Faces, and other luminaries, as well as capturing Curtis Mayfield, Humble Pie, Peter Frampton, KISS, and the entire Woodstock festival live. Kramer's crowning accomplishment, however, was his extraordinary work with Jimi Hendrix—work that didn't go unnoticed by one James Patrick Page.

Page's professional relationship with Kramer spanned three studio and two live Led Zeppelin albums, beginning with *Led Zeppelin II*. Kramer continued to work on *Houses Of The Holy* and *Physical Graffiti* as well as *The Song Remains The Same* and *How The West Was Won*.

Unlike the band's debut album, which Page has said was recorded and mixed in some thirty hours, *Led Zeppelin II* took eight months to complete, as it was recorded piecemeal in studios located in London (Olympic and Morgan), Los Angeles (A&M, Quantum, Sunset, Mirror Sound, and Mystic), Memphis (Ardent), New York (A&R, Juggy Sound, Groove, and Mayfair), and Vancouver (a "hut"), whenever Page and the other bandmembers could schedule brief getaways from their incessant touring.

That approach to recording meant that the rhythm tracks might be recorded in one studio, guitar overdubs in another, and vocals in yet another. What is more, sometimes only sections of a song would be completed in a single location, requiring that they be edited together later. Examples include inserting Page's unaccompanied guitar solo on "Whole Lotta Love" into pre-existing tracks and patching together sections

of "Moby Dick"—one of several songs that reveal less-than-perfect splices upon careful listening. Kramer is credited with recording three cuts—"Heartbreaker," "Ramble On," and "Bring It On Home"—though he almost certainly also recorded at least parts of other songs.

Once the tracks were recorded, however, Page and Kramer took the master tapes to A&R Studio in New York City, where they mixed the album in a mere two days. They used a Scully 280 one-inch eight-track machine and a custom-built mixing console with a dozen or fewer channels and only two pan pots. They put those pan pots to good use, though, both in terms of dramatically moving instruments and vocals from one side of the stereo field to the other—such as during the middle section of "Whole Lotta Love" and toward the end of "What Is And What Should Never Be"—and also for creating more subtle stereo effects using reverb and delay.

When discussing the effects used on *Led Zeppelin II*, it is important to note that while the studio was equipped with Pultec equalizers, Teletronix limiters, and other now-legendary gear, there were no "effects processors" in the modern sense. Reverb effects were generated via three giant EMT 140 plates located in the stairwells, and delay effects were achieved using a three-head reel-to-reel tape recorder (the delay results from the time it takes the tape physically to travel between the record head and the playback head). Page may also have used an Echoplex tape-delay while recording, but the device was not employed as an "outboard" processor while mixing the album.

Kramer has said that Page was very much in charge at all times and had quite specific ideas about every aspect of production—but Page also had his reasons for enlisting Kramer, not least of all the engineer's reputation for innovative thinking. The most frequently recounted example of this creative symbiosis is the story of how the ghost-like vocal lines that appear four minutes into "Whole Lotta Love" came to be. Although details vary in different accounts, the gist is that a guide vocal recorded on one of the eight tracks was bleeding into the mix due to a faulty fader or other problem; Kramer and Page decided to add reverb to it, transforming a liability into a special effect. (That you can clearly hear the ghost vocal itself repeating—"Way down inside . . . way down inside . . . you need . . . you need," etc., suggesting that it was actually processed with a long delay, is never accounted for by either Page or Kramer.)

Another example of creative treatments include the warbling vocal sound on the choruses of "What Is And What Should Never Be" produced by tape-phasing Plant's voice with two synchronized reel-to-reel tape recorders. The same track is played back simultaneously on the two recorders, and then

one machine is manipulated so that its playback speed falls slightly behind that of the second, producing watery effects as the sound modulates in and out of phase.

Less obvious production techniques used throughout the album include panning a guitar or other instrument to one side of the stereo field and a reverberated version of the same sound to the other (as on the opening riff to "Whole Lotta Love") and layering three guitars with two panned to either side and the third down the middle (as on the extended solo section before the final verse of "Heartbreaker"). Page was also fond of "backwards reverb," where the tape is flipped over and reverb recorded to an empty track while it is playing in reverse; then, when the tape is turned back over, the backwards reverb is heard starting *before* the sound it was applied to. Page has said he used it on the slide part during the chorus of "Whole Lotta Love," but it is likely also used on the middle section of the song, and at other points on the album.

On future Led Zeppelin albums, Kramer and Page would take advantage of sixteen- and twenty-four-track tape machines and incorporate all sorts of new effects devices as they became available. But it is both sobering and instructive to realize what can be accomplished with minimum resources when those resources are at the disposal of a pair of creative geniuses.

At work in the studio during one of the sessions that made up *Led Zeppelin II*, spring 1969.
Charles Bonnay/Time & Life Pictures/Getty Images

TOUR DATES

6.13.69	Town Hall, Birmingham, England
6.15.69	Free Trade Hall, Manchester, England
6.20.69	City Hall, Newcastle, England
6.21.69	Colston Hall, Bristol, England
6.26.69	Guilde Hall, Portsmouth, England
6.27.69	Playhouse Theatre, London, England
6.28.69	Bath Festival, Shepton Mallet, England
6.29.69	First London Gala Pop Festival, Royal Albert Hall, London, England
7.5.69	Atlanta Pop Festival, Atlanta International Raceway, Atlanta, GA
7.6.69	Newport Jazz Festival, Newport, RI
7.11.69	Laurel Jazz Festival, Laurel Race Track, Laurel, MD
7.12.69	Summer Pop Festival, Spectrum Stadium, Philadelphia, PA
7.18–19.69	Kinetic Playground, Chicago, IL
7.20.69	Musicarnival, Cleveland, OH
7.21.69	Schaefer Music Festival, Wolman Rink, Central Park, New York, NY
7.25.69	Mid-West Rock Festival, State Fairgrounds, West Allis, WI
7.26.69	PNE Agrodome, Vancouver, BC
7.27.69	Seattle Pop Festival, Gold Creek Park, Woodinville, WA
7.29.69	Kinsmen Field House, Edmonton, AB
7.30.69	Terrace Ballroom, Salt Lake City, UT
8.1.69	Fairgrounds Arena, Santa Barbara, CA
8.2.69	Civic Auditorium, Albuquerque, NM
8.3.69	Houston Music Hall, Houston, TX
8.4.69	State Fair Coliseum, Dallas, TX
8.6.69	Memorial Auditorium, Sacramento, CA
8.7.69	Community Theatre, Berkeley, CA
8.8.69	Swing Auditorium, San Bernardino, CA
8.9.69	Anaheim Convention Center, Anaheim, CA
8.10.69	Sports Arena, San Diego, CA
8.15.69	HemisFair Arena, San Antonio, TX
8.16.69	Convention Hall, Asbury Park, NJ
8.17.69	Oakdale Musical Theater, Wallingford, CT
8.18.69	The Rock Pile, Toronto, ON
8.20.69	Aerodrome, Schenectady, NY
8.21.69	Carousel Theatre, Framingham, MA
8.22–23.69	Pirates' World, Dania, FL
8.24.69	Veterans' Memorial Coliseum, Jacksonville, FL
8.27.69	Casino Ballroom, Hampton Beach, NH
8.29–30.69	Singer Music Festival, Flushing Meadow Park, Queens, NY
8.31.69	Texas Int'l Pop Festival, Dallas Motor Speedway, Lewisville, TX
10.3.69	Circus Theatre, Scheveningen, Netherlands
10.4.69	De Doelen, Rotterdam, Netherlands
10.5.69	Concertgebouw, Amsterdam, Netherlands
10.10.69	Olympia, Paris, France
10.12.69	The Lyceum, London, England
10.17.69	Carnegie Hall, New York, NY
10.18.69	Olympia Stadium, Detroit, MI
10.19.69	Kinetic Playground, Chicago, IL
10.20.69	Paramount Theater, Seattle, WA
10.21.69	Electric Factory, Philadelphia, PA
10.24.69	Public Auditorium, Cleveland, OH
10.25.69	Boston Garden, Boston, MA

10.30.69	Kleinhans Music Hall, Buffalo, NY
10.31.69	Rhode Island Auditorium, Providence, RI
10.31.69	Springfield Municipal Auditorium, Springfield, MA
11.1.69	Onondaga War Memorial, Syracuse, NY
11.2.69	O'Keefe Centre, Toronto, ON
11.4.69	Kitchener Memorial Auditorium, Kitchener, ON
11.5.69	Memorial Hall, Kansas City, KS
11.6–8.69	Winterland Ballroom, San Francisco, CA
12.6.69	Chatenay Malabry, Paris, France
1.7.69	Town Hall, Birmingham, England
1.8.70	Colston Hall, Bristol, England
1.9.70	Royal Albert Hall, London, England
1.13.70	Guildhall, Portsmouth, England
1.15.70	City Hall, Newcastle, England
1.16.70	City Hall, Sheffield, England
1.24.70	Leeds University, Leeds, England
2.17.70	Usher Hall, Edinburgh, Scotland
2.23.70	Kulttuuritalo, Helsinki, Finland
2.25.70	Konserthuset, Göteberg, Sweden
2.26.70	Konserthuset, Stockholm, Sweden
2.27.70	Concertgebouw, Amsterdam, Netherlands
2.28.70	KB Hallen, Copenhagen, Denmark
3.7.70	Casino de Montreux, Montreux, Switzerland
3.8.70	Circus Krone Bau, Munich, Germany
3.9.70	Konserthaus, Vienna, Austria
3.10–11.70	Musikhalle, Hamburg, Germany
3.12.70	Rheinhalle, Dusseldorf, Germany
3.21.70	Pacific Coliseum, Vancouver, BC
3.22.70	Seattle Center Arena, Seattle, WA
3.23.70	Memorial Coliseum, Portland, OR
3.25.70	Denver Coliseum, Denver, CO
3.26.70	Salt Palace, Salt Lake City, UT
3.27.70	The Forum, Inglewood, CA
3.28.70	Memorial Auditorium, Dallas, TX
3.29.70	Hofheinz Pavilion, University of Houston, Houston, TX
3.30.70	Civic Arena, Pittsburgh, PA
3.31.70	The Spectrum, Philadelphia, PA
4.1.70	Boston Gardens, Boston, MA
4.2.70	Civic Center, Charleston, SC
4.3.70	Macon Coliseum, Macon, GA
4.4.70	Coliseum, Indianapolis, IN
4.5.70	Civic Center, Baltimore, MD
4.7.70	Charlotte Coliseum, Charlotte, NC
4.8.70	Dorten Arena, Raleigh, NC
4.9.70	Curtis Hixon Hall, Tampa, FL
4.10.70	Miami Beach Convention Center, Miami, FL
4.11.70	Kiel Auditorium, St. Louis, MO
4.12.70	Met Center, Bloomington, MN
4.13.70	Montreal Forum, Montreal, PQ
4.14.70	Ottawa Civic Centre, Ottawa, ON
4.16.70	Roberts Stadium, Evansville, IN
4.17.70	Mid-South Coliseum, Memphis, TN
4.18.70	Veterans' Memorial Coliseum, Phoenix, AZ

TOUR DATES

Unledded
1970

Led Zeppelin was hurtling on, if you excuse the mixed metaphor, liked a runaway locomotive. In 1970, the group grossed a whopping $5 million in the States, and *Led Zeppelin II* topped 2 million in U.S. sales, a heady figure for even rock's heaviest band. The only other Atlantic Records act ever to top that mark was Iron Butterfly with the interminable *In-A-Gadda-Da-Vida*.

Of course, Zep had already started writing material for its third album. "It's all acoustic, folks," Robert Plant confided to *Melody Maker*. "You can see it, can't you: 'Led Zeppelin go soft on their fans' or some crap like that." Then he promised that he and Jimmy Page would hide away in an isolated cabin in the mountains—perhaps Marin County outside San Francisco—to write more material. Instead, they ended up in Wales at Bron-Yr-Aur, a cottage with no electricity or running water that Plant's family had rented in summers of his childhood.

Two roadies went along to help out. The working holiday also included Plant's wife, Maureen, and daughter, Carmen, as well as Page's lady, Charlotte Martin. (For inquiring minds who want to know, word is that their daughter, Scarlet, was conceived on this Bron-Y-Aur getaway.) Despite the small entourage, the two musicians managed to steal away to the trees that echoed with laughter and music.

"It was time to step back, take stock, and not get lost in it all," Plant told *Rolling Stone* in 1975. "Hence, the trip into the mountains and the beginning of the ethereal Page and Plant.... It was a great place. 'The Golden Breast' is what the name means. The place is in a little valley and the sun always moves across it."

Page felt that the duo's communing at the cottage in April "was the first time I really came to know Robert. Actually, living together at Bron-Y-Aur, as opposed to occupying nearby hotel rooms," he told U.S. journalist Cameron Crowe. "The songs took us into areas that changed the band, and it established a standard of traveling for inspiration . . . which is the best thing a musician can do."

Bath Festival, Shepton Mallet, England, June 28, 1970.

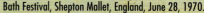

KB Hallen, Copenhagen, Denmark, February 28, 1970. Jorgen Angel/Redferns

Said Plant to British journalist Nigel Williamson: "We wrote these songs and walked and talked and thought and went off to the abbey where they hid the grail. No matter how cute and comical it might be now to look back at that, it gave us so much energy because we were really close to something. We believed. It was absolutely wonderful, and my heart was so light and happy. At that time, at that age, 1970 was like the biggest blue sky I ever saw."

In June, Page and Plant took the songs to the rest of the band, rehearsed, and then began recording with the Rolling Stones' portable equipment. Zeppelin's sound began to change: A taste of country music, some traditional English folk sounds, a nod to U.S. folk-rock (think Crosby, Stills & Nash), and even some East Indian scales. Banjo, pedal steel guitar, dulcimer, and mandolin were added to the mix. In short, it was less heavy blues and more acoustic and folk. In other words, Page and Plant tried to preserve the spirit of Bron-Yr-Aur.

Not that Zeppelin had tired of the blues. "Playing the blues is actually the most challenging thing you can do," Page told *Guitar World*. "It is very hard to play something original. 'Since I've Been Loving You' is a prime example. That was the only song on the third album that we had played live prior to our sessions, yet it was the hardest to record. We had several tries at that one. The final version is a live take with John Paul Jones playing organ and foot bass pedals at the same time. Because we rented the Rolling Stones' mobile recording studio, we could relax and take our time and develop the songs in rehearsals. We didn't have to worry about wasting studio time."

All four members contributed ideas. "Out On The Tiles" was inspired by an old drinking song Bonzo Bonham used to sing. Page told *Guitar World*, "John Bonham used to do a lot of, sort of, rap stuff. He would just get drunk and start singing things like what you hear in the beginning of 'The Ocean' [on 1973's *Houses Of The Holy*]. He would stomp his feet, and his fingers would get going. I think he originally had some lyrics about drinking pints of bitter, you know: Now I'm feeling better because I'm out on the tiles."

Page brought the Indian influences. During a rare break when he was with the Yardbirds, he had traveled to India and bought a sitar—before George Harrison even had one, he often proudly pointed out. With *III*, he finally introduced those sounds he'd adored into the music he played.

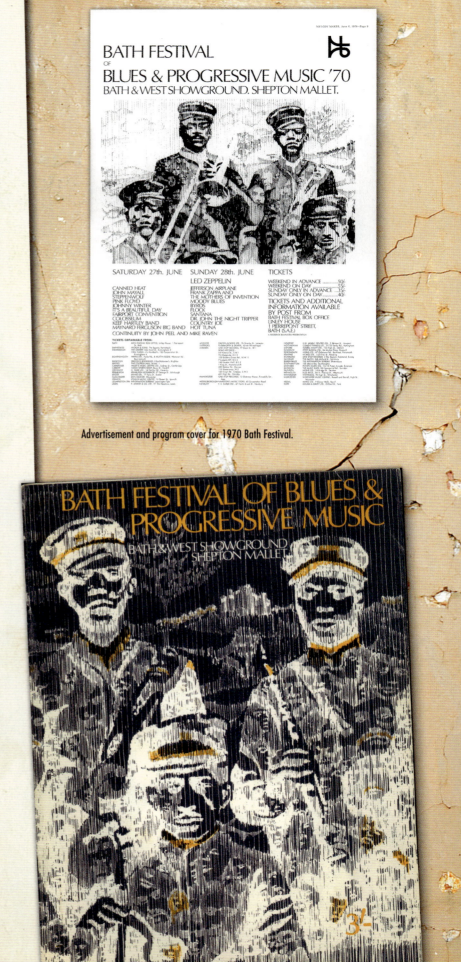

Advertisement and program cover for 1970 Bath Festival.

"I like to play it heavy, but with a lot of light and shade."

—*Jimmy Page, quoted in Cameron Crowe's "Led Zeppelin: Light And Shade"*

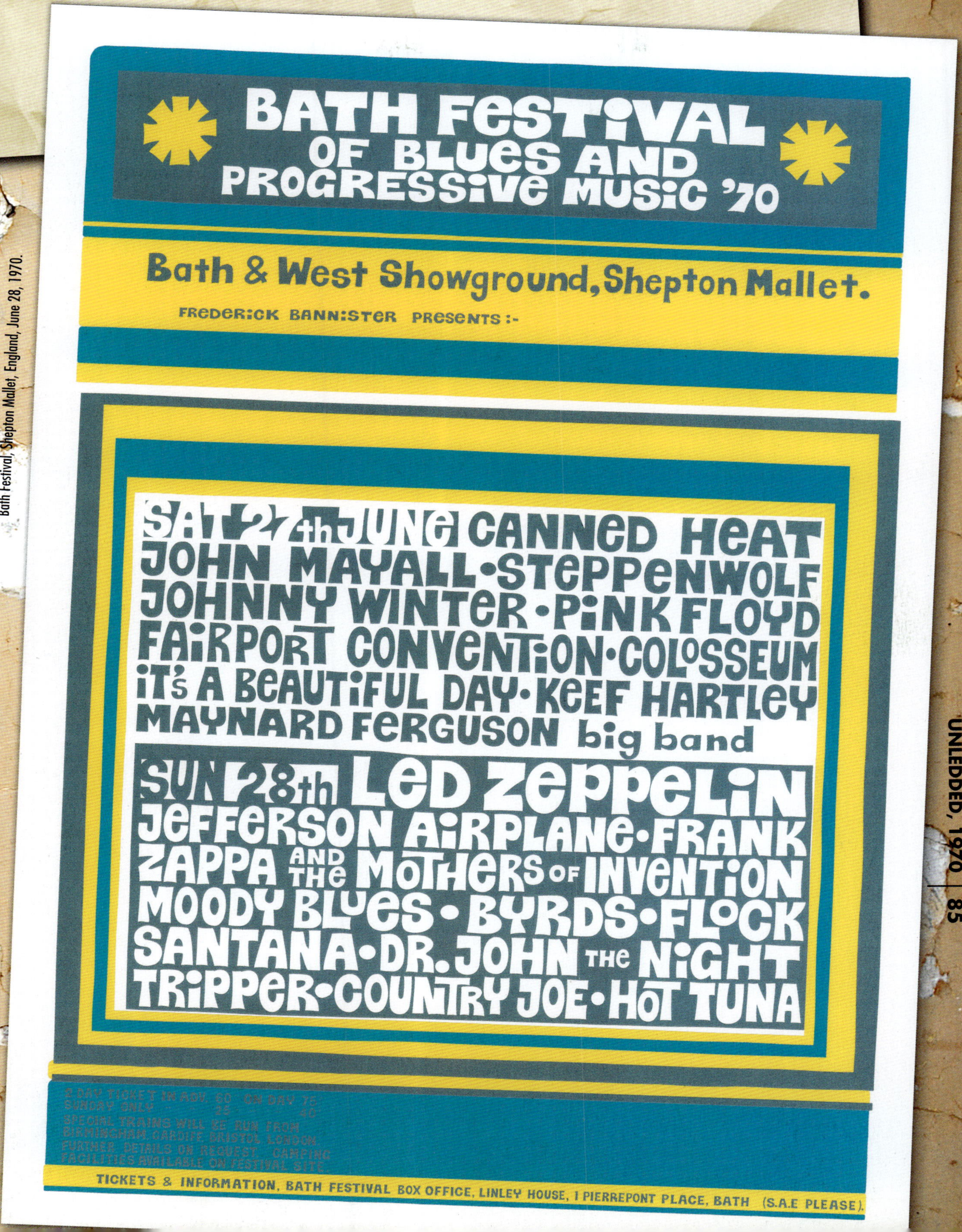
BATH FESTIVAL
OF BLUES AND
PROGRESSIVE MUSIC '70
Bath & West Showground, Shepton Mallet.
FREDERICK BANNISTER PRESENTS :-
SAT 27th JUNE CANNED HEAT
JOHN MAYALL · STEPPENWOLF
JOHNNY WINTER · PINK FLOYD
FAIRPORT CONVENTION · COLOSSEUM
IT'S A BEAUTIFUL DAY · KEEF HARTLEY
MAYNARD FERGUSON big band
SUN 28th LED ZEPPELIN
JEFFERSON AIRPLANE · FRANK
ZAPPA AND THE MOTHERS OF INVENTION
MOODY BLUES · BYRDS · FLOCK
SANTANA · DR. JOHN THE NIGHT
TRIPPER · COUNTRY JOE · HOT TUNA
2 DAY TICKET IN ADV. 60 ON DAY 75
SUNDAY ONLY 25 40
SPECIAL TRAINS WILL BE RUN FROM
BIRMINGHAM, CARDIFF, BRISTOL, LONDON.
FURTHER DETAILS ON REQUEST. CAMPING
FACILITIES AVAILABLE ON FESTIVAL SITE.
TICKETS & INFORMATION, BATH FESTIVAL BOX OFFICE, LINLEY HOUSE, 1 PIERREPONT PLACE, BATH (S.A.E PLEASE).

Bath Festival, Shepton Mallet, England, June 28, 1970.

BILL · GRAHAM · PRESENTS · IN · SAN · FRANCISCO

THE BYRDS
POCO
COMMANDER CODY
BROTHERHOOD OF LIGHT
THURS · FRI · SAT · SUN
AUGUST 13 14 15 16

OUTSIDE PRODUCTIONS
VAN MORRISON
JOHN LEE HOOKER
SUNDAY
AUGUST 30
BERKELEY COMMUNITY CENTER
AND
LED ZEPPELIN
WEDNESDAY
SEPTEMBER 2
OAKLAND COLISEUM

ALBERT KING
COLD BLOOD
MASON PROFFIT
LIGHTS · CRIMSON MADNESS
THURS · FRI · SAT · SUN
AUGUST 20 21 22 23

IRON BUTTERFLY
WITH PINERA AND RHINO
NUM
BLACK OAK ARKANSAS
LIGHTS · LITTLE PRINCESS 109
MON · TUES · WED
AUGUST 24 25 26

FILLMORE · WEST

SEATTLE CENTER COLISEUM
SEPT. 1 8 PM

LED ZEPPELIN

PRESENTED BY
CONCERTS WEST
TICKETS
$3.50 FIDELITY LANE $4.⁵⁰5.⁵⁰6.
SUBURBAN OUTLETS

Seattle Center Coliseum, Seattle, WA, September 1, 1970.

Atlantic Records print advertisement for *Led Zeppelin III*, released October 5, 1970, in the U.S.

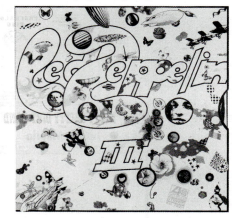

Led Zeppelin III
is here...

and after you play the album,
play the jacket

On Atlantic Records & Atlantic Tapes (Tapes Distributed by Ampex)

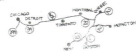

Living for pockets full of gold, manager Peter Grant kept Led Zeppelin on tour between recording sessions. He also arranged a performance in Iceland as part of a British cultural festival, which was to be filmed for the Zeppelin documentary that had begun at Royal Albert Hall in January. Then, to assuage the band's guilt about not gigging enough in jolly old England, Grant secured the quartet a key slot at the huge Bath Festival on June 28, 1970, featuring Donovan, Santana, Frank Zappa, the Byrds, and others. "This is home and it's very important to do well in your own country," Bonham told *Record Mirror* before Bath. "In the very early days, I suppose we did lose faith in England. After all that rehearsing, it was disarming to find you couldn't get a gig. It was the Fillmores in America that made us, and the kids have been great ever since."

Believing that timing is everything, Grant wanted Zeppelin to take the Bath stage at dusk, leaving Jefferson Airplane, the ostensible headliner, to close the night. So Zep was scheduled to go on between the Flock and Hot Tuna. The crowd of 150,000 went wild for the Flock, a jazz-rock band from Chicago, and its fiery violinist Jerry Goodman (who would later join the Mahavishnu Orchestra), and demanded two encores. At the end of the second encore, Grant ordered Zeppelin's roadies to remove the Flock's equipment, and the startled U.S. band protested. Suddenly, on stage, "it was sheer pandemonium," Zep tour manager Richard Cole wrote in his book, *Stairway To Heaven: Led Zeppelin Uncensored*. Grant had proved once again that he put the heavy in Led Zeppelin. The band cleaned up with its performance at Bath, from the opener, a new number called "Immigrant Song," to its—count 'em—four encores.

In August, plans for Zeppelin's U.S. tour got derailed temporarily when Jones' father, pianist Joe Baldwin, became terminally ill and the son wanted to be home. Page went to America anyway to mix *Led Zeppelin III* at the famous Ardent Studios in Memphis with engineer Terry Manning, whom he'd befriended in his Yardbirds days. Manning decided to have some fun by inscribing little sayings on the lead-out groove spaces on the masters inspired by the writings of the late Aleister Crowley (the world's "first hippie," according to Manning), whose books Page had given to the engineer. "I wrote 'Do What Thou Wilt' on one side of one set and 'Shall Be The Whole of the Law' on the other side of the same set," Manning said in a 2008 interview. "I remember writing 'So Mote It Be' on one side of another, but I've forgotten the rest. We joked that with the different things written on different lacquers, real fans would have to buy two or more records to complete the set. This was absurdly funny to us, as we couldn't imagine anything like that might really happen."

Advertisement for the Strawberry Fields Festival, Moncton, NB, August 7–9, 1970, at which Led Zeppelin were erroneously billed. It was one of a string of cancelled August shows.

In late August, the tour resumed (with a brief respite to return to England for Mr. Baldwin's funeral) as the band previewed tunes from *Led Zeppelin III*. Some U.S. fans acted like a lover who had unexpectedly slapped them in the face. "We've started doing the acoustic things onstage and it's been going off well, especially in [Los Angeles]. Some places, though, it's been a bit of a shock," Page told *Rock* magazine in 1970. "I relate it back to the period after we'd done the first album, but the second one hadn't come out, and the reaction was a bit cold, really. A similar thing has happened with the acoustic things, for the moment, there not being any association. The audience is hearing them fresh, and there has been mixed reactions. They've always gone down OK, but you get the feeling that people prefer to hear the heavier stuff."

In September, England's *Melody Maker* published its annual readers' poll and Led Zeppelin was voted best band, displacing the Beatles, who had held that slot every year since 1963. On October 5, *Led Zeppelin III* was issued. Not only was the sound controversial, so was the album jacket. Perhaps inspired by a preoccupation with San Francisco, the cover featured pseudo-psychedelic artwork with butterflies, airplanes, and assorted random objects, with a cutout notch that revealed a spinning wheel featuring an even more colorful collage of photos of the band, pop art doodads, and images of the famous zeppelin ship. Page called the cover a disappointment.

"I will take responsibility for that one," he told *Guitar World* in 1993. "I knew the artist and described what we wanted with this wheel that made things appear to change. But he got very personal with this artwork and disappeared off with it. We kept saying, 'Can we take a look at it? Can we see where it is going?' Finally, the album was actually finished, and we still did not have the art. It got to the point where I had to say, 'Look, I have got to have this thing.' I was not happy with the final result—I thought it looked teeny-bopperish. But we were on top of a deadline, so, of course, there was no way to make any radical changes to it."

Page, the finicky architect, did order one change, according to Manning. "When the album covers came back from the printing plant, to be joined with the vinyl pressings, Jimmy looked at them for approval and found that they had left off the credit for me that he had written to be there," the engineer recalled. "So he had them all destroyed and completely reprinted to include my credit. What a guy! And these were pretty expensive and involved covers, with the spinning photo wheel and all." ◆

Behind The Board:
Terry Manning
by Jon Bream

Don't always believe the fine print on albums. The liner notes sometimes get it wrong—like on *Led Zeppelin III*. The band was running so far behind on the recording that Jimmy Page and company had to do some emergency sessions in the United States during a concert tour. On days off, Page, manager Peter Grant, and whoever else was necessary flew to Memphis.

Page had befriended engineer Terry Manning in 1966 when the guitarist was with the Yardbirds on a Dick Clark Caravan of Stars tour and Manning was in a Memphis band. They'd stayed in touch over the years; in fact, Page had invited Manning to relocate to London to help set up a recording studio for Zeppelin, but Manning declined because he had so much work in Memphis with Isaac Hayes, the Staples Singers, and other Stax Records acts.

"I would pick them up at the airport and drive directly to the old Ardent studio at 1457 National Street," Manning recalls of his work with the band on *Led Zeppelin III*. "We overdubbed things, tracked some things and edited and mixed everything. As nostalgic, vintage, or mythological as it may seem to people now to have worked in these supposedly golden days with all that vintage gear, it just wasn't thought of in that way at that time. We just used what we had and did the best we could."

Not surprisingly, Page and his partners were particular about some of their recording techniques. Drummer John Bonham wanted "as few microphones as possible" on his kit. "He would say that *he* would control the levels and dynamics, not the engineer. And he could," says Manning, who has gone on to work with ZZ Top, George Thorogood, Lenny Kravitz, and Shakira, among others.

At one session, Page wanted to use a little trick that Andy Johns, his engineer in London, had employed. "Jimmy said Andy had some secret technique to get doubling effects, or delays, that Jimmy didn't remember but he wanted to use it," Manning remembers. "So I called Andy to find out. He really didn't want to divulge this, but Jimmy insisted. So Andy finally told me that he'd turn the tape around backwards and 'pre-delay' a sound with a tape delay, then turn the tape back right and 'un-delay' it with vari-speed tape delay to get the right timing. Worked like a charm."

During the mixing sessions, Manning experienced a magic moment. "I remember that the first time I got that feeling that this was something special—and I never think much about this sort of thing while in the recording or mixing process because there's just too much to do. It was when I went to the bathroom down the hall while 'Since I've Been Loving You' was playing out of the mastering room door. It sounded pretty good, and I realized that Robert Plant's vocal was awfully distinctive on this one."

Manning finished the mastering without Page. He put the masters in boxes and drove them to Nashville, where Led Zeppelin was performing. "There, I gave them to Peter Grant, who had them delivered by hand to the various pressing plants," Manning recalls. "Atlantic [Records] never saw them nor had anything to do with them—at Peter's insistence." ◆

The Voice Is Strong

Ann & Nancy Wilson On Robert Plant

By Gene Stout

Ann and Nancy Wilson's deep admiration for Led Zeppelin has had a profound influence on their careers. Heart's first hit, "Crazy On You," featuring Ann's soaring vocals, reflected that influence.

"Led Zeppelin became such a big, important band in pop culture at the same time that we were putting Heart together," Ann says. "And so we went from a bar band that did radio covers to a band that could do Led Zeppelin songs. And I went from being the chick in the band who sang 'Superstar' by Karen Carpenter to the lead singer who sang 'Whole Lotta Love' or 'Communication Breakdown.'"

Ann and Nancy met Robert Plant for the first time in the mid-eighties.

"We were playing in Leeds, England, and he came to our show," Ann continues. "At that time, we were doing 'Rock And Roll' in our set. . . . I was really near-sighted and I couldn't really see the good-looking blond guy standing on the left side of stage, just checking us out. And nobody wanted to tell me because they didn't want me to freak out. They knew what a big fan I was.

"After the show, he came back and we said 'hi' and everything. He really has a vibe around him. Nancy and I used to joke that the air moves around him as he walks."

Ann remembered Plant as a gentleman.

"Let's face it, Zeppelin is a boy's club, and it must have been something for them to accept these two women playing their stuff with all this confidence."

Plant's vocal range still amazes her.

"I don't know how they were able to achieve his upper range way back in the *Houses Of The Holy* days, whether they were speeding up tape or whether he actually sang that high. It sounded so beautiful that I don't even care," Ann says. "And then of course every guy in every hair band had to try and copy him, but nobody ever succeeded in sounding that good."

"No Quarter" and "The Rain Song" are among Ann's favorite Zeppelin songs.

"People always think of Plant as this big blues shouter, and they don't give him credit for the ballads he does. He does them in a way that's just as intense."

Though Nancy is more guitarist than singer, she learned a lot from Plant—as well as from her sister—about expressing herself vocally.

"I think part of what was happening with Plant's voice is something that Ann actually gave me advice about. She said, 'Stop thinking about pitch, stop thinking about the technical aspects of your singing, [and] just tell a story. Talk . . . and use your words to tell your story. Don't sing it, tell it. And I think that's what Plant knew from the very beginning. He has a voice that's like a bolt from heaven. He's a born singer, as Ann is. It comes completely from the gut. You feel completely familiar with Plant when he's singing, because he's talking to you, he's not just singing at you." ❧

Concerts West

presents

An Evening Of
LED ZEPPELIN

SEPTEMBER 4th at 8:30 P.M.

THE FORUM

—TICKETS—

**FORUM BOX OFFICE
TICKETRON — 878-2211
All Mutual Agencies,
Wallich's Music Stores**

The Forum, Inglewood, CA, September 4, 1970.

"Immigrant Song" b/w "Hey, Hey, What Can I Do," the latter of which was the only non-LP Zeppelin song released from 1968 to 1990, the same year it was included in the *Led Zeppelin* box set.

The Forum, Inglewood, CA, September 4, 1970. *Michael Ochs Archives/Getty Images*

"Jimmy was incredible, because he was the classic rock star with the moated castle, the velvet clothes, the fabulous cars that he couldn't drive and the eighty thousand rare guitars."

—Michael des Barres, quoted in Stephen Davis' Hammer Of The Gods

the LPs:

Led Zeppelin III
By William McKeen

It was torture. We barely made it back to school in time after the frantic lunch-hour drive to the record store. And now I had to sit all afternoon in algebra and then government, just looking at it, unable to play it. But I had to have it first, the day it came out.

I held it before me, suspending it on fingertips over my desk, while my oblivious teacher spewed gibberish about algebraic number theory. Behind me I heard a whisper: "Check it out. He's got the new album." I'd removed the cellophane and started playing with the cover. Inside the front of the gatefold jacket, there was a rotating wheel. Windows cut into the cover (which featured an assortment of airplanes, flowers, butterflies, and teeth) showed glimpses of a colorful, spinning world underneath. Every time I turned the wheel, I saw something different.

And perhaps that is the obvious metaphor for the music within that splendid album cover. Every time I played *Led Zeppelin III*—which I first did later that afternoon, and many times in the four decades since—I heard something different: fear, exaltation, majesty, delight. Even today, each time I play it, I'm back in that time: an innocent fifteen-year-old boy so eager for this music that I begged a ride from Birdman, my true-believer friend with a driver's license. Both of us had Zeppelin disease.

After all, Led Zeppelin was our band. We loved the Beatles and the Stones and Dylan, but that was the music of our big brothers and sisters. When I discovered *Led Zeppelin* and played it endlessly, it was my older sister who banged on my bedroom door, telling me to turn it down. Those guitar solos hurt her hair, she said.

I was so happy—I had found something that was mine.

The first album was a jolt, the next step in rock 'n' roll's evolution. *Led Zeppelin II* was that skull-crunching rock multiplied, with all the noises, effects, and dream-sequence glimpses of Jimmy Page's otherworld, wrapped in a sound collage. The word we used at the time was *heavy*. Led Zeppelin drew a line in the sand with a blowtorch. The first two Zeppelin albums were Holy Writ to us.

To say that millions of American teenage boys anticipated that third album is like saying rain is occasionally wet. We wanted rock 'n' roll, of course, but we got something more.

After school that day, Birdman and I went to our homes to listen, vowing to talk later. I shut myself into my second-floor bedroom sanctuary and was with *Led Zeppelin III* for many disturbing hours thereafter.

It began with Robert Plant's hellish death scream of "Immigrant Song," one step away from the heart-stopping thunder chords of the first albums. The song came riding over the hillside, the musical equivalent of a pillaging, rampaging Viking horde. *So this is what it sounds like right before you die*, I thought. I would come to appreciate the richness and mythology in Zeppelin lyrics, but as an innocent fifteen-year-old, they frightened me. "We are your overlords," Plant bellowed. "On we sweep with threshing oar!"

"What do you think?" Birdman asked when he called.

"Kind of scary," I said. "They come from the land of ice and snow? Sounds like they want to conquer us or kill us. Maybe both."

"Huh?" Of course, Birdman had tuned out the words and was trying to learn Page's guitar parts on "Since I've Been Loving You."

I had found the soundtrack for my nightmares. Beyond "Immigrant Song," there were John Paul Jones' disturbing strings on "Friends," towering, shape-shifting music that still stalks my dreams. There was the glorious, grinding "Since I've Been Loving You," the album's centerpiece. Although there was still traditional Zeppelin rock ("Out On The Tiles"), my strongest feeling was that this wasn't the Led Zeppelin me and my boys had come to know and love.

It took me a few years to realize the album was a career masterstroke, and to appreciate the courage it took to so violently shake up what could have become rock-by-numbers. *Led Zeppelin II ½* would have kept all of us squirming adolescent boys happy with groin-level riffs. They could have made those first two albums again and again and gotten away with it.

Instead, they took us someplace new. I later learned that those first two albums were made on the run, largely written and recorded on the road. But after the band had some success and could finally take a break, they decided to make their third album under different circumstances. They found a small cottage in South Wales called Bron-Yr-Aur, where most of the songs were written in a more comfortable place than the cramped airplane seats and anonymous hotels that gave birth to the first two albums. When it came time to record this third album, the band passed on the time-tested studios of London, New York, and Los Angeles, and rented a two-hundred-year-old home in the country southwest of London. The drawing room of the Headley Grange estate had the acoustics that Jimmy Page wanted, and a mobile recording unit was summoned.

The music reflected this origin. Page's guitar still thundered, but the serenity of Bron-Yr-Aur came through in all of the softer stringed instruments Page had mastered. The lovely "That's The Way" would not have been out of place on an album by one of those wimpy Southern California singer-songwriters Birdman

and I loathed. The country lilt "Tangerine" gave us Zeppelin with the moan of a steel guitar. "Bron-Y-Aur Stomp" (the misspelling allegedly immortalized in the process of filing the copyright) was a chiming acoustic run showing the band's gentleness beneath the blood and bluster. But they could still build electric drama unlike any other band. The deceptive quiet that opened "Gallows Pole" (was that a lute in the second verse?) built with demented John Bonham windshield-wiper time to the ending, when we realize the narrator is a rotting corpse.

Not that it mattered to us in the Zeppelin Generation, but critics were not kind to the album. They never liked the band much, but the fans made Zeppelin critic-proof.

Today, I teach rock 'n' roll history at a university. When I ask the eighteen-year-olds what they listen to, it's Zeppelin, the Doors, the Grateful Dead, and Dylan. That music does not sound dated. Even to my fifty-plus ears, *Led Zeppelin III* still sounds brilliant, at turns frightening and magnificent. I recall it fondly as something that taught me about taking chances, trying something new, always changing.

Every time I turn the wheel, I see something different.

Birdman and I both morphed into quiet, scholarly types and recently saw each other for the first time in thirty years. He was at an academic conference downstate and rented a car for the long drive, figuring it was finally time to see me again and meet the family.

"What did you listen to on the way up?" I asked in the driveway.

"Zeppelin, man," he said. "Of course."

Two American teenage boys, so happy to finally have something that belonged to us.

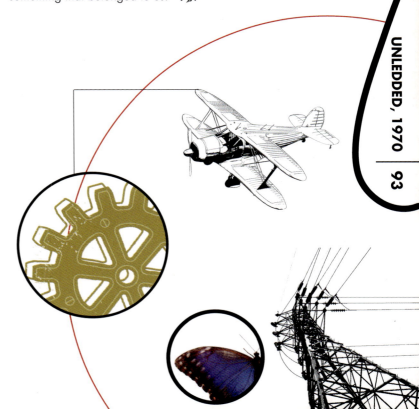

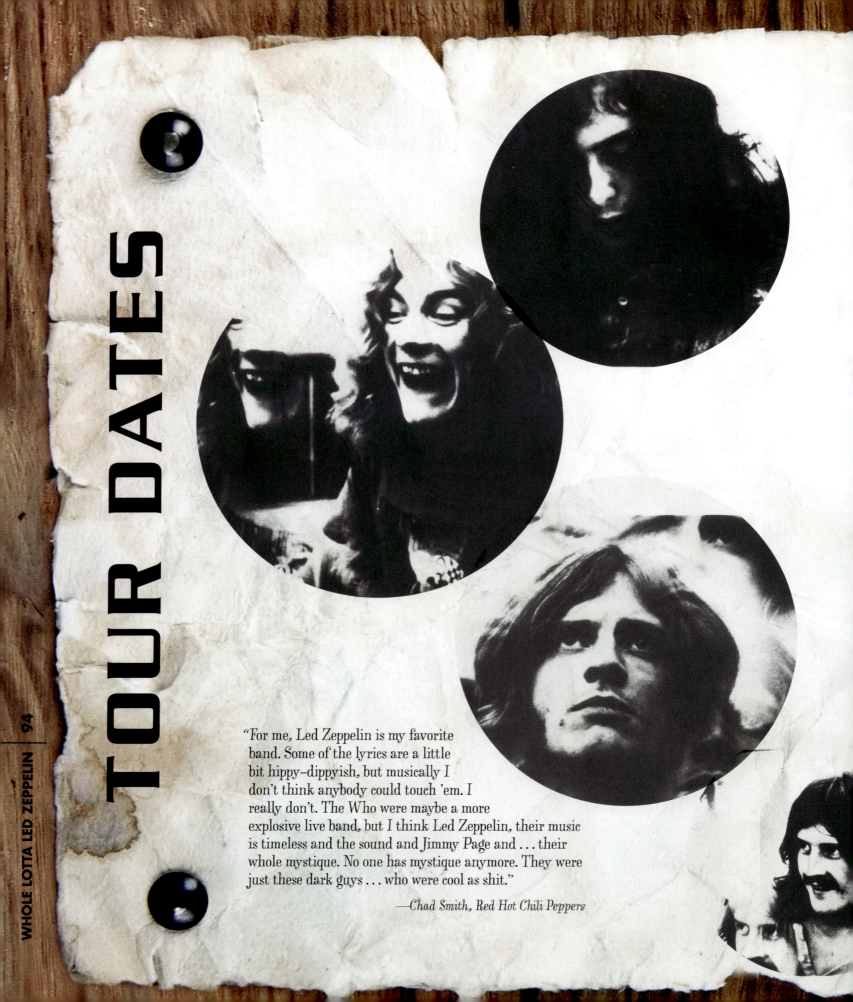

TOUR DATES

"For me, Led Zeppelin is my favorite band. Some of the lyrics are a little bit hippy–dippyish, but musically I don't think anybody could touch 'em. I really don't. The Who were maybe a more explosive live band, but I think Led Zeppelin, their music is timeless and the sound and Jimmy Page and . . . their whole mystique. No one has mystique anymore. They were just these dark guys . . . who were cool as shit."

—Chad Smith, Red Hot Chili Peppers

"I think it was based in the blues but also in Anglo–Celtic folk traditions that were first-hand to those guys. I think that was important. Plant was listening to the Incredible String Band and Joni Mitchell and he knew who Richard Thompson was and Sandy Denny and those people. They were very heavily rooted in stuff that's really, really primal and always works and always pushes buttons that people who listen to music have."

—*Steve Earle*

TOUR DATES

6.22.70	Laugardalsholl Hall, Reykjavik, Iceland
6.28.70	Bath Festival, Shepton Mallet, England
7.16.70	Sporthalle, Cologne, Germany
7.17.70	Grugahalle, Essen, Germany
7.18.70	Festhalle, Frankfurt, German
7.19.70	Deutschlandhalle, Berlin, Germany
8.15.70	Yale Bowl, New Haven, CT
8.17.70	Hampton Roads Coliseum, Hampton, VA
8.19.70	Municipal Auditorium Arena, Kansas City, MO
8.20.70	Oklahoma City Fairgrounds Coliseum, Oklahoma City, OK
8.21.70	Assembly Center, Tulsa, Oklahoma, OK
8.22.70	Tarrant County Convention Center, Fort Worth, TX
8.23.70	HemisFair Arena, San Antonio, TX
8.25.70	Municipal Auditorium, Nashville, TN
8.26.70	Public Auditorium, Cleveland, OH
8.28.70	Olympia Stadium, Detroit, MI
8.29.70	Man Pop Festival, Winnipeg Arena, Winnipeg, MB
8.31.70	Milwaukee Arena, Milwaukee, WI
9.1.70	Seattle Center Coliseum, Seattle, WA
9.2.70	Oakland Coliseum, Oakland, CA
9.3.70	Sports Arena, San Diego, CA
9.4.70	The Forum, Inglewood, CA
9.6.70	International Center Arena, Honolulu, HI
9.9.70	Boston Garden, Boston, MA
9.11.70	Olympia Stadium, Detroit, MI
9.12.70	Municipal Auditorium, Cleveland, OH
9.19.70	Madison Square Garden, New York, NY

Untitled
1971

Even though *Led Zeppelin III* scaled to No. 1 in the United States, it was the slowest selling of the band's early albums. Once again, in the States, the band promoted a single, "Immigrant Song," with a non-album B-side, a mid-tempo mandolin ballad called "Hey Hey What Can I Do." "Immigrant Song" peaked at a middling No. 16 in *Billboard*, and the album received mostly inauspicious reviews, not that many British hard-rock bands earned glowing write-ups from *Rolling Stone* or other U.S. publications at the time.

Lester Bangs, the idiosyncratic critic who was bemused by his veer-from-the-critical-norm appreciation of Zeppelin, wrote in *Rolling Stone*: "I keep nursing this love/hate attitude toward Led Zeppelin. Partly from genuine interest and mostly indefensible hopes, in part from that conviction that nobody that crass can be all bad. . . . When I first heard the album, my main impression was the consistent anonymity of most of the songs. . . . Finally I mention a song called 'That's the Way,' because it's the first song they've ever done that's truly moved me. Son of a gun, it's beautiful. Above a very simple and appropriately everyday acoustic riff, Plant sings a touching picture of two youngsters who can no longer be playmates because one's parents and peers disapprove of the other because of long hair and being generally from the dark side of town. The vocal is restrained for once—in fact, Plant's intonations are as plaintively gentle as some of the Rascals' best work."

The lack of supportive press in both the United States and the United Kingdom would weigh upon Zeppelin's next album. Once again, Robert Plant and Jimmy Page repaired to Bron-Yr-Aur in Wales for more bucolic bonding and songwriting. Then they convened with John Paul Jones and John Bonham at Headley Grange, a supposedly haunted former workhouse, to rehearse. Those sessions are where things came together as a group. "I suppose we're all capable of putting a trademark on an album, marking just one person, but none of us are so narrow-minded," Jones told

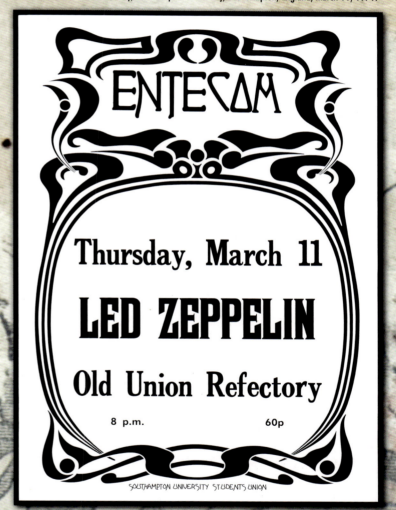

Old Refectory, Southampton University, Southampton, England, March 11, 1971.

Marquee Club, London, England, March 23, 1971.

John Barnett/4 Eyes Design

Disc & Music Echo magazine in 1970. "That wouldn't be the group, and the group's always played what comes out, and what comes out goes down. If it sounds good to everybody, then it's played."

The British press being the British press, that fall *Melody Maker* and *New Musical Express* reported rumors of Led Zeppelin disbanding. The group not only denied the notion but booked a return-to-their-roots club tour of England and Ireland in March, including the celebrated, tiny Marquee club in London where Zep had last played in December 1968. On March 5 in Belfast, Led Zeppelin played "Stairway To Heaven" for the first time in concert, complete with Page's double-neck guitar but without the recorders that would be heard on the forthcoming fourth album. On April 1, "Stairway" was performed at London's Paris Theatre, a concert heard on DJ John Peel's BBC *In Concert* program. On tour, the band was offering other new numbers, including "Going To California" and "Black Dog," also from its as-yet unreleased fourth album.

In other countries, Zeppelin continued to play big gigs. One memorable show occurred on July 5, 1970, in Milan at the Vignorelli Velodrome—just two days after Doors frontman Jim Morrison had died in Paris. Outside the Velodrome were two thousand police officers anticipating left-wing political protesters among the fifteen thousand fans on hand for the show. The ruckus moved into the auditorium as tear gas filled the room while Led Zeppelin took the stage. Plant called for calm as the band worked its way through its repertoire. But as the crowd rioted, manager Peter Grant ordered the band off stage during John Bonham's "Moby Dick" drum solo. Plant is still bothered by that evening. "We escaped down an access route and the troops pumped gas canisters at us," the singer told British journalist Nigel Williamson. "We managed to get in a dressing room and I barricaded the door with a medicine cabinet and got everybody in there with wet towels around our heads. Then they broke the windows and popped a couple of canisters in from the street." Led Zeppelin would never perform again in Italy.

The band took a rare six weeks off that summer, which afforded Page an opportunity to deal with mixing the upcoming album and designing its cover. It turned out that there had been a problem with mixing sessions at Los Angeles' Sunset Sound, so the task would have

to be redone at Olympic Studio in London. Meanwhile, still reeling from the awful artwork on *Led Zeppelin III*, Page decided he wanted an untitled album a là the Beatles' so-called "White Album" in 1968. He also had been bothered by the critics' reaction to the third album. "After all we had accomplished, the press was still calling us a hype," Page later told *Guitar World*. "So that is why the fourth album was untitled. It was a meaningless protest really, but we wanted to prove that people were not buying us for the name."

Page had a concept for the cover to complement the folk-myth lyrics Plant had written for "Stairway To Heaven," the centerpiece of the new LP. "Robert and I came up with the design of *IV* together," the guitarist said in *Guitar World*.

(continued on page 100)

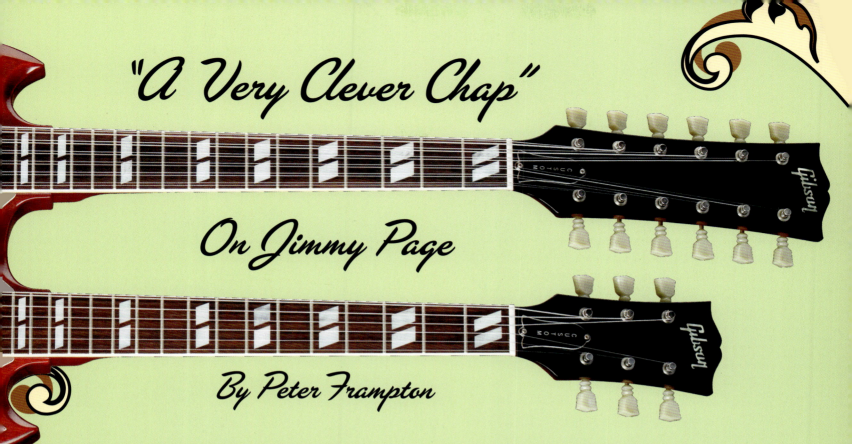

"A Very Clever Chap"

On Jimmy Page

By Peter Frampton

I think people think of Jimmy "the great guitar player" and all these signature solos that he's done . . . "Stairway To Heaven" on down. But I see him much more as an arranger, an orchestrator. That was the big deal for me, the way he would orchestrate the guitar parts. I'm sure between all of them they did the arrangements, but his stacking of guitar parts was the real interesting part of what he did.

I did sessions with John Paul Jones as a music director before Led Zeppelin or even during the time they were getting together. So you're talking about one of the top musical directors of rock stuff for sessions in London being John Paul Jones, and then you're talking about Jimmy as one of the top session players way back to the early and mid-sixties when he played on the Kinks' records and all that sort of stuff. So you had someone who had cut their teeth, obviously, on the blues but was also very, very influential in what was played on a lot of pop records, too. So he's a very well-rounded player. His technique on acoustic [guitar] is phenomenal, and he uses various different open tunings and this special kind of "Jimmy Page tuning" you heard on a lot of the earlier stuff. He was obviously pretty damn good technically pretty early on.

It's the whole picture with him. It's not just that he's a great blues player or a great acoustic player or a great slide player or whatever. It's the arranger in him that plays right into how he played, as well, because to me he was always thinking of that final picture, the audio picture, and it seemed to me he was always looking ahead and knew what he wanted, and then was building it up all the time within the tracks. It would be like a folky acoustic guitar underneath, and then he would come in and do a slide part or a blues slide part for a solo, and then there were the orchestrated lines he would do. He knew how to put the song together. But the thing was, he had all these amazing parts, but they were all perfect for that particular song or piece of music they appeared on. Just a very clever chap.

And they were not your normal harmonies, either. He would go for the obtuse harmony, like the Everly Brothers—it sounds normal but it was very different. The Everlys would put the melody on top and harmonize underneath, and then the Beatles stole from the Everlys and instead of harmonizing, the melody goes up and down underneath [the melody] or below it, creating very unique harmonies. They weren't what you'd call your Andrews Sisters kind of cluster harmonies. And Jimmy would do that on the guitar as well. It would make them very obtuse and therefore not run-of-the-mill.

For a while there it seemed like every time I made a solo record [Led Zeppelin] was recording at the other studio at Olympic. So I got to see Jimmy, virtually in darkness, with, like, this wall of amplifiers, and he would end up using this little tiny thing most of the time. And he'd orchestrate all those wonderful, classic tracks of theirs with all these numerous guitar parts that he would put on laboriously himself. But if you listen to them it was just like an orchestra. And I took a lot from that. There's a track on my *Something's Happening* album called "Magic Moon," and it's almost . . . Jimmy could've written that riff. I was trying so hard at that point to do a decent Led Zeppelin type of tribute. So he was definitely an inspiration and an influence, and just so unique that you just can't overstate what he did.

—As told to Gary Graff

(continued from page 98)

"Robert had actually bought the print that is on the cover from a junk shop in Reading. We then came up with the idea of having the picture—the man with the sticks—represent the old way on a demolished building, with the new way coming up behind it. The illustration on the inside was my idea. It is the Hermit character from the Tarot, a symbol of self-reliance and wisdom, and it was drawn by Barrington Colby. The typeface for the lyrics to 'Stairway' was also my contribution. I found it in a really old arts ad crafts magazine called *Studio*, which started in the late 1800s. I thought the lettering was so interesting, I got someone to work up a whole alphabet."

Page also asked his bandmates each to choose a symbol, or rune, to represent himself. As a possible source, he showed them *The Book Of Signs* by Rudolph Koch. Jones opted for a circle covered with three interlocking arcs, which according to the Koch book wards off evil. Bonham picked up a rune with three overlapping rings, which symbolized his family. (It's also, coincidentally, similar to the Ballantine beer logo.) Plant and Page went for custom designs. The singer's feather inside a circle is inspired by Native American symbolism while Page's rune, stylized letters that read like "ZoSo," is just a doodle, he has insisted. Others speculate that it refers to sorcerer Austin Osman Spare's cult, Zos.

The long-delayed album was not released when Led Zeppelin made its first foray into Japan in September. In unusual spirits, the band unexpectedly threw in snippets from the standards "Smoke Gets In Your Eyes" and "The Lady Is A Tramp," as well as the Rolling Stones' "Honky Tonk Women" and Simon & Garfunkel's "59th Street Bridge Song." But Zeppelin didn't have smooth sailing. On stage in Osaka, Plant and Bonham got into a row, with the singer receiving a fat lip. The drummer left the stage, reluctantly returned, and then refused to play "Moby Dick." Bonham added another infamous incident to Zeppelin's legacy at the Tokyo Hilton when he and tour manager Richard Cole took samurai swords and chopped down the door to Jones' room and then carved up the interior. That redecorating got Led Zeppelin banned from the Hilton chain for life. There was a bonus to the Japan junket, however, Page and Plant got to stop in India on their way back to England to check out some Bombay discos and music clubs.

The quartet's seventh North American tour featured many new tunes, prompting ever-vigilant manager Peter

Japanese tour program, Budokan, Tokyo, Japan , September 23–24, 1971.

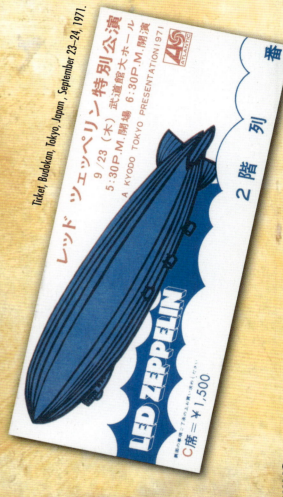

"When I first heard ['Stairway To Heaven'], I thought it was about some materialistic person who thought they could buy everything with money, and they didn't really care about their soul or their spirituality. As years went by, I heard a lot of it was about the Queen of England. It's funny how you interpret it. It's a very abstract song. I always thought it was about somebody trying to save their soul. I always thought of it as a spiritual song; that's why I used the choir."

–Dolly Parton, who recorded "Stairway To Heaven" for her 2002 release, Halos & Horns

"[Led Zeppelin] wasn't really a huge influence. I was more into hearing stories, and that ethereal lyric kind of thing wasn't doing it for me. But I had the poster of the 747 [*sic*] on my wall, and *Led Zeppelin IV* and a couple of the records would make the turntables. They were unavoidable, y'know?"

—*Jon Bon Jovi*

BUFFALO CONCERT PRESENTATIONS in association with PETER GRANT presents LED ZEPPELIN plus supporting acts to be announced EMPIRE POOL, WEMBLEY. SAT 20 NOV. tickets available at all branches of harlequin records on fri. 5th nov at 11 am ~75p all seats

"The reason why we are us is because of them—their records influence us more than [anything] It was just like a new planet coming into the solar system. They just broke new ground and affected everybody on earth. I think a person can come out of a mud hut in the middle of Vietnam and know 'Stairway To Heaven.' It's everywhere."

—*David Bryan, Bon Jovi*

Grant to be on the lookout for bootleggers taping the band's concerts. In Vancouver, after Cole spotted a man holding a recording device, he dispatched some roadies to smash the man's equipment. It turns out that he was a government official trying to monitor the band's decibel levels in response to a citizen's complaint. Police showed up, but Grant managed to smooth all the ruffled feathers.

Bonham, for one, thought this was one of the band's more successful North American jaunts. "The American tour was good in actual fact," he told *Melody Maker* that year. "We played really well and had some great things happen. I think I enjoyed it more than any other tour of America. You see, we had a lot of time at home to think, and we grew a lot closer together."

Finally, on November 8, 1971, nearly six months after the recordings had been completed, Led Zeppelin released its fourth album. The LP started with two blasts of rock 'n' roll, "Black Dog" and "Rock And Roll," before launching into "The Battle Of Evermore" and the epic, eight-minute "Stairway To Heaven," which would become the band's signature and the most played—or overplayed, depending on your perspective—song of all time on rock radio. Page had started composing the piece at his home studio and played the track for Jones one night at Headley Grange when Plant and Bonham had gone out. "I worked really hard on the thing," Page told Cameron Crowe. "Jonesy and I then routined it together, and later we ran through it with the drums and everything. Robert was sitting there at the time, by the fireplace, and I believe he came up with 80 percent of the lyrics at that time. He was just sort of writing and suddenly there it was."

"Yeah, I just sat there next to Pagey while he was playing it through," Plant told Crowe. "It was done very quickly. It took little working out, but it was a very fluid, unnaturally easy track. It was almost as if—uh, oh—it just had to be gotten out at that time. There was something pushing it, saying 'you guys are OK, but if you want to do something timeless, here's a wedding song for you.'"

Years later, Page reflected to *Guitar World*:

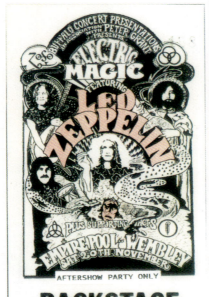

"To me, I thought "Stairway" crystallized the essence of the band. It had everything there and showed the band at its best. . . . It was a milestone for us. Every musician wants to do something of lasting quality, something which will hold up for a long time, and I guess we did it with "Stairway." [Pete] Townshend probably thought that he got it with "Tommy." I don't know whether I have the ability to come up with more. I have to do a lot of hard work before I can get anywhere near those stages of consistent, total brilliance. I don't think there are too many people who are capable of it. Maybe one. Joni Mitchell. That's the music that I play at home all the time, Joni Mitchell."

Some of the fourth album was simply carry-you-back-to-basics rock 'n' roll, like "Black Dog," inspired by an old black Labrador that hung out at Headley Grange where Zeppelin was rehearsing. Plant told *Rolling Stone*: "Not all my stuff is meant to be scrutinized, though. Things like 'Black Dog' are blatant let's-do-it-in-the-bath-type things, but they make their point just the same. People listen. Otherwise, you might as well sing the menu from the Continental Hyatt House."

Jones came up with the riff for "Black Dog," he explained in an AOL chat in 1997: "It came to me on a train coming back from rehearsal at Jimmy Page's house. I'd been listening to a song on a Muddy Waters' record called 'Electric Mud,' which had a long, rambling blues riff and I thought I'd like to try something with a similar form."

With those four runic symbols decorating the stage, Led Zeppelin celebrated the release of its fourth album with seventeen concerts in the United Kingdom. Two London shows, billed as "Electric Magic," featured circus acts and pigs in costumes. The album went to the top of the British charts, but stalled at No. 2 in the States, blocked variously by *Santana III*, Sly & the Family Stone's *There's A Riot Goin' On*, and Carole King's singer-songwriter blockbuster *Tapestry*, which resided on top for fifteen weeks. Not to fret, though— Led Zeppelin's fourth long-player still ranks as the fourth best-selling album in the States of all time. ●

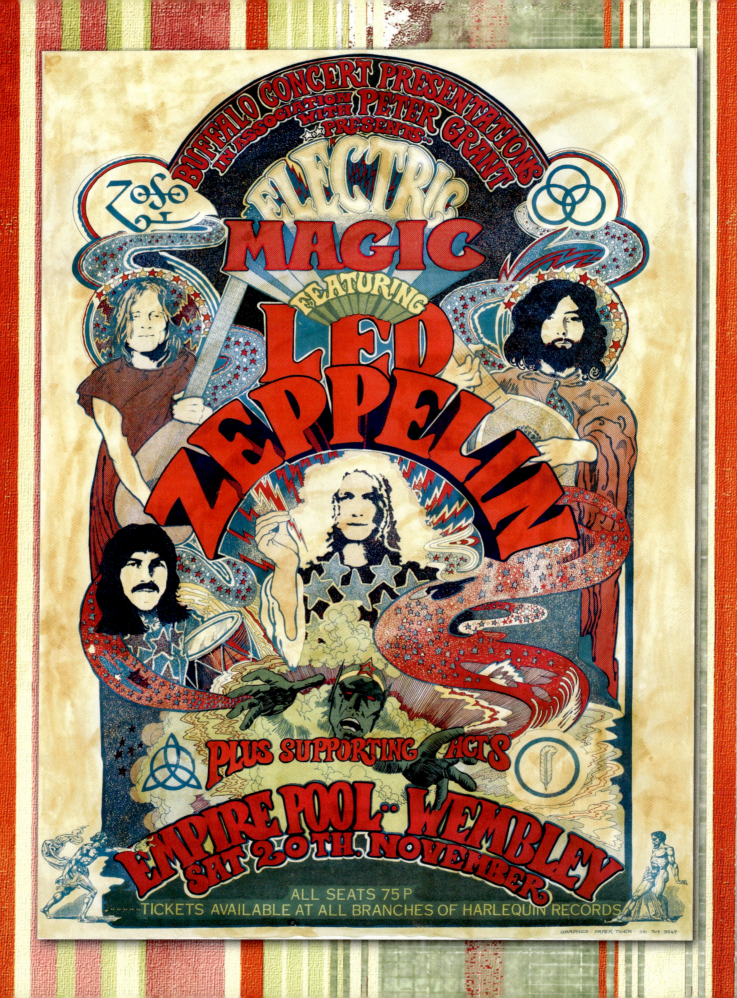

"I wanted to try an electric blues with a rolling bass part. But it couldn't be too simple. I wanted it to turn back on itself. I showed it to the guys, and we fell into it. We struggled with the turn-around, until Bonham figured out that you just count four-time as if there's *no* turn-around. That was the secret. Anyway, we titled it after a dog that was wandering in and out of the studio. The dog had no name, so we just called the song 'Black Dog.'"

—*John Paul Jones on "Black Dog," quoted in Cameron Crowe's "Led Zeppelin: Light And Shade"*

TO A CASTLE I WILL TAKE YOU

BY JON BREAM

Aleister Crowley in divine mood.

Jimmy Page's interest in astrology and the occult have been well documented. (Dude, the runes on the fourth album were inspired by occult sources.) Page became fascinated with infamous British occultist Aleister Crowley (1875–1947), who was known as "the wickedest man in the world" for practicing black magic, experimenting with drugs, and hosting sex orgies. Page collected Crowley's manuscripts and paintings and even purchased a robe Crowley wore during black magic rituals. In 1971, he delved deeper into Crowley's world by buying the mystic's former home in Scotland on the shores of Loch Ness. Legend had it that murders had taken place in the house, and one of Page's caretakers reportedly committed suicide there.

"Magic is very important if people can go through it," Page told *Disc & Music Echo* magazine in 1972. "I think Crowley's completely relevant to today. We're seeking for truth: the search still goes on. Crowley didn't have a very high opinion of women—I don't think he was wrong. Playing music is a very sexual act, an emotional release, and the sexual drive comes in along with all the other impulses.

. . . At least as musicians we aren't doing any environmental or moral damage. In fact, musicians can ask some of the ugly questions that politicians don't want to answer."

Page also studied others who wrote about black magic and related topics. "You can't ignore evil if you study the supernatural as I do. I have many books on the subject and I've also attended a number of séances," the guitarist is quoted as saying in Nigel Williamson's *The Rough Guide To Led Zeppelin*.

Rock singer Michael Des Barres, whose band Detective recorded two LPs for Zep's Swan Song label, used to visit his friend Page. "He'd pull out Crowley's robes, Crowley's Tarot deck—all the Crowley gear that he'd collected," Des Barres told Ritchie Yorke in *Led Zeppelin: From Early Days To Page & Plant*. (Des Barres was married to ex-groupie Pamela Des Barres for fourteen years.) "I thought: 'this is great!' It was all so twisted and debauched, their whole thing. That's what Jimmy represented to me. I don't know what I represented to Jimmy; I always thought that Jimmy liked me because I happened to say 'Rimbaud' at the right time." 🦅

"Yeah, I just sat next to Pagey while he was playing it through. It was done very quickly. It took a little working out, but it was a very fluid, unnaturally easy track. It was almost as if—uh-oh—it just had to be gotten out at that time. There was something pushing it, saying 'you guys are okay, but if want to do something *timeless*, here's a wedding song for you.'"

—Robert Plant on *"Stairway To Heaven,"*
quoted in Cameron Crowe's *"Led Zeppelin: Light And Shade"*

Wembley Empire Pool, London, November 20, 1971. *Fin Costello/Redferns*

the LPs:
Untitled
By Barney Hoskyns

Led Zeppelin's untitled fourth album remains the band's most perfectly realized display of sheer power and stylistic range. (Note: Unlike the Beatles' "White Album" or the Byrds' *(Untitled)*, it is also one of the few truly "untitled" albums in rock history, released as such because, in Jimmy Page's words, "names, titles, and things like that don't mean a thing." I refer to it as *IV* here solely out of convenience; others have called it *ZoSo*, *Runes*, or *Four Symbols*. Marrying the carnal heaviness of *II* to the acoustic lacework of *III*, the album balances the blues-rock grind of "Black Dog" against the sun-dappled utopianism of "Going To California"; the swampy stomp of "When The Levee Breaks" against the chiming mandolins of "The Battle Of Evermore"; the retro-R&B blast of "Rock And Roll" against the bucolic intro to "Stairway To Heaven."

True, Zeppelin stretched out still further on 1975's double *Physical Graffiti*. But while "Kashmir" and "In My Time Of Dying" and "Ten Years Gone" are undeniable Zep peaks, *Graffiti* contains too many weak links, too many off-the-cuff sketches, to rival *IV*.

Just eight tracks long, *IV* is a blueprint for the journey every great album should take you on, from bone-shredding blues-metal to plangent California dreaming, via Fairport folk convention and medieval prog-rock. The fourth biggest-selling long player of all time, it boasts in "Stairway To Heaven" the most-played track in American FM radio history.

Opener "Black Dog" is one of the most fearsomely powerful tracks in the Zeppelin catalog. Notwithstanding its awkward B-verse section—wherein Page's fiddly guitar riff is brazenly out of synch with John Bonham's straight 4/4 drum pattern—the track grips the listener from the outset and never lets go as it moves through a series of churning interlinked riffs unfolding in one continuous sequence. The only real punctuations in the song are the *a capella* vocal phrases inspired by Fleetwood Mac's "Oh Well"—bloodcurdling Robert Plant hollers that suggest a man possessed by demonic lust.

"Rock And Roll" is a departure for Zeppelin. For all their stated love of rockabilly and R&B, the band had never genuflected at the altar of fifties America(na) the way they do here. Kicking off with a quotation—a stab at Earl Palmer's rifle-shot snare-and-cymbal intro to Little Richard's 1957 hit "Keep-A Knockin' "—they pummel their way through the full-throttle boogie riff, channeling not only Chuck Berry but such R&B vocal groups as the Drifters and the Montones. With "sixth Rolling

Stone" Ian Stewart tickling the ivories like Johnnie Johnson, the song more than holds its own next to anything Berry or Little Richard ever recorded.

Picking up where *Led Zeppelin II*'s "Ramble On" left off, "The Battle Of Evermore" references Tolkien's *Return Of The King* in its allusions to the Dark Lord and the Ringwraiths. Riding on John Paul Jones' strummed mandolin and featuring the richly lustrous tones of Fairport Convention's Sandy Denny in call-and-response counterpoint to Plant's narrative lead, it's one of the band's great acoustic outings.

"Stairway To Heaven" slowly builds from pastoral acoustic prettiness to driving electric intensity. The medieval feel of Page's intro is underscored by the recorders Jones plays alongside him, transporting us to some hazy scene out of Edmund Spenser's *The Faerie Queene*. When Page brings in his 12-string electric, the feel shifts instantly, as though ushering us out of the misty past into the amplified present. The song then begins the ascent to its frenzied climax, complete with a passionate Page solo played over chords borrowed from Dylan's "All Along The Watchtower." For some, "Stairway" is a colossal joke, a pseudo-classical epic that's impossible to take seriously. For those who can suspend their cynical disbelief for eight minutes, the song remains the greatest epic track in all of rock.

Built on Jones' electric piano chords, the pounding "Misty Mountain Hop" is another Tolkien-inspired song, one that draws allegorical parallels between hippies and the dwarves in *The Hobbit*. Hippie boy Plant sings of a free-festival drug bust and a consequent longing to flee to a place "where the spirits go now/Over the hills where the spirits fly. . . ."

Next up, "Four Sticks" is a trance-like raga with Indian overtones, Bonham playing the song's strange meter with the double drumsticks of the title and Jones overdubbing a VCR synth solo in the second middle-eight section. The track just about works as an exotic oddity, its crabbed oriental feel making it a missing link between *III*'s "Friends" and *Physical Graffiti*'s "Kashmir" while anticipating the sound of Perry Farrell's Jane's Addiction by some twenty years.

The premise of "Going To California" is simple enough: it's a love song to the Golden State's more bucolic side, specifically the canyons of Los Angeles. Specifically, the song pays tribute to Joni Mitchell, the brilliant Canadian songstress who made Laurel Canyon her home early in 1968. Jones pulls out his mandolin again and darts magically around Page's resonant acoustic picking. The Zeppelin songbook doesn't get any softer than "Going To California," which became an integral part of the acoustic mini-set the group inserted into its early-seventies live repertoire as a sort of musical sorbet.

Written by blues singers Memphis Minnie and Kansas Joe McCoy before they left Tennessee for Chicago in the economically disastrous year of 1929, "When The Levee Breaks" tells of the devastating floods that swamped the South in the 1920s.

IV's finale also stands with "Black Dog" as a vital counterweight to the album's more ethereal moments. Grungily primeval, it's a second dose of heavy blues that returns the band to their 12-bar New Yardbirds roots, taking Minnie's Delta woes and turning them into a driving hulk of a track. Page's grinding slide meshes with Plant's squalling harmonica, forced forward by the mightiest drum sound ever captured on tape. The primordial thwack of the song's beat, with its fat booming echo, is almost industrial in its density. No wonder the band delays the entrance of Plant's vocal for almost a minute and a half.

IV was not an overnight phenomenon. Though it sold in huge numbers and swiftly outstripped sales of 1970's *III*, it was only with Zeppelin's 1973 U.S. tour that the album began to attain its *Thriller*-esque status. Much of that had to do with the burgeoning popularity of "Stairway To Heaven," a song that turned Zeppelin's fans into a global cult of suburban stoners doubling as disciples of darkness.

To date, *IV* has sold 23 million copies in the United States alone. It remains a monument in the musical landscape, the benchmark against which all other rock albums must be judged.

"Bonzo and Robert had gone out for the night, and I worked really hard on the thing. Jonesy and I then routined it together, and later we ran through it with the drums and everything. Robert was sitting there at the time, by the fireplace, and I believe he came up with 80 percent of the lyrics at that time. He was just sort of writing away and suddenly there it was...."

—Jimmy Page on "Stairway To Heaven,"
quoted in Cameron Crowe's "Led Zeppelin: Light And Shade"

"The first song I played all the way through must have been 'Stairway To Heaven.' I remember getting through the fingerpicking and just cursing Jimmy Page"

—Johnny Depp

Sheet music to "Stairway To Heaven," 1972.

3.5.71	Ulster Hall, Belfast, Ireland
3.6.71	National Boxing Stadium, Dublin, Ireland
3.9.71	Leeds University, Leeds, England
3.10.71	UKC Students Union, University of Kent, Canterbury, England
3.11.71	Old Refectory, Southampton University, Southampton, England
3.13.71	Bath Pavilion, Bath, England
3.14.71	Trentham Gardens, Stoke-On-Trent, England
3.18.71	Mayfair Ballroom, Newcastle, England
3.19.71	Union Buildings, Manchester University, Manchester, England
3.20.71	The Belfry, Sutton Coldfield, England
3.21.71	Nottingham Boat Club, Nottingham, England

3.23.71	Marquee Club, London, England
4.1.71	Paris Cinema Theatre, London, England
5.3.71	KB Hallen, Copenhagen, Denmark
5.4.71	Fyns Forum, Odensen, Denmark
5.10.71	Liverpool University, Liverpool, England
7.5.71	Vigorelli Velodrome, Milan, Italy
8.7–8.71	Casino de Montreux, Montreux, Switzerland
8.19.71	Pacific Coliseum, Vancouver, BC
8.20.71	Seattle Coliseum, Seattle, WA
8.21–22.71	The Forum, Inglewood, CA
8.23.71	Tarrant County Convention Center, Fort Worth, TX
8.24.71	Memorial Auditorium, Dallas, TX
8.25.71	Sam Houston Coliseum, Houston, TX
8.27.71	Municipal Auditorium, San Antonio, TX
8.28.71	Arena, St. Louis, MO
8.29.71	Municipal Auditorium, New Orleans, LA
8.31.71	Sports Stadium, Orlando, FL
9.1.71	Hollywood Sportatorium, Hollywood, FL
9.3.71	Madison Square Garden, New York, NY
9.4.71	Maple Leaf Gardens, Toronto, ON
9.5.71	Chicago International Ampitheater, Chicago, IL
9.7.71	Boston Garden, Boston, MA
9.9.71	Hampton Roads Coliseum, Hampton, VA
9.10.71	Onondaga War Memorial, Syracuse, NY
9.11.71	War Memorial Auditorium, Rochester, NY
9.13–14.71	Community Theatre, Berkeley, CA
9.16–17.71	Civic Auditorium, Honolulu, HI
9.23–24.71	Budokan, Tokyo, Japan
9.27.71	Shiei Taikukan Hall, Hiroshima, Japan
9.28–29.71	Festival Hall, Osaka, Japan
11.11.71	City Hall, Newcastle, England
11.12.71	Mecca Ballroom, Newcastle, England
11.13.71	Caird Hall, Dundee, Scotland
11.16.71	St. Matthew's Baths Hall, Ipswich, England
11.17.71	Kinetic Circus, Birmingham, England
11.18.71	Union of Students, Sheffield University, Sheffield, England
11.20–21.71	Wembley Empire Pool, London, England
11.23.71	Public Hall, Preston, England
11.24.71	Free Trade Hall, Manchester, England
11.25.71	Leicester University, Leicester, England
11.29.71	Liverpool Stadium, Liverpool, England
11.30.71	Kings Hall, Belle Vue, Manchester, England
12.2.71	Starkers, Royal Ballrooms, Bournemouth, England
12.7.71	Locarno Ballroom, Coventry, England
12.9.71	Polytechinc, Lanchester, England
12.15.71	City Hall, Salisbury, England

LOCARNO Coventry
Smithford Way Tel. 24570
THURSDAY, 9th DECEMBER
KINETIC CIRCUS presents
LED ZEPPELIN
at 8 p.m.
Admission Ticket
A
0415

Where's That Confounded Bridge?
1972–1973

Following the release of the fourth album, Led Zeppelin encountered difficulties on tour as well as in their attempts to bridge the gap to critical accolades and even fan acceptance of new material that would help comprise their next LP.

The band did not immediately tour the United States to promote the fourth album. Instead, manager Peter Grant booked the quartet's first tour of Australia and New Zealand for February 1972, with a warm-up show in Singapore en route. Alas, the opening concert was scratched because the Singapore government made a big hairy deal about grooming, refusing admission to men with long hair. The band didn't even get off the plane when it stopped for refueling in Singapore.

Things were a little rocky Down Under as well. After the band's first Australian concert in Perth, its hotel was raided the next morning by a police drug unit (the cops came up empty-handed). After more successful shows in Australia and New Zealand, John Paul Jones and John Bonham, whose wife was expecting a baby in April, returned to London, and Jimmy Page and Robert Plant returned to Bombay. Like the Rolling Stones' Brian Jones before him, the guitarist was obsessed with marrying eastern and western music, so he revisited some of the same haunts from his previous trip. At a disco Page and Plant jammed with Indian musicians on "Rock And Roll" and "Black Dog." During the day, locals drove the rock stars around so they could listen to and tape-record street musicians. The highlight, though, was when the two visitors went to a local studio to record "Four Sticks" and "Friends" with an Indian orchestra led by Bollywood film conductor Vijay Ragav Rao. Even though the experimental recordings were never released, the collaboration had a profound effect on Page and Plant.

Zeppelin took a break from business as usual while Bonham's daughter, Zoe, and Plant's son, Karac, were born. Then the quartet began work on its fifth album at Olympic Studio in London and later Stargroves, Mick Jagger's rural retreat.

Seattle Coliseum, Seattle, WA, June 18, 1972. *Robert Knight/Redferns*

New Musical Expresses confirms the band's 1972–1973 U.K. tour, a string of 24 dates.

Green's Playhouse, Glasgow, Scotland, December 4, 1972.

Budokan, Tokyo, Japan, October 2–3, 1972.

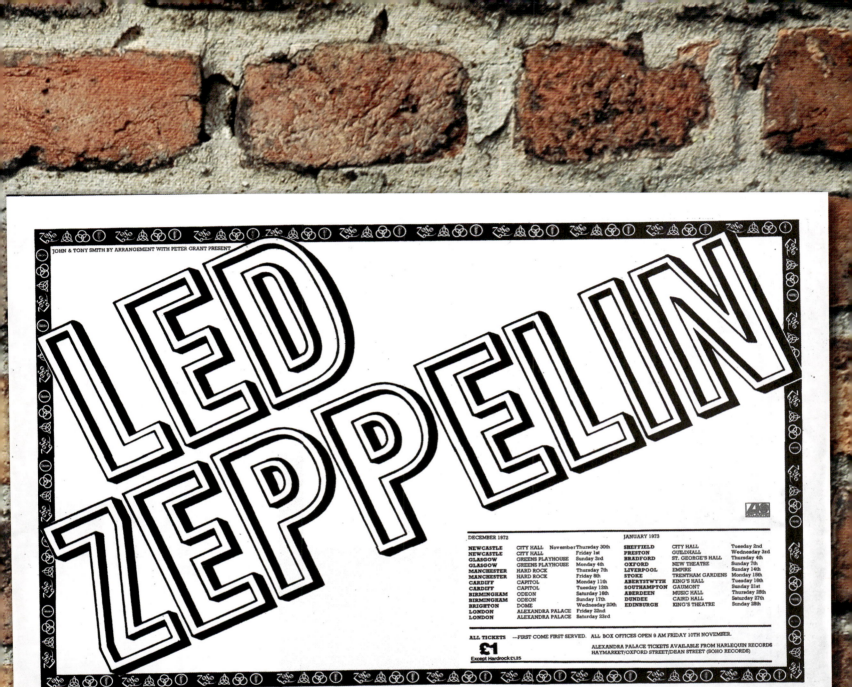

U.K. tour poster, winter 1972–1973.

Naturally, the United States beckoned for Zep's eighth tour there. Things were different this time around. Grant hired a built-for-comfort private jet and negotiated an unprecedented deal for concert payments—the band would take 90 percent of the ticket receipts, the promoter 10 percent, compared with the familiar 50/50 split.

The shows featured new material, including "The Crunge" and "Over The Hills And Far Away" from the forthcoming fifth album. In Baltimore, the band squeezed in a couple of Elvis Presley tunes. During a Los Angeles Forum concert featuring a seven-song encore, Zep covered "Hello Mary Lou," "Louie Louie," John Lee Hooker's "Boogie Chillun," Willie Dixon's "Bring It On Home" and Eddie Cochran's "Weekend," among others. Parts of the Forum show, including a twenty-three-minute treatment of "Whole Lotta Love," ended up on 2003's *How The West Was Won*, which Page pronounced on its liner notes as "Led Zeppelin at its best."

Despite triumphs on stage and at the box office, Led Zeppelin was still sore about the lack of press support in the United Kingdom and the United States, especially compared with the attention lavished on the self-proclaimed world's greatest band, the Rolling Stones, who, on their first U.S. tour since 1969, were being fawned over by Andy Warhol, Jack Nicholson, Norman Mailer, and other A-list celebrities. Zeppelin hired its first press agent, B. P. Fallon, who had worked with the Beatles at Apple Records and Joe Cocker and Traffic at Island Records. Fallon arranged for some British reporters to attend U.S. concerts, but the band still acted like the dogs of doom were howling.

Bonham carped to *New Musical Express*: "Look, we've just toured the States and done as well as if not better than the Stones, but there was hardly anything about it in the British press. All we read was the Stones this, and the Stones that, and it pissed us off, made us feel what the hell, here we are flogging our guts out and for all the notice being given to us, we might as well be playing in bloody Ceylon. Because the kids in England didn't even know we were touring the States."

Plant complained to *Melody Maker*: "Our egos have been hurt, they really have. For some reason, English critics have never told the truth about us. For some reason, they've been out to get us, a bit. So things are clouded over and nobody gets to know what's really happening."

(continued on page 122)

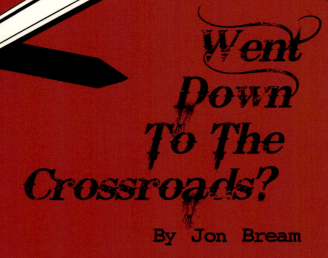

Went Down To The Crossroads?

By Jon Bream

Jimmy Page's interest in black magic and the supernatural, coupled with Zeppelin's rise to the upper stratosphere of rock 'n' roll with rocket-like speed has led some to ponder: Did Page make a pact with ol' Lucifer?

Here's what Robert Plant told *New Musical Express* about that subject in 1985: "Jimmy had his moments when he played his games, but none of them with a great deal of seriousness, and through his own choice, he never really tried to put the story straight. Now maybe he's fully aware of the fact that it's gone on a little longer than it needed to. . . . Pagey liked the idea of being considered a man of mystery. He really should have been a San Francisco version of Simon Templar, hiding in shadows and peeping round corners. He got some kind of enjoyment out of people having the wrong impression of him. He's a very meek guy, shy to the point where sometimes it's uncomfortable. But he let it all go on; and it's his choice whether it all continues. It's not up to me to start saying the guy plays cricket."

Over the years, there were rumors that if you played the classic "Stairway To Heaven" from Zeppelin's fourth album backward, you could hear Satanic messages. Bollocks, Plant once told *Q* magazine with a laugh: "You can't find anything if you play that song backwards. I know because I've tried. There's nothing there. . . . We never made a pact with the devil. The only deal I think we ever made was with some of the girls' high schools in the San Fernando Valley."

In other words, Jimmy Page shouldn't be confused with U.S. bluesman Robert Johnson, who really did make a deal with the devil. Honest, it's in all the music encyclopedias. ✦

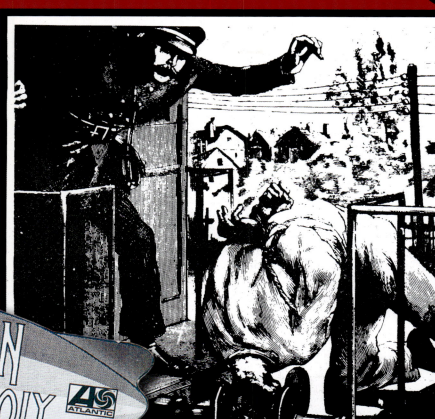

"Led Zeppelin was always the focus of death threats because of their occult association and their big success. The '73 tour was the first time that significant death threats had been directed toward Led Zeppelin, so it was taken very seriously. Later, the death threats became routine."

—*Danny Goldberg, quoted in Stephen Davis'* Hammer Of The Gods

LED·ZEPPELIN · HOUSES ₒf THE·HOLY

DOES THINGS TO PEOPLE...

U.S. print ad announcing *Houses Of The Holy*, released March 18, 1973, in the U.S.

"*Houses Of The Holy* was a very inspired time. I think the material is very much to the point, very focused and strong. I think 'The Crunge' was great; 'Rain Song' was really good. There was a lot of imagination on that record. I prefer it much more than the fourth album. I think it's much more varied, and it has a flippance which showed up later again on in *In Through The Out Door*, with stuff like 'Hot Dog' and 'Candy Store Rock' on *Presence*—which was a total thing of me trying to be Elvis or something.

—*Robert Plant on his favorite Zeppelin album,* High Times, *1991*

THIS SPREAD: KB Hallen, Copenhagen, Denmark, March 2, 1973. *Jorgen Angel/Redferns*

"My take on this period [1973] was that it was sometimes boring. They were *tired*. One of the stories that doesn't get told was how many times there *weren't* wild parties, and how lonely and exhausted they would get, and how they would be so worried about what they looked like in a picture and would their wives be mad at them."

—*Danny Goldberg, quoted in Stephen Davis'* Hammer Of The Gods

(continued from page 118)

Even John Paul Jones weighed in to *Melody Maker*: "They say Jethro Tull are brilliant on stage; well, they do the same bloody thing every night, the same gags, everything the same. Each of our gigs is treated differently, we don't have any set religiously rehearsed thing."

Upon their return to the United Kingdom, Page continued to work on the fifth album's overdubs and graphic design. He also was distracted by a side project: composing a soundtrack (on a newly acquired synthesizer) for director Kenneth Anger's film, *Lucifer Rising*, a project that would drag on fruitlessly for three years, leading to a war of words in the media between the two who had originally bonded when they'd found themselves bidding against each other for a rare Aleister Crowley manuscript at auction.

In October 1972, Led Zeppelin headed to Japan for a second time, with Jones bringing along a synthesizer for the first time (for "Stairway To Heaven"). Next up was a twenty-four-concert U.K. tour, during which *NME's* Nick Kent accompanied the band for a bit. While he wrote auspicious reports at the time, he later ranted about the boorish behavior of tour manager Richard Cole and drummer John Bonham. In Nigel Williamson's *The Rough Guide To Led Zeppelin*, Kent later recalled, "I once saw them beat a guy senseless and then drop money on his face. It makes me feel sick when I hear Plant talking about what a great geezer Bonzo was, because the guy was a schizophrenic animal."

In March, Zeppelin rocked the European continent, where the individual members made quite an impression on Benoit Gautier of Atlantic Records' Paris office, which helped with tour security. He told Stephen Davis in *Hammer Of The Gods* that Page was "the mastermind of it all and very much in control" despite his predilection for cocaine. Plant "never harmed anybody, had good manners, was always smiling," Gautier further observed. He figured "the bright, intelligent and cultured" Jones was the smartest member. "He never got caught in an embarrassing situation. He would always show at the very last minute for anything. You'd never even know where he was staying. He drove himself and was independent from the rest of the band. It upset them that they couldn't manipulate him." As for the complex Bonham, he "would cry when talking about his family. Then the roadies would start to push him to do something and he'd go crazy. He would throw drinks or dump food on somebody if Jimmy told him to. He had no natural defense against being manipulated and nothing to protect him."

(continued on page 126)

Tellin' All Of Your Lies: Plant And Page On *Hammer Of The Gods*

by Jon Bream

If you crave tales from Zeppelin's depraved side, read Stephen Davis' colorful 1985 band bio *Hammer Of The Gods*, which draws heavily on the memories of Zep tour manager Richard Cole, or Cole's own 1992 tell-all, *Stairway To Heaven: Led Zeppelin Uncensored.*

Jimmy Page disses Cole's book (he also has claimed to reading only two pages of it). Page takes exception to Cole's account of Page and Plant, at their first fruitful meeting, discussing Joan Baez's rendition "Babe I'm Gonna Leave You." The book says that Plant picked up a guitar and showed Page a proposed arrangement. In reality, Page says, it was the other way around. "That has made me completely ill," Page told *Guitar World* in 1993. "I'm so mad about it that I can't even bring myself to read the whole thing. The two bits that I have read are so ridiculously false that I'm sure if I read the rest I'd be able to sue Cole and the publishers. But it would be so painful to read that it wouldn't be worth it."

Robert Plant similarly dismisses *Hammer Of The Gods*, while claiming not to have read it. In 1985, he told *New Musical Express:* "The mood of what has been related to me is grossly deceptive because I would think that about 97 percent of the time over a 12-year period, it was maximum smiles. We held together and we had a great time—and without affecting anybody else particularly and without becoming sadistic morons. . . . Over the years, we've all sat back and watched it and smiled. If you get stuck into denying things and setting stories right, then you're a party to it, you're prey to these people. Now I look at it with scorn. I find it funny that people should have waited so long until the heat's gone and the book can't sell to lie so furiously, to paint a picture that's grayer than it was blue.

"[Davis] did a lot of investigations with a guy who used to work with Led Zeppelin, Richard Cole. . . . He was tour manager, and he had a problem which could have been easily solved if he'd been given something intelligent to do rather than check the hotels, and I think it embittered him greatly. He became progressively unreliable and, sadly, became a millstone around the neck of the group.

"These stories would filter out from girls who'd supposedly been in my room when in fact they'd been in his. That sort of atmosphere was being created, and we were quite tired of it. So eventually we relieved him of his position. . . . And in the meantime he got paid a lot of money for talking crap. A lot of the time he wasn't completely . . . well. And so his view of things was permanently distorted one way or another."

The Forum, Inglewood, CA, June 3, 1973. *Michael Ochs Archives/Getty Images*

"The dressing room of the San Diego Sports Arena was a madhouse. The band changed into its stage clothes amid a jumble of roadies, well-wishers, and local record and radio executives trying to introduce their children. Robert called for tea and honey, ignoring the mountain of fried chicken, fresh fruit, and crates of fans' gifts piled in a corner. Just as they were about to go on, Led Zeppelin piled into a washroom for a bit of blow in private. Then they hit the stage with 'Rock And Roll' and the San Diego Sports Arena erupted. The crowd immediately flattened the seats and pressed up close to the stage like netted fish. As the show heated up, dozens of girls were hoisted on their boyfriends' shoulders. Many of the girls took off their halter tops and wiggled their bare breasts at the band, causing a stampede backstage as the roadies scrambled to get a look. Gradually Zeppelin's avowed Apollonian intent reverted to a Dionysiac bawdiness. People fainted and were either trampled underfoot or passed over the crowd to the security men in front of the stage. The sheer body heat inspired the band. Jimmy whanged into the rarely played 'The Crunge' and manipulated the theremin with wild shamanistic gestures. Robert constantly pleaded for order, and the show turned into a masterpiece. As the band left the stage for the last time after an hour of encores, a huge white-hot neon sign at the rear of the stage lit up the hall with its undeniable message: LED ZEPPELIN."

—*Stephen Davis on the 1973 tour,* Hammer Of The Gods

"I actually went to see them in about '73 or '74, something like that. They were a band my mates were into more than myself; I didn't go out and buy Zeppelin records 'cause a lot of my friends were into the band and had them already. But I thought that rhythm section and Page's guitar work was just phenomenal at the time."

—Bruce Foxton, The Jam

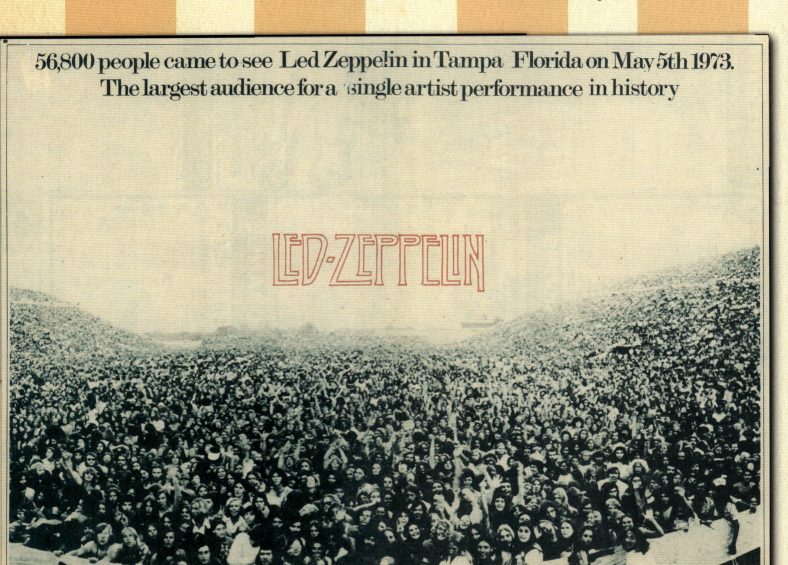

56,800 people came to see Led Zeppelin in Tampa Florida on May 5th 1973.
The largest audience for a single artist performance in history

LED-ZEPPELIN

Congratulations from Concerts West & Atlantic Records

"It was really the Led Zeppelin records that first got me standing on my bed strumming a tennis racket. It was the riffology of Jimmy Page that fused with my DNA; and the barometer in my head of whether a riff was a good one or a bad one was certainly determined by songs like 'Black Dog' and 'Out On The Tiles' and 'The Ocean.' There's really hardly a better band than Led Zeppelin."

—Tom Morello, aka the Nightwatchman, Rage Against the Machine, Audioslave

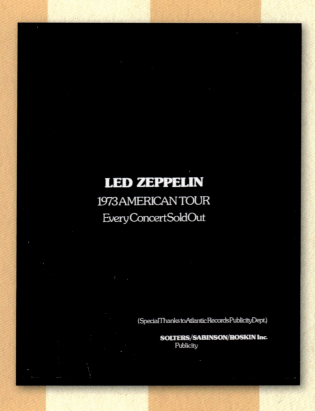

LED ZEPPELIN

1973 AMERICAN TOUR

Every Concert Sold Out

(Special Thanks to Atlantic Records Publicity Dept.)

SOLTERS/SABINSON/ROSKIN Inc.
Publicity

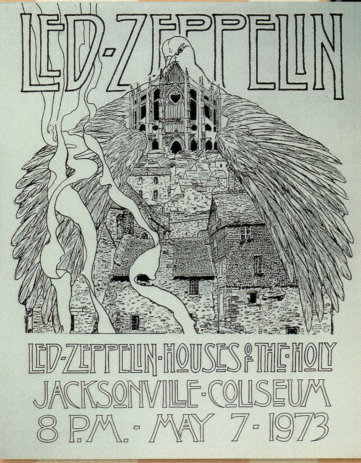

(continued from page 122)

On March 18, 1973, *Houses Of The Holy* was released a staggering seventeen months after the release of the fourth album. There were lighthearted numbers, including the ska-tinged "D'yer Mak'er" and the R&B jaunt "The Crunge," as well as some heavier, more atmospheric pieces such as "The Song Remains The Same." Page talked about the making of that number with *Guitar World*: "It was originally going to be an instrumental—an overture that led into 'The Rain Song.' But I guess Robert had different ideas. You know, 'This is pretty good, better get some lyrics—quick!' [laughs]. . . . I had all the beginning material together, and Robert suggested that we break down into half-time in the middle. After we figured out that we were going to break it down, the song came together in a day."

"The Crunge," which seemed like a goof or an R&B spoof, was played on a Stratocaster. "I wanted to get that tight James Brown feel," Page explained. "You have to listen closely, but you can hear me depressing a whammy bar at the end of each phrase. Bonzo started the groove on 'The Crunge,' then Jonesy started playing that descending bass line and I just came in on the rhythm. You can really hear the fun we were having on *Houses* and *Physical Graffiti*. And you can also hear the dedication and commitment."

And the change, which was necessary for Zeppelin. "Our music may change so much in times to come that our audience does diminish," Plant told *CREEM* magazine. "Because I know we won't become passé, we might take things beyond what people are prepared to accept from us. For example, our third album wasn't immediately accepted, but it was a signpost for the continuity of the internal stimulus of the band. It had to be, it was the next step, and people didn't take to it too quickly. They were more interested in where's 'Whole Lotta Love.' Had we not done it, we would probably have stayed together for only one more album. When you think you've reached a dead end, you have to get off the horse."

For Zeppelin's ninth U.S. tour, the show would not remain the same. The band upped the ante and the arsenal: lasers, explosions, stage fog, mirrored balls, and American publicist Danny Goldberg, who had written for *Rolling Stone* magazine. In the course of eighty-seven days (with a break in June), Zep stormed the States, grossing a record $4 million, topping the Stones' mark of 1972. Crowds at stadium shows were huge—fifty thousand in Atlanta and in San Francisco, and fifty-six thousand in Tampa, the latter mark breaking, as Zep's publicist was quick to point out, the Beatles' 1965 record at Shea Stadium.

LED ZEPPELIN

Los Angeles, 1973.

Reportedly inspired by a white-knuckle bout with air turbulence aboard a small private jet, Zeppelin leased a Boeing 720 known as *The Starship* with LED ZEPPELIN painted on the fuselage and an organ in the cabin on which Jones entertained the entourage. (The plane enabled the group to base its tour in large cities such as Chicago, Los Angeles, and New York and fly back after every gig.)

The tour's three-night stand at New York's Madison Square Garden was filmed for a documentary that became *The Song Remains The Same*. Filmmaker Joe Massot asked the musicians to wear the same outfits all three nights so he could edit footage, but Jones, usually the goody-goody, stubbornly refused to cooperate.

The tour was an unquestionable triumph, but Zeppelin returned to England with some holes in the balloon. The hard-working, hard-partying Page was malnourished, sleep-deprived, and downright exhausted. Jones informed Grant of his intentions to quit to spend more time with his family, and Plant's voice problems necessitated surgery. In 1988, the singer revealed to Williamson that he couldn't talk for three weeks. Zeppelin, the hardest-touring band in rock 'n' roll, took an eighteen-month hiatus from the stage. ●

Danny Goldberg was there in the eye of the hurricane as Led Zeppelin's press agent for the 1973 U.S. tour and, from 1974 to 1976, as vice president of the band's own label, Swan Song. He agreed to this exclusive interview for Whole Lotta Led Zeppelin *in 2008.*

EDITOR: When did you begin working with Led Zeppelin?

DANNY GOLDBERG: I was hired in 1973 by a public relations firm called Solters & Roskin, Inc., an old-school, show-biz PR firm: Lee Solters and Sheldon Roskin had worked with Barbra Streisand and another one of their clients was Frank Sinatra. They hired me specifically because I was in my early twenties and had long hair. I had been a rock writer, had written a little bit for *Rolling Stone* and *CREEM*, knew a lot of the rock press; I understood rock 'n' roll. So, I was hired by Solters & Roskin specifically to be a publicist that would handle rock bands because that was the growing segment of the PR business. When Led Zeppelin became a client of Solters & Roskin, my boss, Lee Solters, immediately assigned them to me because he knew it wasn't his thing.

EDITOR: And was this your first job doing press work with a band? Was it the first band you had represented?

DANNY GOLDBERG: Led Zeppelin wasn't the first client I worked with, but on the other hand I had only been there for a few months when Zeppelin came in.

I became Led Zeppelin's North American publicist for the '73 tour. *Houses Of The Holy* had just came

out, and they toured in the United States from May through June and then the month of July 1973. And then in '74 they hired me to work for them full time as vice president of their new record label, Swan Song. I continued to work with them until the middle of 1976.

At the time, I had certainly been around rock 'n' roll a lot, but there was nothing like Led Zeppelin. They were the biggest band in the world. And they had a reputation.

EDITOR: What were your first impressions of the band and of Peter Grant?

DANNY GOLDBERG: They were nothing like you might expect. Lee Solters and I flew over to Paris because the band was in the middle of doing a European tour and they were playing at the Palais du Sport in Paris. We met Peter before we met the band. We saw the show, and the next day we met with the band and Peter. In that situation, they were very, very thoughtful and polite—not the rock 'n' roll wild men that their reputation would have predicted. They knew they were meeting with American PR people and they wanted to make a good impression.

They had made a decision that they wanted to get more high-profile press, a different kind of press. They had been around for several years already. *Houses Of The Holy* was their fifth album, and they already were a huge band. They had accomplished a lot without getting very good press and they wanted to add to their accomplishments by expanding their visibility more into the mainstream media and the music press. I mean they were not beloved by the *music* press then either.

EDITOR: And why do you think that is? The band seemed to almost have had a fear of dealing with the press, in my impression.

DANNY GOLDBERG: I don't think there was a *fear*. To understand this, you need to step back to the band's beginnings. Led Zeppelin had came along in January '69 with their first record. At the time, they were really kind of a second wave of hard rock album groups. Cream had come out several years before; the Stones had been around since '63. Jimmy Page himself was one of three great guitarists to come out of the Yardbirds, and Eric Clapton and Jeff Beck already had bigger reputations with the public. As part of this second wave of hard rock, they were not viewed as new and unique by the music press.

But another thing was happening by the time Zeppelin's first record came out—the development of rock radio. For about three or four years from the mid '60s to the late '60s, rock critics had been really essential in introducing a lot of the rock artists to their audiences. Now, when rock radio came along, the role of the rock critics was tremendously diminished. Zeppelin's first album was one of the first albums in the United States to break big over the airwaves rather than in the music press. Rock stations like WBCN in Boston, KMET in L.A., and KSAN in San Francisco really made Zeppelin very big, very fast. And the rock press was not part of this. A lot of the rock writers were now in their mid twenties and the audience for Zeppelin was in their teens. So, these rock writers were already a generation removed, and one thing we know about older people is they always have a low opinion of the music of younger people.

So, for those various reasons—both the changes in the business and a slight generational shift—the rock critics were brutal to Led Zeppelin. They gave them terrible reviews on the first couple of albums. And so after that, the band said, "Fuck 'em! If they're not going to appreciate or respect us, then let's just not talk to them." So Zeppelin developed a hostile attitude toward the rock critics because of the fact that they weren't well received.

The same thing happened in England. The press didn't like them there, too. I don't know if it was so much radio or whether it was the generational thing. But whatever it was, they were not embraced by critics. So therefore, they hated them.

EDITOR: And what was your strategy to turn that around?

DANNY GOLDBERG: There were three elements. First was to beg for favors. Second was to get Zeppelin to meet the writers. I told the rock critics, "Look, you may or may not like them, but the audience *loves* them—and you can't be serious about covering this cult and ignore the audience." My belief was that the band that I met was articulate and smart, and I thought that if they met people they'd win them over. Also, there were younger writers coming along—people like Cameron Crowe.

And we got lucky.

The first two concerts Zeppelin did on the '73 U.S. tour were both stadium shows. The first was at Atlanta Stadium.

EDITOR: Which you were able to promote as the biggest thing to hit Atlanta since *Gone With The Wind*.

DANNY GOLDBERG: Right. The second was at Tampa Stadium and it sold out. 56,800 people came to see Zeppelin, which was just a little bit more than the 55,000 that saw the Beatles at Shea Stadium in 1965. Tampa Stadium happened to have more seats than Shea, thus it could physically seat more people. So I spread the story that Zeppelin had broken the Beatles record—Led Zeppelin was now bigger than the Beatles were in their heyday. (At Woodstock, of course, there were all sorts of huge events that drew more than 56,000 people, but for a concert headlined by one band it was the largest at the time. And was no government agency or truth squad was out there to correct us.) So, that Tampa Stadium concert was the biggest single-artist show ever in the history of the United States. That became a gimmick by which to make the larger point that Led Zeppelin was the most popular band in America right then. If you like rock 'n' roll you better know about them. And if you write about rock 'n' roll, you at least should cover them.

Robert Hilburn, the music editor at the *L. A. Times*, was sympathetic to this notion of the generational myopia of some of the older rock writers. He had the idea of assigning a high school student to write about Led Zeppelin, and that high school student's name was Cameron Crowe. So, Cameron did the story for the *L. A. Times*. And that opened doors.

Then, *Rolling Stone* calls and says they want to do a cover spread on the band. They had already given *Houses Of The Holy* another horrible review, calling the album a "limp blimp." But now, as they hear all the publicity about how big the band is, *Rolling Stone* wants to do a cover story. So I talk to the band about it, and they say, "No fucking way. Fuck them, they hate us." I said, "All right, cool. We'll tell everyone you turned down *Rolling Stone* for the cover. That's a PR angle: You're so big you don't need *Rolling Stone*."

Now in '75, *Rolling Stone* calls again. This time they say, "Look, we'll do a Q&A so there can't be any sarcastic commentary by the writer. It'll be just the questions and answers. And you can choose the writer." Jimmy says, "OK, we'll do it. And have Cameron Crowe be the writer." That cover story was the turning point in getting respect from the critics.

EDITOR: Did you see yourself as a sort of spin doctor? Did you work to dispel all of the stories surrounding—the tales of groupies, the band throwing televisions out hotel windows, the infamous Shark Episode, all that kind of stuff?

DANNY GOLDBERG: I just kind of allowed it.

EDITOR: Just let the stories build into legends?

DANNY GOLDBERG: Well, those stories—those *particular* stories—already existed.

When I met the band, I said to them, "You know, you have the reputation of being barbarians." And Peter Grant replied, "Yes, but we're only *mild* barbarians."

Robert said, "Look, we were young then, but we're not like that any more. We just want to play music." And my experience with them was always good. I mean, John Bonham got drunk a couple of times and kind of—well, those stories have all been told in *Hammer Of The Gods* and elsewhere. Of course there were a lot of girls around and rowdiness, but it wasn't anything that interfered with people getting a good story. And, as far as the earlier stuff goes, it was kind of legendary in the sense that it was edgy, but it was in the past.

EDITOR: You didn't try to cover up any of the past.

DANNY GOLDBERG: No, no. It was about focusing on the music, that's all.

EDITOR: Right.

DANNY GOLDBERG: No one was denying anything. "We were young then," they'd tell writers. "Now we're older. Now we're in our *mid* twenties!"

EDITOR: Ha! And so what was the hardest thing about working with them?

DANNY GOLDBERG: Well, there was often a lot of stress, as parts of the entourage were tightly wound. There was always a general air of tension, of threatened violence. I never saw any violence, but Peter Grant and road manager Richard Cole, these were tough guys. Just the sheer magnitude of what they were trying to do created a lot of pressure. And the band had a high level of expectations to go with it all. So, it could be exhausting, and there were days when I just couldn't please them. It was all exciting, but it was certainly tense.

EDITOR: What was the most fun part?

DANNY GOLDBERG: Controlling the backstage access, handing out photo passes—all of that was exciting.

And getting to know Led Zeppelin as people was great. They were all brilliant people and it was a privilege to spend time with them. I knew then that they were important musicians.

John Paul Jones was the most shy. He was the quietest of the band, yet he is one of the most brilliant arrangers and bass players in the history of rock music

John Bonham is, I think, by consensus the greatest rock drummer ever. At the very least, he's in everybody's top five list.

I got to know Robert better than the others: he was articulate, enthusiastic.

Peter Grant was an incredible guy to work for. He was a genius when it came to the rock 'n' roll business. He changed the paradigm in many ways in favor of the artist. He understood how valuable they were. He got Led Zeppelin a bigger percentage of concert money than any bands had before, and this permanently changed the economics of the business. He carried himself in a way that made everyone understand that Led Zeppelin was what was driving all of these businesses and they'd better be treated with respect. I really internalized that, and for the rest of my career have always tried to look at artists the way he looked at his artists. So, Peter was a great teacher to me.

And of course the music was great. The shows were mostly fabulous. They tended to improvise some at every show. I never was a big fan of drum solos, but Bonham's drum solos varied from night to night and were really magical.

EDITOR: So you had a real sense you were making history?

DANNY GOLDBERG: Well, *they* were making history—and I was trying to cram my way into the picture. But I knew Led Zeppelin was a very important band. There was nothing like them. They really did things their own way and never pandered to the radio station formats. They didn't copy themselves. Jimmy and Robert were both determined to keep the creativity going to change their style, to use new instruments, to find new words—they were real artists. They weren't just a commercial band. And they had tremendous—and serious—purpose about what they did. They were almost agonizing about it. It was really a privilege to be around such brilliant people.

EDITOR: What place do you think Led Zeppelin will have in rock 'n' roll history? Are they the "heaviest band ever," as *Rolling Stone* called them? Are they the true originators of the rock 'n' roll lifestyle? What do you think?

DANNY GOLDBERG: In the end, I don't think there's anybody in any country in the world where rock 'n' roll has been played, no matter what their personal taste is, who wouldn't include Led Zeppelin among the most important rock bands of all time.

"WE WERE ONLY MILD BARBARIANS."

—Peter Grant

THE STARSHIP

By Richard Cole with Richard Trubo

In his memoir Stairway To Heaven: Led Zeppelin Uncensored, *tour manager Richard Cole described the jet-setting 1973 US tour in all of its mile-high excesses.*

As the band headed for England for their planned hiatus, I spent most of the remainder of June trying to find a jet that would meet their extravagant tastes and ease their extravagant anxieties while making traveling more comfortable.

I contacted Lou Weinstock of Toby Roberts Tours, who used to arrange for planes for Elvis. Lou passed on a brochure to me about a Boeing jet called the *Starship*. It was a 720B—a forty-seater that had been customized specifically for rock stars, although no one had yet taken a long-term lease on it. Frankly, I doubted that anyone could afford it.

The Starship was owned by singer Bobby Sherman and one of the creators of the Monkees. And it was elegant. A lengthy bar. Televisions. An artificial fireplace in the den and a fur-covered bed in the bedroom. A Thomas organ built into the bar. A kitchen for preparing hot food. "It's like Air Force One with satin sheets," I told Peter.

"See what kind of price you can negotiate," Peter said. "It sounds like a great way to travel. And Danny Goldberg can probably get us some great publicity out of it."

After several lengthy phone calls, I finalized the deal. The price: $30,000 for the remaining three weeks of the American tour. Yes, it was expensive. But once the band got used to the convenience, comfort, and luxury, the price wasn't important. As Robert said on our first flight, "It's like a floating palace."

When we picked up the jet at Chicago's O'Hare airport in early July, it was parked next to Hugh Hefner's plane. Thanks to Goldberg, the rock press was swarming all over the tarmac as we boarded the *Starship* for the first time. One reporter asked Peter, "How does your plane compare to Mr. Hefner's?"

Peter thought for a second, and even though he had barely seen the interior of our own plane, he answered, "The *Starship* makes Hefner's plane look like a dinky toy."

The comment made headlines in the rock press, although Bonham later told me, "I'd like to get some of those Hefner girls on the *Starship*!"

"Don't worry," I told him. "We'll have plenty of girls. I'll see to that."

The band not only fell in love with the *Starship*, but they enjoyed the status of having such an elegant plane, something that other rock bands would envy. Maybe the Stones got a lot more media attention, but no one had a jet quite like this one.

To take full advantage of the *Starship*, I devised a strategy to minimize the exhaustion—physical and mental—that had become an almost inevitable part of touring. For this and the remaining American tours, we based ourselves in a limited number of U.S. cities—New York, Chicago, New Orleans, Dallas, Miami, and Los Angeles—in hotels where we felt comfortable. From those launching pads, we would use the *Starship* to fly to concerts in Milwaukee, Cleveland, Philadelphia, Boston, and other nearby cities. There was no longer a need to move to a new, unfamiliar hotel every night.

On the flights to the concerts, the mood on the *Starship* was relatively quiet. But pandemonium reigned on the post-concert flights. No matter what the hour, no matter how tired we may have been, no one slept, not when there were hot meals to eat, beer to drink, and flight attendants and girls to flirt with.

Ironically, at a time when Zeppelin was firmly entrenched as the world's biggest band, there were fewer groupies throwing themselves into our taps than during the early days. One seventeen-year-old blonde who we met at the Riot House in Los Angeles during that '73 tour told me, "My friends didn't even want to try to get to you guys. Your security is becoming so tight that they just figured they'd never get near you."

Many of the old groupies had disappeared. Some had simply grown up. A few had gotten married. Too many had died of drug overdoses. Still, we would meet girls, often in L.A. clubs like the Rainbow Bar and Grill, and few of them ever turned down the invitation for a ride on the *Starship*. When they were willing, the bedroom gave us some privacy, too.

Among its other toys, the *Starship* had an on-board telephone, and whenever we'd be flying into Los Angeles, I'd call from the air to let the Rainbow know we were on the way. I'd usually get Tony or Michael, who ran the Rainbow, on the phone, and tell them, "We'll be landing at nine-thirty, and then we'll have a twenty-five-minute limo ride from the airport. Please have our tables cleared and some Dom Perignon ready for us." The Rainbow never said no. They spoiled us rotten, but at this point in the band's career, we expected—and almost always got—special treatment.

Linda and Charlotte, who were our favorite Rainbow waitresses and "den mothers," would cordon off an area for Led Zeppelin, and no one got beyond the line of demarcation unless one of us signaled for her safe passage. Usually, adolescent girls with layers of makeup, tight-fitting tops, short skirts, and spike heels had the best chance of winning admission to our asylum.

There were other diversions on the *Starship*. The refrigerators were always well stocked—plenty of champagne, beer, wine, Scotch, Jack Daniels, and gin. The belly of the plane was crammed with cases of Dom Perignon (1964 and 1966 vintage) and Singha beer. We'd drink just about anything, but at times we'd be in the mood for a particular type of alcohol—or drug—and that would become the "substance of choice" for that particular tour.

When he wasn't in a corner playing backgammon, John Paul often would sit at the Thomas, and, with the booze flowing, we'd sing pub songs. We'd encourage the flight attendants—two girls and a guy—to join the partying, and while they took their in-flight responsibilities seriously, they began to feel like part of the Zeppelin family. We didn't fuck around with the stewardesses, Susie and Bianca, because they wouldn't stand for it. But there was a lot of teasing.

Relaxing in-flight before the fireplace aboard the *Starship*. Michael Brennan/Scope Features.com

Susie was an attractive eighteen-year-old blonde; Bianca was twenty-two years old, with a dark complexion and a good sense of humor. Years later, Susie told me, "Back in nineteen seventy-three, when you guys would get off the plane and we'd be straightening things up, we'd find one-hundred-dollar bills rolled up with cocaine inside them. We knew we weren't on a chartered flight for the Queen of England, but in the beginning I was shocked."

One afternoon, on a flight to Cincinnati for a concert at Riverfront Stadium, the *Starship* had been in the air only fifteen minutes when I heard banging and shouts coming from the bathroom.

"Get me out! Get me out!"

It was Bonzo. The bathroom door was locked. I hit it with a couple of Bruce Lee kicks. The door trembled, then it collapsed. There, before my eyes, sat Bonzo, perched on the can with his pants down, literally unable to move.

"Help me, damn it!"

As hard as he was trying, Bonzo couldn't stand up. Apparently, a mechanic had not properly sealed the vent beneath the toilet, and air pressure was literally sucking him down, keeping his ass anchored to the seat.

I grabbed Bonham by the arms and pulled him free. "Oh, my God!" he gasped, feeling terribly shaken but not hurt. He pulled up his pants and didn't seem the least bit embarrassed by what had happened. He was probably just happy to be alive. As he returned to the main cabin of the plane, he mumbled, "I'm never gonna trust a toilet seat again."

The Starship became a symbol of just how high Led Zeppelin was flying. Yes, it was extravagant, pretentious, and snobbish. But the band felt they had earned it.

the LPs:
Houses Of The Holy
By Jim DeRogatis

By January 1972, few were the horizons left for Led Zeppelin to conquer. Like the marauding Vikings of "The Immigrant Song," the four Brits had stormed the music industry, deflected the trifling arrows of hostile critics, and secured a dominant position as the biggest-grossing concert act to that point, as well as the creators of what would become one of the best-selling recordings in history: their officially untitled fourth album, which has sold more than 23 million copies in the United States alone since its release in November 1971.

On the climb to these rarefied misty mountaintops, the two accomplished session musicians and two startlingly talented Black Country newcomers had taken the blues into the Space Age on their first two albums, setting the sonic standard for much of the hard rock and heavy metal to follow. They had showed their range by highlighting a more genteel and melodic side on *Led Zeppelin III*. And, on their fourth trip into the recording studio, they had brought these disparate elements together, producing the twin pillars that would stand as their definitive artistic statements: "When The Levee Breaks" and "Stairway To Heaven."

With nothing left to prove, Jimmy Page, John Paul Jones, Robert Plant, and John Bonham were free to do whatever the hell they wanted—and what they wanted to do was have some fun. "We had no set ideas. We just recorded the ideas each one of us had at that particular time," Page told Ritchie Yorke, perhaps the band's most reliable biographer. "It was simply a matter of getting together and letting it out." Asked three decades later whether there'd been pressure to duplicate the success of the fourth album, Page told *Guitar World* magazine, "Of course, but we didn't let it get in the way. My main goal was to just keep rolling."

To be sure, there are moments of extreme heaviosity and concepts as ponderous as any the band would tackle on the album that became *Houses Of The Holy*. The title referred to the concert venues where the faithful gathered in what Plant called an air of spirituality (though that may have just been the pot smoke). Coupled with the extraordinary cover art by Hipgnosis, allegedly inspired by the Arthur C. Clarke novel *Childhood's End*, it was hard not to think of pagan rituals, virgin sacrifices, and other dark and unholy deeds—those are a real five-year-old boy and seven-year-old girl on the cover, captured in multiple exposures over the course of a week by photographer Aubrey Powell, who would probably be busted for child pornography in these more politically correct times. ("You probably couldn't get away with that now," former child model Stefan Gates told *The Daily Mail* in 2007, when he was forty-two. "I personally have no idea what it means, though there's something about it that is disturbing and haunting, perhaps more so because I am in it.")

And yes, the album does boast two epics, both clocking in at seven minutes or longer, and these can hardly be called lighthearted. "The Rain Song" is an oddity among Zep tunes: a defiantly lush and languorous love song, apparently written as a response to a comment by George Harrison, who allegedly told Bonham that the problem with his band was that it didn't write any ballads. The strengths of this one are a vocal performance that Plant considers one of his best and the glorious orchestrations by Jones. There also is "No Quarter," the creepiest of the band's forays into the swords-and-sorcery realm of J. R. R. Tolkien. Some fans have discerned supposed references to Aragorn and his army traversing the Paths of the Dead en route to Mordor while dodging the Wargs or "dogs of doom" sent by the Dark Lord Sauron. Whether or not that reading is accurate, the lyrics certainly give you something to consider while passing the bong and submersing yourself in the delightfully devilish, proto-Goth ambience of Jones' Mellotron.

Overall, though, *Houses Of The Holy* is characterized by a sunny, carefree, and almost relentlessly optimistic vibe. Here is a group of musicians, each at the peak of their powers, who've achieved a rare and synergistic connection, and they are simply reveling in playing together as they pay homage to more of the artists who inspired them—in the genres of doo-wop (the ending of "The Ocean"), R&B (the blatant James Brown riff of "The Crunge"), folk rock (via the gorgeous 12-string guitar of "Over The Hills And Far Away"), reggae ("D'yer Mak'er"), and other world rhythms (if not exactly musically, then at least in the lyrics of "The Song Remains The Same," which explore Plant's notion that music is the one universal force with the potential to unite mankind).

One by one, the virtuosos take their turns to shine in the spotlight: Page with the regale guitar orchestra he created via an intricate pastiche of overdubs on "The Song Remains The Same," and Plant swinging from one melodic hook to another

on the celebratory "Dancing Days," a vocal performance so ebullient that you even forgive hippie-dippy lyrics such as, "I got my flower, I got my power/I got a woman who knows" and "I saw a lion, he was standing alone/With a tadpole in a jar." Above all there are Jones and Bonham, undeniably the most influential rhythm section in rock history, grooving potently but fluidly through the 4/4 to 7/8 transitions of "The Ocean," sounding like the hardest-hitting and most propulsive dance band ever on "Dancing Days" and "The Crunge" and coming up with something unique and wonderful even as they magnificently maul that reggae beat on "D'yer Mak'er" (pronounced, if you have a British accent, as "jah-may-kah" and nodding to that hoary old joke, "My wife went on vacation to the West Indies." "Jamaica?" "No, she went of her own accord!").

There isn't a rock drummer in the world who hasn't at some point attempted to hammer out Bonzo's dramatic opening assault on his snare drum in "D'yer Mak'er," and so esteemed is his place in the pantheon that many will even wax rhapsodic about how you can hear his bass drum pedal squeak on "The Ocean" (which, fittingly enough, is a song about the sea of fanatically devoted followers in Led Zeppelin's wake).

The making of the band's fifth album couldn't have been all fun and games. The recording sessions dragged on for nine long months, from January through August 1972, hinting that there was at least some hesitation, consideration, and consternation. But there also are the comments that recording engineer Eddie Kramer made to Stephen Davis for *Hammer Of The Gods*: "The general feeling was excellent. For instance, I have a very strong vision, from my perspective in the mobile with the doors to the truck wide open, of all four of them dancing in single file on the lawn [at Stargroves] during the first playback of 'Dancing Days.' It was Robert, Bonzo, Jonesy, and Jimmy dancing in a line on a green lawn, celebrating this incredible thing they'd just recorded."

Whether or not Kramer's story is true, this is the sort of joyous reaction that *Houses Of The Holy* continues to prompt from this listener and many others thirty-five years after the creation of what may be Led Zeppelin's most casual but most inspired and uplifting sounds.

TOUR DATES

2.16.72	Subiaco Oval, Perth, Australia
2.19.72	Memorial Drive, Adelaide, Australia
2.20.72	Kooyong Stadium, Melbourne, Australia
2.25.72	Western Springs Stadium, Auckland, New Zealand
2.27.72	Showground, Sydney, Australia
2.29.72	Festival Hall, Brisbane, Australia
5.27.72	Oude Rai, Amsterdam, Netherlands
5.28.72	Vorst Nationaal, Brussels, Belgium
6.6.72	Cobo Hall, Detroit, MI
6.7.72	Montreal Forum, Montreal, PQ
6.9.72	Charlotte Coliseum, Charlotte, NC
6.10.72	Buffalo Memorial Auditorium, Buffalo, NY
6.11.72	Civic Center, Baltimore, MD
6.13.72	The Spectrum, Philadelphia, PA
6.14–15.72	Nassau Coliseum, Uniondale, NY
6.17.72	Memorial Coliseum, Portland, OR
6.18–19.72	Seattle Coliseum, Seattle, WA
6.21.72	Denver Coliseum, Denver, CO
6.22.72	Swing Auditorium, San Bernardino, CA
6.23.72	Sports Arena, San Diego, CA
6.25.72	The Forum, Inglewood, CA
6.27.72	Long Beach Arena, Long Beach, CA
6.28.72	Tucson Community Center, Tucson, AZ
10.2–3.72	Budokan, Tokyo, Japan
10.4.72	Festival Hall, Osaka, Japan
10.5.72	Kokaido, Nagoya, Japan
10.9.72	Festival Hall, Osaka, Japan
10.10.72	Kaikan Hall, Kyoto, Japan
10.28–29.72	Pavillon, Montreux, Switzerland
11.30–12.1.72	City Hall, Newcastle, England
12.3–4.72	Green's Playhouse, Glasgow, Scotland
12.7–8.72	Hard Rock, Manchester, England
12.11–12.72	Capitol Theatre, Cardiff, Wales
12.16–17.72	Birmingham Odeon, Birmingham, England
12.20.72	Brighton Dome, Brighton, England
12.22–23.72	Alexandra Palace, London, England
1.2.73	City Hall, Sheffield, England
1.7.73	New Theatre, Oxford, England
1.14.73	Liverpool Empire, Liverpool, England
1.15.73	Trentham Gardens, Stoke-On-Trent, England
1.16.73	King's Hall, Aberystwyth, Wales
1.18.73	St. George's Hall, Bradford, England
1.21.73	Gaumont Theatre, Southampton, England
1.22.73	Old Refectory, Southampton University, Southampton, England
1.25.73	Aberdeen Music Hall, Aberdeen, Scotland
1.27.73	Caird Hall, Dundee, Scotland
1.28.73	King's Theatre, Edinburgh, Scotland

1.30.73	Guildhall, Preston, England
3.2.73	KB Hallen, Copenhagen, Denmark
3.4.73	Scandanavium Arena, Göteberg, Sweden
3.6–7.73	Kungliga Tennishallen, Stockholm, Sweden
3.14.73	Messenhalle, Nuremburg, Germany
3.16.73	Stadthalle, Vienna, Austria
3.17.73	Münchner Olympiahalle, Munich, Germany
3.19.73	Deutschlandhalle, Berlin, Germany
3.21.73	Musikhalle, Hamburg, Germany
3.22.73	Gruga-Halle, Essen, Germany
3.24.73	Orthenauhalle, Offenburg, Germany
3.26.73	Palais de Sport, Lyon, France
3.27.73	Parc des Expositions, Nancy, France
4.1–2.73	Palais des Sports, Paris, France
5.4.73	Atlanta Stadium, Atlanta, GA
5.5.73	Tampa Stadium, Tampa, FL
5.7.73	Jacksonville Coliseum, Jacksonville, FL
5.10.73	Memorial Coliseum, University of Alabama, Tuscaloosa, AL
5.11.73	Kiel Auditorium, St. Louis, MO
5.13.73	Municipal Auditorium, Mobile, AL
5.14.73	Municipal Auditorium, New Orleans, LA
5.16.73	Sam Houston Coliseum, Houston, TX
5.18.73	Memorial Auditorium, Dallas, TX
5.19.73	Tarrant County Convention Center, Fort Worth, TX
5.22.73	HemisFair Arena, San Antonio, TX
5.23.73	University of New Mexico, Albuquerque, NM
5.25.73	Denver Coliseum, Denver, CO
5.26.73	Salt Palace, Salt Lake City, UT
5.28.73	Sports Arena, San Diego, CA
5.31.73	The Forum, Inglewood, CA
6.2.73	Kezar Stadium, San Francisco, CA
6.3.73	The Forum, Inglewood, CA
7.6–7.73	Chicago Stadium, Chicago, IL
7.8.73	Market Square Arena, Indianapolis, IN
7.9.73	Civic Center, St. Paul, MN
7.10.73	Milwaukee Arena, Milwaukee, WI
7.12–13.73	Cobo Hall, Detroit, MI
7.15.73	Buffalo Memorial Auditorium, Buffalo, NY
7.17.73	Seattle Center Coliseum, Seattle, WA
7.18.73	Pacific Coliseum, Vancouver, BC
7.19.73	The Spectrum, Philadelphia, PA
7.20.73	Boston Garden, Boston, MA
7.21.73	Civic Center, Providence, RI
7.23.73	Civic Center, Baltimore, MD
7.24.73	Three Rivers Stadium, Pittsburgh, PA
7.27–29.73	Madison Square Garden, New York, NY

TOUR DATES

Moving Through Kashmir
1974-1975

Absence from the stage didn't mean inactivity. Led Zeppelin had to finish a concert film, get its own record label off the ground, and record a double album.

First the film. Each of the four musicians and Peter Grant, the fifth member (at least in his mind), conceived and shot fantasy sequences, entrusting the project to director Joe Massot, a Page pal who had written the hippie western *Zachariah* and directed *Wonderwall* about a peeping-Tom professor. The mighty Zeppelin film and attendant live album wouldn't be released for another three years, however.

In January 1974, the ever-visible Grant and Ahmet Ertegun, founder of Atlantic Records, announced that Led Zeppelin would form its own record label. In May, the band settled on a name, Swan Song Records. Surprisingly, Zeppelin signed mostly old cronies rather than new faces. The first year, Swan Song released new LPs by the Pretty Things, first-wave British rockers who started in 1964, and Bad Company, a supergroup featuring former members of Mott the Hoople, King Crimson, and Free (namely lead singer Paul Rodgers). Swan Song also would later sign Grant's pal and subsequent client Maggie Bell, who had powerful pipes, and pub-rock stalwart Dave Edmunds.

Sessions for Led Zeppelin's sixth album began in late 1973 at Headley Grange and later continued from February through May 1974. Early in the process, Page had a strong sense of direction, as he explained to *Circus* magazine in 1973: "The last album was difficult to get into because it was so complex. We used intricate rhythm patterns and hid a lot of ideas in the lyrics. The next one will still have complex songs, and will have an acoustic guitar piece based on a solo I used to do with the Yardbirds during a song called 'White Summer.' But most of the album will get back to something people think we've been drifting away from—straightforward rock 'n' roll."

With the launch of Swan Song Records, the band's new label recycled old Atlantic Records publicity images.

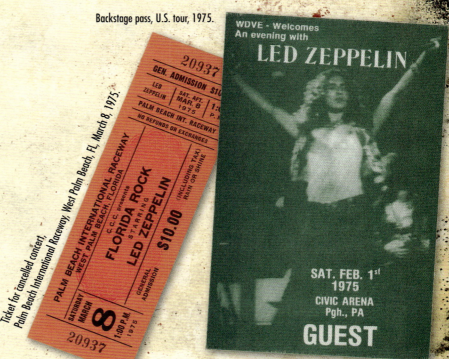

Backstage pass, U.S. tour, 1975.

Ticket for cancelled concert, Palm Beach International Raceway, West Palm Beach, FL, March 8, 1975.

Olympia Stadium, Detroit, MI, January 31, 1975. *Charles Auringer/BackstageGallery.com*

Still, the album—a double disc with fifteen songs—would be a long time coming. "We haven't yet got around to our six-month decision on covers yet," Robert Plant joked in late March 1974, according to Keith Shadwick's *Led Zeppelin: The Story Of A Band And Their Music 1968–1980*. There was some truth in his jest. It really did take months to create the complicated cover, which was more befitting the Rolling Stones than Led Zeppelin. The cover didn't depict mystical mountains but rather gritty reality: a photo of a four-story brownstone, walk-up apartment building in New York's Greenwich Village. On the front cover, the apartment windows were cut out to reveal letters that spelled the band's moniker; on the back, the shades were drawn in the windows. Actually, the lettering and the window shades were on the album's two inner sleeves; flip the sleeves over and the windows reveal a Sgt. Pepper–like mish-mash of historical images: Elizabeth Taylor in *Cleopatra*, Queen Elizabeth II's coronation, King Kong, presidential assassin Lee Harvey Oswald, The Wizard of Oz, a U.S. spaceman walking on the moon, a crashing blimp, Jean Harlow, a Leonardo da Vinci painting, and, among others, the individual members of Led Zeppelin. Whew!

On October 31, 1974, Swan Song threw an extravagant party for the release of its first title, Pretty Things' *Silk Torpedo*, in southeast London, complete with ever-flowing booze, food fights, and strippers dressed as nuns. That night it dawned on Plant that Zeppelin hadn't been on stage for more than a year. "I realized that I really missed the unity of the four of us," he told *New Musical Express*. "I realized that, above everything else, above record companies, above films, we were Led Zeppelin. . . . From that moment on, we started rehearsing and getting into full gear."

One of the tour rehearsals was used to provide additional footage for the film project. Filmmaker Peter Clifton had replaced the sacked Joe Massot. Clifton told Chris Welch in *Peter Grant: The Man Who Made Led Zeppelin*: "I got them all on the stage together in their outfits [they had worn in New York City] and they suddenly realized they were back on stage together for the first time since Madison Square Garden. They started playing 'Black Dog' just for me, and we all got such a shock. They were so hot and tight and fueled up with you know what. There had been a huge argument just minutes beforehand, and then suddenly they began playing, and it was an extraordinarily electric moment between them." Actually, it wasn't as simple as the director made it sound —the band never knew which rehearsals would be filmed and, hence, which outfits to wear, and Page had dramatically restyled his hair, so he had to wear a wig for the filming.

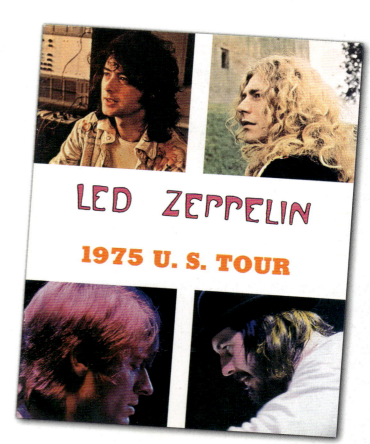

LED ZEPPELIN

1975 U. S. TOUR

Program, U.S. tour, 1975.

SWAN SONG in association with
CONCERTS WEST · JERRY WEINTRAUB
presents AN EVENING WITH
"LED ZEPPELIN"
SAM HOUSTON COLISEUM
HOUSTON, TEXAS
THURSDAY, FEBRUARY 27, 1975 · 8:00 P.M.
ADMIT ONE
GEN. ADM.
NO REFUNDS
$7.50
$7.50
GLOBE TICKET CO. HOUSTON $260
011569
011569

Ticket, Sam Houston Coliseum, Houston, TX, February 27, 1975.

Olympia Stadium, Detroit, MI, January 31, 1975. *Michael Brennan/Scope Features.com*

Then, after warm-up gigs in Holland and Belgium for a winter U.S. tour, Page inadvertently caught the middle finger on his left hand in the door as he was exiting a train at crowded Victoria Station in London en route to a band rehearsal. "It's the one that does all the leverage and most of the work, and it really came as a blow because I just couldn't play with it," he told *New Musical Express*. He had to devise a new fretting technique, which meant he couldn't play "Dazed And Confused." On tour, the band substituted "How Many More Times," which hadn't been played live in nearly four years.

It was nobody's fault but his, and Page was obviously flummoxed by his finger. "I have no doubt that the tour is going to be good, it's just, dammit, I'm disappointed that I can't do all I can do," he told Cameron Crowe in what would be Led Zeppelin's first—and only—cover story in *Rolling Stone* until 2007. "I always want to do my very best and it's very frustrating to have something hold me back in the set the very second I'm able to play it. We may not be brilliant for a few nights, but we'll always be good."

Physical Graffiti was released on February 24, 1975, between legs of the U.S. tour. It entered the U.S. charts at No. 3 and soon ascended to No. 1 for six weeks. Page talked about his new masterwork in an interview with *Guitar World* magazine.

GW: If *Houses Of The Holy* was one of your tightest productions, then *Physical Graffitti* is one of your loosest. Did you make a conscious decision to retreat from a highly polished sound?

JP: Yes, but not completely. "In My Time Of Dying" is a good example of something more immediate. It was just being put together when we recorded it. It is jammed at the end and we do not even have a proper way to stop the thing. But I just thought it sounded like a working group. We could have tightened it up, but I enjoyed its edge. On the other hand, "Kashmir," "In the Light," and "Ten Years Gone" are all very ambitious.

GW: The recording, though, does not seem as punchy as some of your previous efforts.

JP: It doesn't? Maybe. I look at it as a document of a band in a working environment. People might say it is sloppy, but I think this album is really honest. *Physical* is a more personal album, and I think it allowed the listener to enter our world. You know, "Here is the door. I am in."

Swan Song Records publicity photo, U.S. tour 1975.

Ticket, Pacific Coliseum, Vancouver, BC, March 19, 1975.

Nassau Coliseum, Uniondale, NY, February 4, 1975. *Paul Michael Quigley*

GW: You and Plant were traveling to places like Morocco and the Sahara Desert around this time, and you can really hear the influence in songs like "Kashmir." Whose idea was it to explore Morocco?

JP: I did a joint interview with William Burroughs for *Crawdaddy* magazine in the early '70s, and we had a lengthy discussion on the hypnotic power of rock and how it paralleled the music of Arabic cultures. This was an observation Burroughs had after hearing "Black Mountain Side," from our first album. He then encouraged me to go to Morocco and investigate the music firsthand, something Robert and I eventually did.

While the soulful strut "Trampled Under Foot" got most of the radio airplay in the United States, the epic eight-and-half-minute "Kashmir," with its classical sweep and drama, operatic vocals, and plodding rhythm, was the double album's masterstroke. It is unquestionably the quintessential Zeppelin song. "It's all there—all the elements that defined the band," John Paul Jones told Cameron Crowe for the liner notes for *The Complete Studio Recordings*.

In a 1990 interview with *Q* magazine, Plant named it his favorite Zep song. "It's so right—there's nothing overblown, no vocal hysterics. Perfect Zeppelin."

Crowe told the song's story in the boxed set's liner notes. The riff came from some work tapes from Page's home studio. "The structure of it was strange, weird enough to continue exploring," the guitarist said. Because Jones was tardy for their recording session, Page worked on the riff with Bonham, Plant added the middle section, and Jones later overdubbed his bass and the string parts. The original title was "Driving To Kashmir," sparked by a long drive in southern Morocco. As Plant recalled:

"The whole inspiration came from the fact that the road went on and on and on. It was a single track road which cut neatly through the desert. Two miles to the east and west were ridges of sandrock. It basically looked like you were driving down a channel, this dilapidated road, and there was seemingly no end to it. 'Oh, let the sun beat down upon my face, stars to fill my dreams.' It's one of my favorites. . . . It was so positive, lyrically."

"Kashmir" was tremendous for the mood. A lot of that was down to Bonzo, what he played. Page and I couldn't have done it without Bonzo's thrift. He was a real thrifty player. It was what he didn't do that made it work. ◣

CIRCUS OF THE L.A. QUEENS

By Jon Bream

Of course, Pamela Des Barres was only one of many Zeppelin groupies. Another was Bebe Buell, Todd Rundgren's longtime girlfriend, who is now best known as the mother of actress Liv Tyler (whose father is Aerosmith's Steven Tyler). In her 2001 book, *Rebel Heart: An American Rock 'n' Roll Journey*, she talks about meeting Page in 1974. According to Buell, she showed up at Page's Hyatt House room with Rundgren's pet raccoon. Page offered Buell some cocaine and suggested that they put the raccoon in the bathroom with a basket of fruit that was in his suite. Later, Zeppelin's overly protective manager, Grant, aroused by noise in Page's suite, showed up. "We dashed into the bathroom and peered in at an incredible mess," Buell wrote. "There was shit smeared all over the walls, and it looked as if somebody had been engaged in a great life-and-death struggle—hence Peter's suspicion that we had been engaged in some torrid orgy." A raccoon, at least according to Buell, had devoured the fruit and spread his business around the bathroom, so Grant moved Page and Buell to another suite. The next morning, the new lovebirds were awakened by a hysterical Lori Maddox, Page's longtime L.A. girl, who had to be dragged away by tour manager Richard Cole. Just another night at the Riot House.

In her book, Buell also discussed the violence surrounding Zeppelin, especially the rough-and-tumble tactics of the bear-sized Grant, reportedly a former wrestler. "Peter Grant brought the gangster image to the rock 'n' roll scene, and he prospered," she wrote. "Richard [Cole] and Peter were not to be tangled with. They were rough players, and if you got in their faces, or tried to fuck with their band, or did anything to disrupt or harm any member of the band, you would get a knuckle sandwich. It was a little like hanging out with the Mafia. Everybody hung out in a pack and catered to those boys and their whims. They were living the rock and roll cliché to the hilt."

So was Buell. In her book, she fantasized about Page as her Sir Lancelot, taking her on horseback to his castle. "He was my type—very dashing, very English, very Renaissance. He had that otherworldly, other-time vibe. . . . He was a lot like Henry VIII, only a lot more handsome and Jimmy was slim, of course. He had a medieval attitude—not macho, but manly. The image he projected was: I would stab—not shoot, but stab—any dragon for you." And if inquiring minds want to know, "he never tried anything but completely straight sex with me, although he had one weird penchant. When he kissed me, he loved to spew his saliva into my mouth."

In the end, Buell, who also dallied with Mick Jagger, Rod Stewart, David Bowie, and Elvis Costello, to name a few, concluded, "The Stones created the prototype for the rock and roll lifestyle; bands like Led Zeppelin were sloppy seconds." Ouch. ⚘

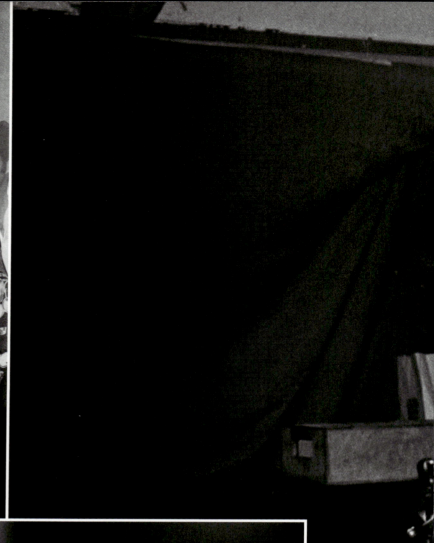

NO STA

"It isn't just a musical thing that takes place, it's a rapport that takes it away from being an earthly thing to almost a little bit above it. . . . This is where you go out on a limb and become King Arthur."

—*Robert Plant*, *quoted in Stephen Davis' Hammer Of The Gods*

Olympic Stadium, Detroit, MI, January 31, 1975. Charles Auringer/BackstageGallery.com

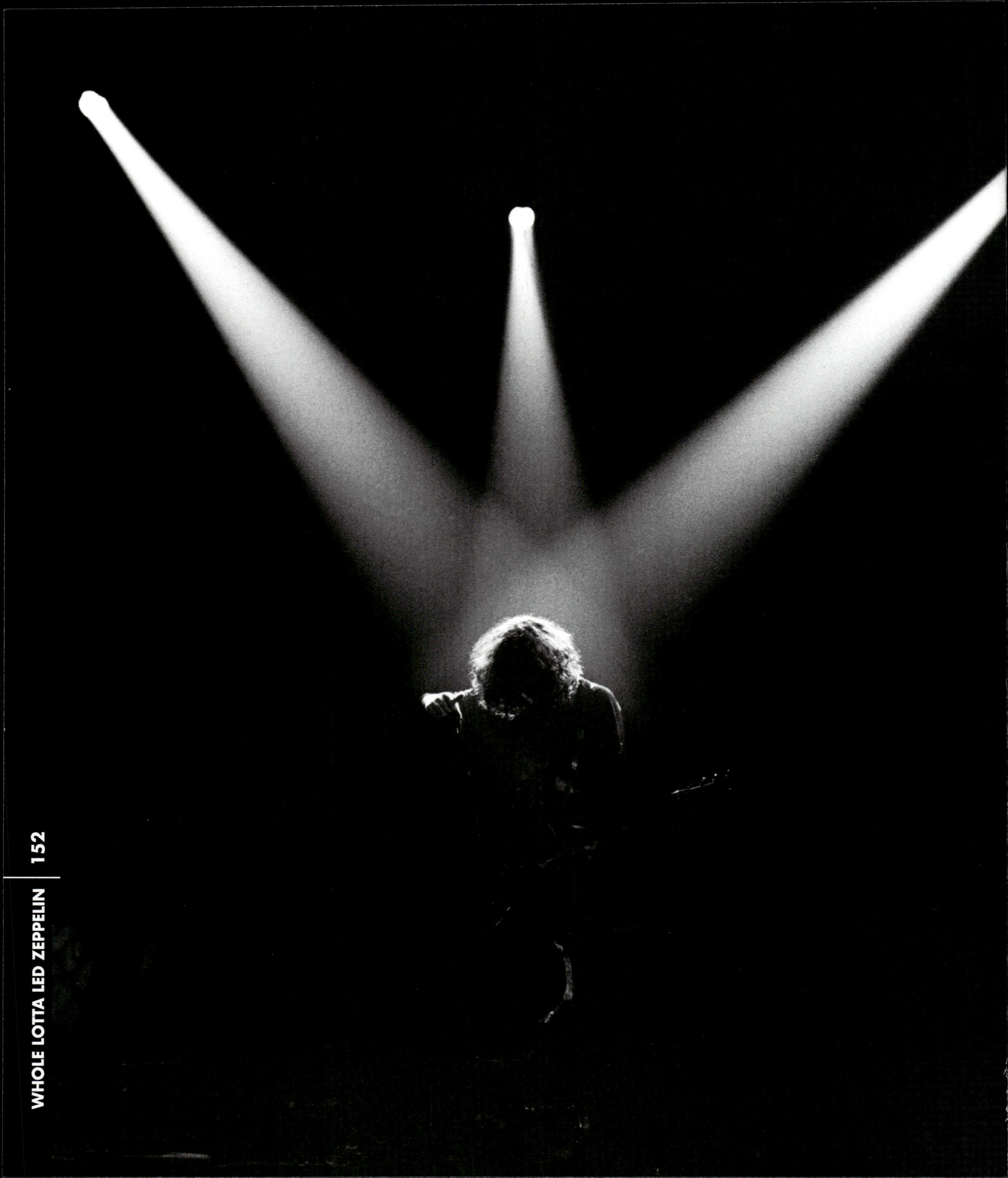

THIS SPREAD: Olympia Stadium, Detroit, MI, January 31, 1975. *Charles Auringer/BackstageGallery.com*

"My vocation is more in composition really than in anything else. Building up harmonies, using the guitar, orchestrating the guitar like an army—a guitar army. I'm talking about actual orchestration in the same way you'd orchestrate a classical piece of music."

—*Jimmy Page,* *quoted in*
Stephen Davis'
Hammer Of The Gods

Olympia Stadium, Detroit, MI, January 31, 1975. *Charles Auringer/BackstageGallery.com*

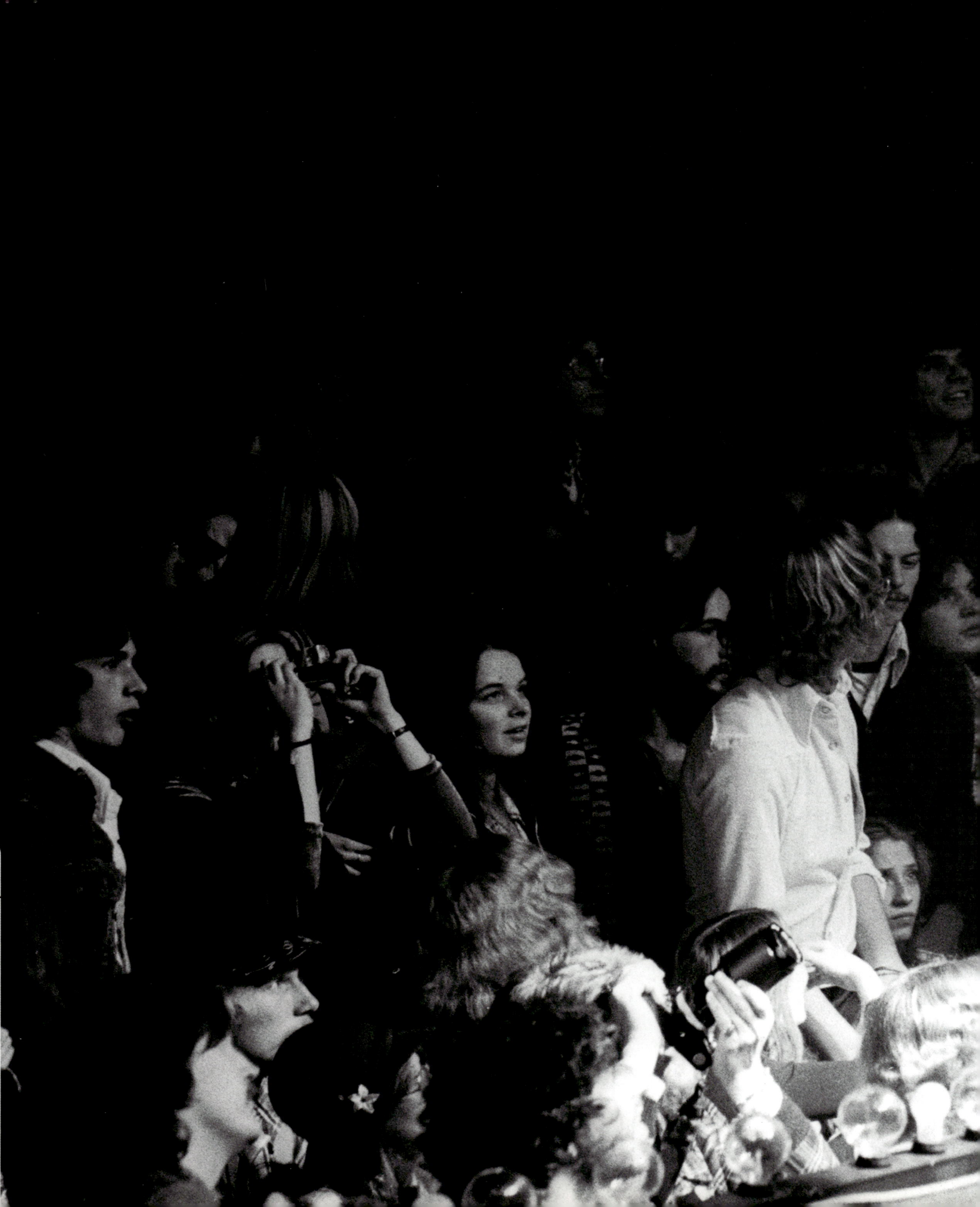

Olympia Stadium, Detroit, MI, January 31, 1975. *Michael Brennan/Scope Features.com*

Olympia Stadium, Detroit, MI, January 31, 1975. *Charles Auringer/BackstageGallery.com*

NAPSHOTS FROM THE FRONT ROW

Madison Square Garden, New York City, February 1975. Led Zeppelin was back in town for three shows on the nights of the 3rd, 7th, and 12th. "Commander Chi" and his sister were there each night, in the front row, with a camera handy.
Images courtesy Commander Chi

ENTER TOWER   GATE
B   11
LOGE $8.50
18A   A   1
LOGE   ROW   SEAT
LED   MON. EVE.   PERF.
ZEPPELIN   FEB. 3   A
8:00 P.M.   1975

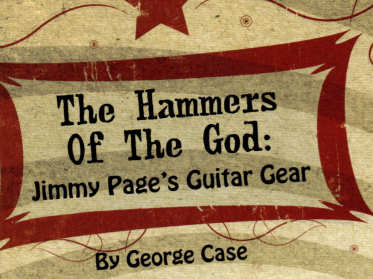

The Hammers Of The God:
Jimmy Page's Guitar Gear

By George Case

Like nearly all rock 'n' rollers of the 1960s and 1970s, Jimmy Page was a working player whose selection of equipment was often based on expediency rather than connoisseurship; between 1968 and 1973 the band was gigging and recording extensively, and more often than not the guitarist chose whatever instruments and accessories he felt comfortable with and could withstand the rigors of transport and performance. During other times in Zeppelin's career, manufacturers would press freebies on Page that he might use a few times without ever endorsing, or he would simply pick up something lying around backstage or in the studio, borrow from someone else, or vaguely request from a roadie or assistant who would then do the legwork of selecting and modifying. That said, Page certainly knew what gear he wanted and, with years of professional experience behind him (particularly as a session hand from 1962 to 1966), he was one of the first rock musicians to acquire a varied arsenal of guitars, amplifiers, and effects, understanding that different pieces were suited for different sounds that could become part of his sonic palette.

Electric Guitars

Page recorded *Led Zeppelin* using a 1958 Fender Telecaster (some sources cite it as a '59). The Tele was given to him by his friend Jeff Beck in 1965 after Page had recommended Beck to take over Eric Clapton's spot in the Yardbirds. The Fender had been Beck's since playing in his early act, the Tridents. Originally a white guitar, it endured some custom decorating by Page when he became a Yardbird ("Everybody painted their guitars back then") and interior rewiring. Its neck was later fitted to another "Botswana Brown" Telecaster body, this one fitted with a "B-bender" tremolo device working off the front strap button, toward the end of the Zeppelin years. A third cream-colored Tele, this one a 1966 and also with a B-bender, was carried on Zeppelin's final European tour in 1980.

From his session years, Page also brought to Zeppelin a 1960 Gibson Les Paul Custom, an ebony three-pickup model equipped with a Bigsby tremolo. Though rarely used on stage, the guitarist did play it at the 1970 Royal Albert Hall gig. Later that year it was stolen during a Zeppelin tour of North America. It has never turned up.

In 1969, Page purchased a 1959 sunburst Gibson Les Paul Standard from Joe Walsh, then of the James Gang. From *Led Zeppelin II* onward, this was the guitar that defined Led Zeppelin's sound—and that of much hard rock in the 1970s and beyond. Armed with this elderly Les Paul, Page wrung a famous stinging "fat" tone from the guitar's two patent-applied-for humbucking pickups. The guitar had already been modified by Walsh, but Page went further. He eventually replaced the tuning heads with sealed Grover units and changed the tone controls to push-pull rotators that could be switched to achieve a "reverse phase" effect. Page subsequently acquired a second 1958 Les Paul, which was nearly identical to his '59.

Guitar buffs debate the origins of both instruments and their usage by Page. The Les Paul gained from Joe Walsh had had its serial number shaved away when its neck was slimmed down, so there's no way of knowing today whether it was indeed a '59, or perhaps a '58. Either way, it is believed to have been Page's "Number One" axe for his Zeppelin tenure. Others say it was the *second* Les Paul that was the Number One and the supposed '59 that was Number Two. If this is the case, the Walsh Les Paul must have been Page's Number One for a while, at least until the '58 was taken up. It was the '59, if it really is a '59, that was copied to produce Gibson's signature Jimmy Page model Les Paul in 2004. Talk about dazed and confused.

Page also briefly used a 1973 Les Paul Standard with a customized crimson finish.

In 1971, Page ordered a custom-built Gibson EDS-1275 6- and 12-string double-neck guitar to replicate the various tones of

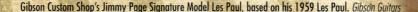
Gibson Custom Shop's Jimmy Page Signature Model Les Paul, based on his 1959 Les Paul. *Gibson Guitars*

Jimmy Page, armed with his Gibson EDS-1275.
Photograph © Neil Zlozower/Gibson Guitars

On Stage With...LED ZEPPELIN

The Jimmy Page
Les Paul

Only a Gibson is Good Enough.

A New Les Paul Designed by Jimmy Page

• 21 legendary sounds!.....the largest selection ever.

• A compound radius neck that feels comfortable right out of the case.

• A figured maple top with a vintage light Honeyburst finish.

Gibson USA

ERNIE BALL PROUDLY HONORS JIMMY PAGE
FIVE DECADES... ONE CONSTANT.
ERNIE BALL STRINGS

> **"The bottom line is that Led Zeppelin leader Jimmy Page's three most important musical utensils were his hands (1944, with later modifications), ears (ditto), and soul (origin unknown)."**

"Stairway To Heaven" onstage; he'd also turn to it for "The Song Remains The Same" and "The Rain Song" live. One of the most iconic instruments in rock history, Page's double-neck is virtually a celebrity itself and cemented Page's reputation as a musical wizard: this guy was so good he seemed to be playing two guitars at once.

For the open-tuned workouts of "Kashmir," "In My Time Of Dying," and the instrumental "White Summer"/"Black Mountain Side," Page used a 1960 Danelectro 3021, a budget-priced solid-body whose high string action and bright tones from its single-coil pickups were well-suited to slide and unconventional tunings.

At Zeppelin's 1975 Earls Court gigs, Page debuted a 1964 Lake Placid Blue Fender Stratocaster. The piercing tone and tremolo arm of the Strat were later prominent throughout *Presence* and *In Through The Out Door* and were also heard at 1979's Knebworth performances. He was also spotted with a 1957 sunburst Stratocaster, Gibson SG, and Gibson RD Artist. A 1965 Fender XII 12-string chimed throughout the studio takes of "Thank You" and "Stairway To Heaven."

Always partial to bluesy bends, Page's electric guitars were strung with light-gauge Ernie Ball Super-Slinky strings. He preferred heavy-duty Herco Flex 75 picks.

Acoustic Guitars

As devoted to folk music as to electric blues, Jimmy Page played a number of acoustic guitars while with Led Zeppelin. He began with a Harmony Sovereign H-1260 (heard on *Led Zeppelin III* and the untitled fourth album), while he'd borrowed a beautiful Gibson J-200 for *Led Zeppelin I*. From the early 1970s, he toted a 1971 Martin D-28 into the studio and on stage, modified with a transducer pickup. Page was also known to have owned a lute-shaped Giannini Craviola, a Gibson "Everly Brothers," and had played Gibson A-2 and A-4 mandolins (as on "Going To California"), a Fender 800 Pedal Steel ("Your Time Is Gonna Come" and "Tangerine") plus a Vega banjo ("Gallows Pole").

Page typically strung his acoustic guitars with Ernie Ball Earthwood strings.

Amplifiers & Accessories

Page tried out a number of studio and onstage rigs in his Zep period. *Led Zeppelin* was recorded with a small Supro

1690T Coronado, turned up to full volume to generate the album's milestone crunch. He later used amps from Fender, Rickenbacker, Univox, and a 100-watt Hiwatt setup before settling on the classic 100-watt 1959 SLP Marshall heads and cabinets with Celestion speakers. As he enthused, "You get a Marshall with a Gibson and it's fantastic, a perfect match." His Marshalls were modified over the years to boost wattage.

Page was an early exponent of outboard signal-altering accessories, aided by innovator Roger Mayer. Page supercharged his electric sounds with a Vox Cry Baby wah-wah pedal and a Sola Sound Tone Bender distortion box, both souped up by Mayer. He also used a Maestro Echoplex reverb unit, Univox overdrive, MXR M-101 phaser, and an Eventide Harmonizer for delay, flanging, and chorus effects. An unusual Gizmotron mechanical contraption was used for the spooky intro to "In The Evening."

One of Jimmy Page's most distinctive audio tools was his theremin. Designed by Russian inventor Léon Theremin in 1919, the theremin was one of the earliest fully electronic instruments. It was also unique in being played without being touched. Two antennae connected to audio oscillators controlling frequency and volume transformed vibrations in the air created by the player's hand gestures. Page moved his hands over his late-model, compact theremin like a magician creating surreal sounds out of thin air. Played through a 100-watt Orange amplifier, the theremin was showcased during the studio and stage recitals of "Dazed And Confused." This epic number also featured Page using an ordinary violin bow on his electric guitar to further his psychedelic solo.

◆ ◆ ◆

The extent to which any of these pieces of gear "made" Jimmy Page the legendary guitar player he became is uncertain. Guitars and amplifiers—made of wood, metal, wires, and tubes—have their own unique temperaments, and even the same instrument can respond differently at different times to particular conditions of age, humidity, and simple wear and tear. Aspiring guitar heroes and members of Zeppelin tribute bands should also be warned that duplicating the collection listed here will cost you well into six figures: a 1958 or '59 sunburst Les Paul alone can easily fetch $100,000 today.

The bottom line is that Led Zeppelin leader Jimmy Page's three most important musical utensils were his hands (1944, with later modifications), ears (ditto), and soul (origin unknown).

Jimmy Page with his Gibson Custom Shop's Jimmy Page Signature Model EDS-1275.
Ross Halfin/Gibson Guitars

Uranium Willie And The Heavy Metal Kid:
A Near-Forgotten 1975 Talk With Jimmy Page

By William S. Burroughs

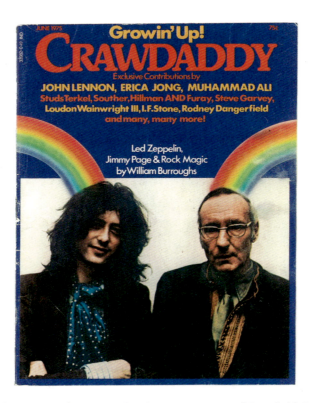

This interview first appeared in the June 1975 issue of Crawdaddy!, *with the introductory apologia, "A friendly conversation over naked lunch. The literary progenitor of verbal anti-materialism and concise print communication meets Jimmy Page, the isometaphysic inventor of physical graffiti. Their interactions exist here, however you cut them up." The article is reprinted here by permission of* Crawdaddy! *editor Peter Knobler and the Burroughs estate.*

When I was first asked to write an article on the Led Zeppelin group, to be based on attending a concert and talking with Jimmy Page, I was not sure I could do it, not being sufficiently knowledgeable about music to attempt anything in the way of musical criticism or even evaluation. I decided simply to attend the concert and talk with Jimmy Page and let the article develop. If you consider any set of data without a preconceived viewpoint, then a viewpoint will emerge from the data.

My first impression was of the audience, as we streamed through one security line after another—a river of youth looking curiously like a single organism: one well-behaved clean-looking middle-class kid. The security guards seemed to be cool and well-trained, ushering gate-crashers out with a minimum of fuss.

We were channeled smoothly into our seats in the thirteenth row. Over a relaxed dinner before the concert, a *Crawdaddy!* companion had said he had a feeling that something bad could happen at this concert. I pointed out that it always can when you get that many people together—like bullfights where you buy a straw hat at the door to protect you from bottles and other missiles. I was displacing possible danger to a Mexican border town where the matador barely escaped with his life and several spectators were killed. It's known as "clearing the path."

So there we sat. I decline earplugs; I am used to loud drum and horn music from Morocco, and it always has, if skillfully performed, an exhilarating and energizing effect on me. As the performance got underway I experienced this musical exhilaration, which was all the more pleasant for being easily controlled, and I knew then that nothing bad was going to happen. This was a safe and friendly area—but at the same time highly charged. There was a palpable interchange of energy between the performers and the audience which was never frantic or jagged. The special effects were handled well and not overdone.

A few special effects are much better than too many. I can see the laser beams cutting dry ice smoke, which drew an appreciative cheer from the audience. Jimmy Page's number with the broken guitar strings came across with a real impact, as did John Bonham's drum solo and the lyrics delivered with unfailing vitality by Robert Plant. The performers were doing their best, and it was very good. The last number, "Stairway to Heaven," where the audience lit matches and there was a scattering of sparklers here and there, found the audience well-behaved and joyous, creating the atmosphere of a high school Christmas play. All in all a good show; neither low nor insipid. Leaving the concert hall was like getting off a jet plane.

I summarized my impressions after the concert in a few notes to serve as a basis for my talk with Jimmy Page: "The essential ingredient for any successful rock group is energy—the ability to give out energy, to receive energy from the audience and to give it back to the audience. A rock concert is in fact a rite involving the evocation and transmutation of energy. Rock stars may be compared to priests, a theme that was treated in Peter Watkin's film *Privilege*. In that film a rock star was manipulated by reactionary forces to set up a state religion; this scenario seems unlikely. I think a rock group singing political slogans would leave its audience at the door.

"The Led Zeppelin show depends heavily on volume, repetition, and drums. It bears some resemblance to the trance music found in Morocco, which is magical in origin and purpose—that is, concerned with the evocation and control of spiritual forces. In Morocco, musicians are also magicians. Gnaoua music is used to drive out evil spirits. The music of Joujouka evokes the God Pan, Pan God of Panic, representing the real magical forces that sweep away the spurious. It is to be remembered that the origin of all the arts—music, painting, and writing—is magical and evocative; and that magic is always used to obtain some definite result. In the Led Zeppelin concert, the result aimed at would seem to be the creation of energy in the performers and in the audience. For such magic to succeed, it must tap the sources of magical energy, and this can be dangerous."

The Interview

I felt that these considerations could form the basis of my talk with Jimmy Page, which I hoped would not take the form of an interview. There is something just basically *wrong* about the whole interview format. Someone sticks a mike in your face and says, "Mr. Page, would you care to talk about your interest in occult practices? Would you describe yourself as a believer in this sort of thing?" Even an intelligent mike-in-the-face question tends to evoke a guarded mike-in-the-face answer. As soon as Jimmy Page walked into my loft downtown, I saw that it wasn't going to be that way.

We started talking over a cup of tea and found we have friends in common: the real estate agent who negotiated Jimmy Page's purchase of the Aleister Crowley house on Loch Ness; John Michel, the flying saucer and pyramid expert; Donald Cammell, who worked on *Performance*; Kenneth Anger, and the Jaggers, Mick and Chris. The subject of magic came up in connection with Aleister Crowley and Kenneth Anger's film *Lucifer Rising*, for which Jimmy Page did the sound track.

Since the word *magic* tends to cause confused thinking, I would like to say exactly what I mean by *magic* and the magical interpretation of so-called reality. The underlying assumption of magic is the assertion of *will* as the primary moving force in this universe—the deep conviction that nothing happens unless somebody or some being wills it to happen. To me this has always seemed self-evident. A chair does not move unless someone moves it. Neither does your physical body, which is composed of much the same materials, move unless you will it to move. Walking across the room is a magical operation. From the viewpoint of magic, no death, no illness, no misfortune, accident, war, or riot is accidental. There are no accidents in the world of magic. And *will* is another word for *animate energy*. Rock stars are juggling fissionable material that could blow up at any time . . . "The soccer scores are coming in from the Capital . . . one must pretend an interest," drawled the dandified Commandante, safe in the pages of my book; and as another rock star said to me, "*You* sit on your ass writing—*I* could be torn to pieces by my fans, like Orpheus."

I found Jimmy Page equally aware of the risks involved in handling the fissionable material of the mass unconscious. I took on a valence I learned years ago from two *Life-Time* reporters—one keeps telling you these horrific stories: "Now old Burns was dragged out of the truck and skinned alive by the mob, and when we got there with the cameras the bloody thing was still squirming there like a worm . . ." while the other half of the team is snapping pictures CLICK CLICK CLICK to record your reactions—so over dinner at Mexican Gardens I told Jimmy the story of the big soccer riot in Lima, Peru in 1964.

We are ushered into the arena as VIP's, in the style made famous by *Triumph of the Will*. Martial music—long vistas—the statuesque police with their dogs on leads—the crowd surging in a sultry menacing electricity palpable in the air—grey clouds over Lima—people glance up uneasily . . . the last time it rained in Lima was the year of the great earthquake, when whole towns were swallowed by landslides. A cop is beating and kicking someone as he shoves him back towards the exit. Oh lucky man. The dogs growl ominously. The game is tense. Tied until the end of the last quarter, and then the stunning decision: a goal that would have won the game for Peru is disqualified by the Uruguayan referee. A howl of rage from the crowd, and then a huge black known as La Bomba, who has started three previous soccer riots and already has twenty-three notches on his bomb, vaults down into the arena. A wave of fans follows The Bomb—the Uruguayan referee scrambles off with the agility of a rat or an evil spirit—the police release tear gas and unleash their snarling dogs, hysterical with fear and rage and maddened by the tear gas. And then a sound like falling mountains, as a few drops of rain begin to fall.

The crowd tears an Alsatian dog to pieces—a policeman is strangled with his tie, another hurled fifty feet down from the top of the stadium . . . bodies piled up ten feet deep at the exits. The soccer scores are coming in from the Capital . . . 306 . . . 318 . . . 352 . . . "I didn't know how bad it was until rain started to fall," said a survivor. You see, it never rains in Lima, or almost never, and when it does it's worse than seeing mules foaling in the public streets . . . trampled ruptured bodies piled in heaps . . .

"*You* know, Jimmy," I said: "The crowd surges forward, a heavy piece of equipment falls on the crowd, security goes mad, and then . . . a sound like falling mountains . . ." CLICK CLICK CLICK: Jimmy Page did not bat an eye.

"Yes, I've thought about that. We all have. The important thing is maintain a balance. The kids come to get far out with the music. It's our job to see they have a good time and no trouble."

And remember the rock group called Storm? Playing a dance hall in Switzerland . . . fire . . . exits locked . . . thirty-seven people dead including all the performers. Now any performer who has never thought about fire and panic just doesn't think. The best way to keep something bad from happening is to see it ahead of time, and you can't see it if you refuse to face the possibility. The bad vibes in that dance hall must have been really heavy. If the performers had been sensitive and alert, they would have checked to be sure the exits were unlocked.

Previously, over two fingers of whiskey in my Franklin Street digs, I had told Page about Major Bruce MacMannaway, a healer and psychic who lives in Scotland. The Major discovered his healing abilities in World War II when his regiment was cut off without medical supplies and the Major started laying on hands . . ." Well Major, I think it's a load of bollocks but I'll try anything." And it turns out the Major is a walking hypo. His psychic abilities were so highly regarded by the Admiralty that he was called in to locate sunken submarines, and he never once missed.

I attended a group meditation seminar with the Major. It turned out to be the Indian rope trick. Before the session the Major told us something of the potential power in group meditation. He had seen it lift a six-hundred-pound church organ five feet in the air. I had no reason to doubt this, since he was obviously incapable of falsification. In the session, after some preliminary exercises, the Major asked us to see a column of light in the center of the room and then took us up through the light to a plateau where we met nice friendly people: the stairway to heaven in fact. I mean we were really *there*.

I turned to Jimmy Page: "Of course we are dealing here with meditation—the deliberate induction of a trance state in a few people under the hands of an old master. This would seem on the surface to have little in common with a rock concert, but the underlying force is the same: human energy and its potential concentration." I pointed out that the moment when the stairway to heaven becomes something actually *possible* for the audience would also be the moment of greatest danger. Jimmy expressed himself as well aware of the power in mass concentration, aware of the dangers involved, and of the skill and balance needed to avoid them . . . rather like driving a load of nitroglycerine.

"There *is* a responsibility to the audience," he said. "We don't want anything bad to happen to these kids—we don't want to release anything we can't handle." We talked about magic and Aleister Crowley. Jimmy said that Crowley has been maligned as a black magician, whereas magic is neither white nor black, good nor bad—it is simply alive with what it is: the real thing, what people really feel and want and are. I pointed out that this "either/ or" straitjacket had been imposed by Christianity when all magic became black magic; that scientists took over from the Church, and Western man has been stifled in a non-magical universe known as "the way things are." Rock music can be seen as one attempt to break out of this dead soulless universe and reassert the universe of magic.

Jimmy told me that Aleister Crowley's house has very good vibes for anyone who is relaxed and receptive. At one time the house had also been the scene of a vast chicken swindle indirectly involving George Sanders, the movie actor, who was able to clear himself of any criminal charges. Sanders committed suicide in Barcelona, and we both remembered his farewell note to the world: "I leave you to this sweet cesspool."

I told Jimmy he was lucky to have that house with a monster in the front yard. What about the Loch Ness monster? Jimmy

Page thinks it exists. I wondered if it could find enough to eat, and thought this unlikely—it's not the improbability but the upkeep on monsters that worries me. Did Aleister Crowley have opinions on the subject? He apparently had not expressed himself.

We talked about trance music. He had heard the Brian Jones record from recordings made at Joujouka. We discussed the possibility of synthesizing rock music with some of the older forms of trance music that have been developed over centuries to produce powerful, sometimes hypnotic effects on the audience. Such a synthesis would enable the older forms to escape from the mould of folk lore and provide new techniques to rock groups.

We talked about the special effects used in the concert. "Sure," he said, "lights, lasers, dry ice are fine—but you have to keep some balance. The show must carry itself and not rely too heavily on special effects, however spectacular."

I brought up the subject of infra-sound, that is, sound pitched below 16 Hertz, the level of human hearing; as ultra-sound is above the level. Professer Gavreau of France developed infra-sound as a military weapon. A powerful infra-sound installation can, he claims, kill everyone in a five-mile radius, knock down walls, and break windows. Infra-sound kills by setting up vibrations within the body so that, as Gavreau puts it, "You can feel all the organs in your body rubbing together." The plans for this device can be obtained from the French Patent Office, and infra-sound generators constructed from inexpensive materials. Needless to say, one is not concerned with military applications however unlimited, but with more interesting and useful possibilities, reaching much further than five miles.

Infra-sound sets up vibrations in the body and nervous system. Need these vibrations necessarily be harmful or unpleasant? All music played at any volume sets up vibrations in the body and nervous system of the listener. That's why people listen to it. Caruso as you will remember could break a champagne glass across the room. Especially interesting is the possibility of rhythmic pulses of infra-sound; that is, *music in infra-sound*. You can't hear it, but you can feel it.

Jimmy was interested, and I gave him a copy of a newspaper article on infra-sound. It seems that the most deadly range is around 7 Hertz, and when this is turned on even at a low volume, anyone within range is affected. They feel anxious, ill, depressed, and finally exclaim with one voice, "I feel TERRIBLE!" . . . last thing you want at a rock concert. However, around the borders of infra-sound perhaps a safe range can be found. Buddhist mantras act by setting up vibrations in the body. Could this be done in a much more powerful yet safe manner by the use of infra-sound rhythms which could of course be combined with audible music? Perhaps infra-sound could add a new dimension to rock music.

Could something be developed comparable to the sonar communication of dolphins, conveying an immediate sonar experience that requires no symbolic translation? I mentioned to Jimmy that I had talked with Dr. Truby, who worked with John

Lilly recording dolphins. Dr. Truby is a specialist in inter-species communication, working on a grant from the government—so that when all our kids are born Venusians we will understand them when they start to talk. I suggested to him that *all* communication, as we know it, is actually inter-species communication, and that it is kept that way by the nature of verbal and symbolic communication, which must be indirect.

Do dolphins have a language? What is a language? I define a *language* as a communication system in which data are represented by verbal or written symbols—symbols that *are not the objects* to which they refer. The word *chair* is not the object itself, the chair. So any such system of communication is always second-hand and symbolic, whereas we *can* conceive of a form of communication that would be immediate and direct, undercutting the need for symbols. And music certainly comes closer to such direct communication than language.

Could musical communication be rendered more precise with infra-sound, thus bringing the whole of music a second radical step forward? The first step was made when music came out of the dance halls, roadhouses, and night clubs into Madison Square Garden and Shea Stadium. Rock music appeals to a mass audience, instead of being the province of a relatively few aficionados. Can rock music make another step forward, or is it a self-limiting form, confirmed by the demands of a mass audience? How much that is radically new can a mass audience safely absorb? We came back to the question of balance. How much new material will be accepted by a mass audience? Can rock music go forward without leaving its fans behind?

We talked about Wilhelm Reich's orgone accumulator, and I showed him plans for making this device, which were passed along to me by Reich's daughter. Basically the device is very simple, consisting of iron or steel wool on the inside and organic material on the outside. I think this was a highly important discovery. Recently a scientist with the National Aeronautics and Space Administration announced an "electrical cell" theory of cancer that is almost identical to Reich's cancer theory put forth 25 years ago. He does not acknowledge any indebtedness to Reich. I showed Jimmy the orgone box I have here, and we agreed that orgone accumulators in pyramid form and/or using magnetized iron could be much more powerful.

We talked about the film *Performance* and the use of cut-up techniques in this film. Now the cut-up method was applied to writing by Brion Gysin in 1959; he said that writing was fifty years behind painting, and applied the montage method to writing. Actually, montage is much closer to the facts of perception than representational painting. If for example you walked through Times Square, and then put on canvas what you had seen, the result would be a montage . . . half a person cut in two by a car, reflections from shop windows, fragments of street signs. Antony Balch and I collaborated on a film called *Cut-Ups*, in which the film was cut into segments and rearranged at random. Nicholas Roeg

and Donald Camel saw a screening of the film not long before they made *Performance*.

Musical cut-ups have been used by Earl Browne and other modern composers. What distinguishes a cut-up from, say, an edited medley, is that the cut-up is at some point random. For example, if you made a medley by taking thirty seconds from a number of scores and assembling these arbitrary units—that would be a cut-up. Cut-ups often result in more succinct meanings, rather than nonsense. Here for example is a phrase taken from a cut-up of this article: "I can see the laser gate crashers with an appreciative cheer from the 13th row." (Actually a gate crasher was extricated by security from the row in front of us; an incident I had forgotten until I saw this cut-up.)

Over dinner at the Mexican Gardens, I was surprised to hear that Jimmy Page had never heard of Petrillo, who started the first musicians' union and perhaps did more than any other one man to improve the financial position of musicians by protecting copyrights. One wonders whether rock music could have gotten off the ground without Petrillo and the Union, which put musicians in the big money bracket, thereby attracting managers, publicity, and the mass audience.

Music, like all the arts, is magical and ceremonial in origin. Can rock music return to these ceremonial roots and take its fans with it? Can rock music use older forms like Moroccan trance music? There is at present a wide interest among young people in the occult and all means of expanding consciousness. Can rock music appeal directly to this interest? In short, there are a number of disparate tendencies waiting to be synthesized. Can rock music serve as a vehicle for this synthesis?

The broken guitar strings, John Bonham's drum solo, vitality by Robert Plant—when you get that many people to get it, very good. Buy a straw hat at the door—the audience all light matches. Cool, well-trained laser beams channeled the audience smoothly. A scattering of sparklers. Danger to a Mexican border town. We start talking over a cup of the mass unconscious—cut to a soccer riot photo in Lima. The Uruguayan referee as another rock star. Sound like falling mountains of the risks involved. It's our job to see trouble and plateau the center of the room—remember the stairway to Switzerland? Fire really there. You can't see it if you refuse—underlying force the same. I mean we were playing a dance hall in heaven at the moment when the stairway actually possible for the audience was unlocked.

Word for Word

WB: I really, really enjoyed the concert. I think it has quite a lot, really, in common with Moroccan trance music.

JP: Yes, yes.

WB: I wondered if you consciously were using any of that. . . .

JP: Well, yes, there is a little on that particular track, "Kashmir"—a lead bass on that—even though none of us have been to Kashmir. It's just that we've all been very involved in that sort of music. I'm very involved in ethnic music from all over the world.

WB: Have you been to Morocco?

JP: No. I haven't, and it's a very sad admission to make. I've only been to, you know, India and Bangkok and places like that through the Southeast.

WB: Well, I've never been east of Athens.

JP: Because during the period when everybody was going through trips over to, you know, Morocco, going down, way down, making their own journeys to Istanbul, I was at art college during that period and then I eventually went straight into music. So I really missed out on all that sort of traveling. But I know musicians that have gone there and actually sat in with the Arabs and played with them.

WB: Yeah, well they think of music entirely in magical terms.

JP: Yes.

WB: And their music is definitely used for magical purposes. For example, the Gnaoua music is to drive out evil spirits and Joujouka music is invoking the God Pan. Musicians there are all magicians, quite consciously.

◆ ◆ ◆

WB: I was thinking of the concentration of mass energy that you get in a pop concert, and if that were, say, channeled in some magical way . . . a stairway to heaven . . . it could become quite actual.

JP: Yes, I know. One is so aware of the energies that you are going for, and you could so easily. . . . I mean, for instance, the other night we played in the Philadelphia Spectrum, which really is a black hole as a concert hall. . . . The security there is the most ugly of anywhere in the States. I saw this incident happen and I was almost physically sick. In fact, if I hadn't been playing the guitar I was playing it would've been over somebody's head. It was a double-neck, which is irreplaceable, really, unless you wait another nine months for them to make another one at Gibson's.

What had happened, somebody came to the front of the stage to take a picture or something and obviously somebody said, "Be

off with you." And he wouldn't go. And then one chap went over the barrier, and then another, and then another and then another, and they all piled on top of . . . you could see the fists coming out . . . on this one solitary person. And they dragged him by his hair and they were kicking him. It was just sickening. Now, what I'm saying is this . . . Our crowds, the people that come to see us are very orderly. It's not the sort of Alice Cooper style, where you actually *try* to get them into a state where they've got to go like that, so that you can get reports of this, that and the other. And the wrong word said at that time could've just sparked off the whole thing.

WB: Yes, there's sort of a balance to be maintained there.

JP: Yeah, that's right.

WB: The audience the other night was very well behaved.

◆ ◆ ◆

WB: Have you used the lasers in all of the concerts?

JP: Over here, yes.

WB: Very effective.

JP: I think we should have more of them, don't you? About 30 of them! Do you know they bounced that one off the moon? But it's been condensed . . . . It's the very one that they used for the moon. I was quite impressed by that.

WB: That isn't the kind of machine that would cause any damage. . . .

JP: Uh, if you look straight into it, yes.

WB: Yes, but I mean . . . it doesn't burn a hole in . . .

JP: No. . . . It's been taken right down. I'm just waiting for the day when you can get the holograms . . . get three-dimensional. The other thing I wanted to do was the Van de Graaff Generator. You used to see them in the old horror films. . . .

WB: Oh yes . . . Frankenstein, and all that.

◆ ◆ ◆

JP: When we first came over here . . . when the draft was really hot and everything . . . if you stayed in the country for more than six months, you were eligible for it . . . they'd drag you straight into the draft.

WB: I didn't realize that.

JP: Yeah.

WB: Oh, I thought you had to be an American citizen.

JP: No. No no. We almost overstayed our welcome. I was producing and having to work in studios here, and the days coming up to the six-month period were just about . . . it was just about neck and neck. And I still had a couple more days left and a couple more days to work on this LP.

WB: Were they right there with the papers?

JP: Well, not quite, I mean obviously it would have taken some time, but somebody would've been there. . . . You know, they do keep an eye on people.

◆ ◆ ◆

WB: Did you ever hear about something called infra-sound?

JP: Uh, carry on.

WB: Well, infra-sound is sound below the level of hearing. And it was developed by someone named Professor Gavreau in France as a military weapon. He had an infra-sound installation that he could turn on and kill everything within five miles. It can also knock down walls and break windows. But it kills by setting up vibrations within the body. Well, what I was wondering was whether rhythmical music at sort of the borderline of infra-sound could be used to produce rhythms in the audience—because, of course, any music with volume will set up these vibrations. That is part of the way the effect is achieved.

JP: Hmm.

WB: It's apparently . . . it's not complicated to build these infra-sound things.

JP: I've heard of this, actually, but not in such a detailed explanation. I've heard that certain frequencies can make you physically ill.

WB: Yes. Well, this can be fatal. That's not what you're looking for. But it could be used just to set up vibrations. . . .

JP: Ah hah . . . A death ray machine! Of course, when radio first came out they were picketing all the radio stations, weren't they, saying "We don't want these poisonous rays" [laughter]. . . .Yes, well . . . certain notes can break glasses. I mean, opera singers can break glasses with sound, this is true?

WB: That was one of Caruso's tricks.

JP: But it is true?

WB: Of course.

JP: I've never seen it done.

WB: I've never seen it done, but I know that you can do it.

JP: I want laser *notes*, that's what I'm after! Cut right through.

WB: Apparently, you can make one of these things out of parts you can buy in a junk yard. It's not a complicated machine to make. And actually the patent . . . it's patented in France, and according to French law, you can obtain a copy of the patent. For a very small fee.

JP: Well, you see the thing is, it's hard to know just exactly what is going on, from the stage to the audience. . . . You can only . . . I mean I've never seen the group play, obviously. Because I'm part of it. . . . I can only see it on celluloid, or hear it. But I know what I see. And this thing about rhythms within the audience, I would say yes. Yes, definitely. And it is . . . Music which involves riffs, anyway, will have a trance-like effect, and it's really like a mantra. . . . And we've been attacked for that.

WB: What a mantra does is set up certain vibrations within the body, and this, obviously does the same thing. Of course, it goes . . . it comes out too far. But I was wondering if on the borderline of infra-sound that possibly some interesting things could be done.

JP: Ah.

◆ ◆ ◆

JP: Last year we were playing [sets] for three hours solid, and physically that was a real . . . I mean, when I came back from the last tour I didn't know where I was. I didn't even know where I was going. We ended up in New York and the only thing that I could relate to was the instrument onstage. I just couldn't . . . I was just totally and completely spaced out.

WB: How long was that you played recently? That was two hours and a half.

JP: That was two and a half hours, yes. It used to go for three hours.

WB: I'd hate to give a three-hour reading. . . .

the LPs:
Physical Graffiti
By Jaan Uhelszki

Almost eighteen months in the making, the double-LP *Physical Graffiti* felt the first stirrings of life in November 1973 when Led Zeppelin descended on Headley Grange in Hampshire, the former workhouse–turned–recording studio and rehearsal complex that the Zeppelin organization purchased from former Faces bassist Ronnie Lane. The band started work on this massive undertaking just as Jimmy Page was finishing up the soundtrack for *Lucifer Rising*, a film by Kenneth Anger (best known for penning *Hollywood Babylon*). During the early stages of preproduction, John Paul Jones fell ill and the recording was postponed until February 1974, a month after the band announced the formation of Swan Song Records.

Unapologetic for the long lapse, Robert Plant told reporters, "On the surface, this band might not appear to be a hive of industry, but when we do get something together it's always something that we're all completely satisfied with."

Once they finally settled in, the band refused to stay at the Grange, preferring a nearby luxury hotel, not only because it was colorless, damp, and filled with wet mold, but because it was reported to be haunted—something which, to no one's surprise, tantalized guitarist Page. He camped out alone among the phantasms and spirits, sharing the historic space with a shrouded lady in gray who flitted about at the top of the second-floor landing. Rather than unnerving him, the mysterious woman fed Page's imagination and no doubt had some impact on the stuff he was writing—most notably the brooding arrangement of "In My Time Of Dying," as well as "Ten Years Gone," wherein his languid, arrhythmic runs provide a near-perfect and almost liquid foil for Plant's ruminations about fleeting love and unwelcome change (reportedly inspired by the singer's first girlfriend, who demanded he choose between her and the music). This song shows how well he chose—and marks one of the first times in their history that Zeppelin allowed their flesh-and-blood foibles to fuel their lyrics. Plant's voice is naked, vulnerable, and not always in key as he uses a series of avian metaphors, culminating in the deathless phrase "on the wings of maybe."

But the band's human side isn't restricted to that track. Even as they lustily wore the thorny crowns of rock legends—and their apocryphal antics and Herculean misbehaviors were hourly whispered among the cognoscenti—*Graffiti* saw them step down off of Olympus to pen songs that were as messy and shambolic as anything on the Rolling Stones' *Exile On Main*

Street and as varied and seemingly incongruent as the Beatles' "White Album." Still, "It wasn't thrown together haphazardly," Page insisted, noting that the running order of the tracks was very important.

The first clue that the songs weren't delivered from on high was the album's title. It was called *Physical Graffiti*, not *The Graffiti Of The Gods*. It was not going to be high art—that was clear. Instead, they intended to record what moved them rather than what would appease a record company. Witness the loose jams "Boogie With Stu" (featuring "sixth Stone" Ian Stewart), "Black Country Woman," and "Bron-Yr-Aur," the latter of which is Page's placid, acoustic, folkloric paean to the holiday home of Robert Plant's family, and also where the band wrote most of their third album, where Page's daughter Scarlet was conceived, and where the austere and stoic guitarist claimed he really got to know Robert Plant.

The most humanizing aspect of *Physical Graffiti*, however, might be the graceful flub during the recording of the eleven-plus-minute "In My Time Of Dying." Drummer John Bonham can be heard to cough and then ask, "That's gonna be the one, isn't it?" Also left in the mix are the sounds of an aircraft in "Black Country Woman," and then the phrase "We gotta get this airplane on." Up until this time, Zep were seemingly inaccessible, rarely giving interviews or stooping to speak to their faithful—four bigger-than-life alpha men swathed in red Turkish robes the moment they left the stage, to be whisked away on their own jet, not to a private island or Idaho, but to their own suite of rooms at New York's fabled Plaza Hotel to sup on chilled lobster and strawberries and ravish willing women. Yet, here they peel back the velvet curtains, cut through the Moroccan incense (well, except on the buzzy exotica of "Kashmir"), throw open the gates to rock Valhalla, and allow themselves to be seen as mere mortals.

Covering a vast expanse of musical territory, Zeppelin undertook *Physical Graffiti* because, with their past successes and now their own label, they could. "At this point we had this beautiful freedom that we could try anything, do anything, which was what the beauty of how the band was, and how the music was made as opposed to how things are today," Jimmy Page told me in 1997. "A band today has to constantly try to keep its head above water."

After six blockbuster albums Zeppelin was almost walking on water and no one was pestering them for another hit. Their canon was swelling with anthemic numbers like "Stairway To Heaven," "Rock And Roll," and "Whole Lotta Love." But ironically, this album, with no obvious hit, was the one that went straight to No. 1, two weeks after its release in February 1975, pulling all of the band's previous five albums in its draft and depositing them back on the *Billboard* album charts, making Zeppelin the first band ever to have six albums on the Top 200 simultaneously. At the time of its release (which garnered over 1 million advance orders), the record was reportedly selling 500-plus copies an hour, even after the long and protracted skirmishes over the album's sleeve art, which originally sported images of Aleister Crowley, Lee Harvey Oswald, and two photos of the band in drag.

But forget the artwork—what was inside is what counted, and the fifteen songs that make up what critics have called the most Zeppelin-ish of all Led Zeppelin albums spanned genres and tempos, and once again contrasted bone-jolting rock-solid tunes alongside mystical spiritual quests, most notably the Eastern-tinged "Kashmir." It was the first song that Page wrote for the album and one that mutated several times before the final version. The first incarnation was titled "Driving To Kashmir," and it chronicled a trip that Page and Plant made to Morocco—not Kashmir—in 1973. At the time of its 1975 release, none of the band members had set foot in the country. Atmospheric, atonal, fractured and disturbing, "Kashmir," along with "The Rover" and "The Wanton Song," epitomized the band's untouchable rock-behemoth reputation and easily could have been on either *Led Zeppelin II* or *IV*.

Page had been contemplating putting out a double disc for sometime, and went on a scavenger hunt of the band's vaults, unearthing outtakes from the Zeppelin's previous albums, grafting them to the band's more recent compositions, and creating a sprawling view of what the band was capable of—the innocence of "Ten Years Gone," the keening mysterious spirituality of "In The Light," the jittery singsong naturalism of "Down By The Seaside," the deceptive simplicity of "Custard Pie," and the mixed metaphors and messages of "Night Flight." Taken together they are, at the very least, a calling card of the band's accomplishments. At best, *Physical Graffiti* is a historical document that chronicles a time when dinosaurs walked the earth. And walked proudly.

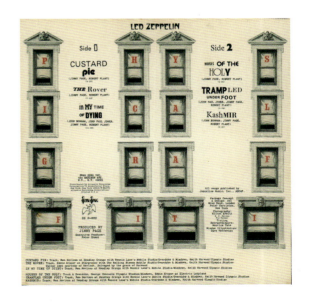

"'Kashmir' was the one for me—an unbeatable riff. I always respected Robert Plant as he goes his own way. He's one of the few."

—Ian Hunter, Mott the Hoople

1.1.75	Ahoy Hallen, Rotterdam, Netherlands
1.12.75	Vorst Nationaal, Brussels, Belgium
1.18.75	Met Center, Bloomington, MN
1.20–22.75	Chicago Stadium, Chicago, IL
1.24.75	Richfield Coliseum, Cleveland, OH
1.25.75	Market Square Arena, Indianapolis, IN
1.29.75	Coliseum, Greensboro, NC
1.31.75	Olympia Stadium, Detroit, MI
2.1.75	Civic Arena, Pittsburgh, PA
2.3.75	Madison Square Garden, New York, NY
2.4.75	Nassau Coliseum, Uniondale, NY
2.6.75	Montreal Forum, Montreal, PQ
2.7.75	Madison Square Garden, New York, NY
2.8.75	The Spectrum, Philadelphia, PA
2.10.75	Capital Centre, Landover, MD
2.12.75	Madison Square Garden, New York, NY
2.13–14.75	Nassau Coliseum, Uniondale, NY
2.16.75	Arena, St, Louis, MO
2.27.75	Sam Houston Coliseum, Houston, TX
2.28.75	Assembly Center, Louisiana State University, Baton Rouge, LA
3.3.75	Tarrant County Convention Center, Fort Worth, TX
3.4–5.75	Memorial Auditorium, Dallas, TX
3.7.75	Events Center, Austin, TX
3.10.75	Sports Arena, San Diego, CA
3.11–12.75	Long Beach Arena, Long Beach, CA
3.14.75	Sports Arena, San Diego, CA
3.17.75	Seattle Center Coliseum, Seattle, WA
3.19–20.75	Pacific Coliseum, Vancouver, BC
3.21.75	Seattle Center Coliseum, Seattle, WA
3.24–25, 27.75	The Forum, Inglewood, CA

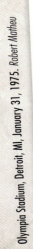

TOUR DATES

Olympia Stadium, Detroit, MI, January 31, 1975. Robert Matheu

A Cry From The Depths
1975

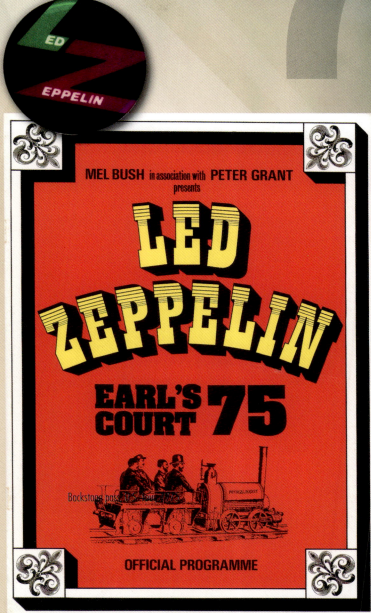

Led Zeppelin was England's biggest band but they couldn't go home whenever they wanted. The ever-shrewd Peter Grant had them living as tax exiles, just like the Rolling Stones, T. Rex's Marc Bolan, and some of the former Beatles. In May 1975, Zeppelin was allowed back in the United Kingdom for five concerts in front of eighty-five thousand fans at Earls Court in London, the group's first homeland gigs since January 1973. During one show, Zeppelin covered Joni Mitchell's "Woodstock," and at some of the gigs, Robert Plant made wisecracks about U.K. tax rules and its chancellor of the exchequer. But the singer and his band would soon be silenced.

On August 4, Plant, his wife, Maureen, and their three children were traveling on the Isle of Rhodes in Greece when their car, driven by Maureen, smashed into a tree. She broke her leg and pelvis, fractured her skull, and needed an immediate blood transfusion. (Luckily, her sister was traveling in the car behind with Page's girlfriend, Charlotte Martin, and their daughter, Scarlet.) Plant, who was in the passenger's seat, broke both of his legs and an arm. (Riding in the backseat, the slightly bruised kids were all right.) After emergency treatment was administered in Greece, a private jet flew the entourage back to London, where Page was working on the documentary movie, and Grant canceled the band's entire U.S. tour, which was set to start in three weeks.

With Page's finger problem and now Plant's shattered legs, it makes you wonder: Was the devil mocking their every step?

While Maureen recuperated, Plant, the tax exile, had to leave the United Kingdom, so he convalesced in a wheelchair in the Channel Islands off France, away from his family and his band. In early September, Plant was moved to Malibu, California, where he met up with Page. Rehearsals began on a seventh album, about the only thing the band could do given Plant's condition. But the sessions

Earls Court program, May 1975. Inside, the uncredited writer notes that Plant "still wears the same boots he wore at Zeppelin's earliest concerts—at the time of their first recordings he had rarely worn [*sic*] headphones." On Page: "Obscene letters sent to him by fans and others distress him inordinately. Death threats are frequent." Jones: "Jones Junior prefers Debussy Preludes Book II and Ravel. . . . 'I had a Rolls' he went on, 'but I sold it. Too ostentatious.'" Bonham, it is stated, "owns twelve dozen pedigree cows . . . his wife calls him 'asbestos guts.'"

Homecoming. John Barnett/4 Eyes Design

weren't smooth. Page complained about John Paul Jones not being around the studio, and Jones, who'd contemplated quitting in 1973, got tired of waiting around for Page, who sometimes didn't show up until 2 A.M. And there was no bedtime for Bonzo. Missing England, John Bonham was drowning his sorrows up and down Sunset Strip. Plant told *Circus* magazine:

"It was really like a cry of survival. I didn't know whether I was going to be able to work with the band again; I didn't know if my leg would heal. We had planned to do a world tour, but obviously that was nipped in the ankle, so to speak. I was stuck in Malibu for a long while, and I said, 'Please, let me do something to do with music; let me do something or otherwise I'm gonna go balmy.' We already had some ammunition from our trip to Morocco; Jimmy and I had put together some epic sort of material, but every time that we started listening and thinking about the ideas that we already had put together, we shied away. We hadn't been back to England in nine or ten months, and consequently I don't think that we were in one of our more mentally stable periods, not in a condition that enabled us to come to grips with what would be a huge accomplishment in our eyes. So we went to S.I.R. [Studio Instrument Rentals a complex of rehearsal facilities] to work on some things. And it was hard in the beginning. I had to sit in an armchair with my leg up in the air while the band was on the stage. And I'd go into another room where Detective were playing and Michael Des Barres was singing, aping all of my movements and looking in the mirror at the same time."

U.S. tax laws also limited the time Led Zeppelin could be in the States. So the group relocated to Munich, Germany, working in Musicland Studio in the basement of a hotel. Accustomed to being leisurely in the studio, Zeppelin reverted to its early years and banged out the next album in a mere eighteen days—with Plant sitting in a wheelchair.

"Against all odds, sitting in a fucking chair, pushed everywhere for months and months, we were still able to look the devil in the eye and say, 'We're as strong as you and stronger, and we should not only write, we should record,' " the singer told *CREEM* magazine in 1977.

Earls Court, London, May 23–25, 1975.

Crazy Ways Are Evident

Ann & Nancy Wilson's On The Music & Page

By Gene Stout

"When you do a Led Zeppelin song, you're really taking a lot on in terms of meter, Ann Wilson explains. "And sometimes they turn the beat around, they drop two or three beats here or there and then pick it up again in the middle, so people are left with one foot in the air. That's the beauty of it. But it's not that easy to learn to play it right and make it all sound fluid. For instance, that song 'The Crunge.' That's a perfect example of a song that is walking all over itself, but somehow it just works."

For Nancy Wilson, discovering Jimmy Page in her teens was transformative.

"When Zeppelin came along, as a guitar player, it was a whole different ball game to sort of download the Jimmy thing. It's definitely bluesy, but then it's translated into its own language," she explains. "When you're a young, impressionable guitar player seeking a seeker, as I was, it's kind of the Holy Grail. Because I had all the folk stuff, some classical chops and a lot of rock 'n' roll under my belt. But Page had a blend of blues and magic. There was sorcery in his playing.

"I think he's a magician, a Merlin, with his guitar. The dissonance and darkness of what he chose to play really goes against the grain of blues and rock 'n' roll."

Nancy continues: "I'm not a dark-side person, but the darkness of Page's music is really appealing. He lived in Aleister Crowley's house, and people say he was conjuring black magic and all that stuff.

"Well, that's what it sounds like to me!"

Led Zeppelin clearly broke a lot of rules.

"That's why they seem so dangerous and so sexy and so over-the-top," Nancy says. "They dared to be personal. They dared to bare their souls with their music. And I think that's part of their greatness." 🜂

After eighteen days of recording, the band headed off for holiday while Page remained in Munich and did overdubs, editing, and mixing—always his task. *Presence* arrived on March 31, 1976, to more positive reviews than Led Zeppelin was accustomed to. Even *Rolling Stone* offered an auspicious write-up.

Uncertainty seemed to have fueled the recording sessions. "There won't be another album like it, put it like that," Plant told *Circus* magazine at the time. "It was an album of circumstances; it was a cry from the depths, the only thing that we could do. I honestly didn't know what was going to happen, and neither did anybody else. If it had been six, seven, or eight years ago, it would probably have been a good deal more raw. It was taken from the balls, you know; that was where it was coming from."

Plant gushed to *Rolling Stone*, borrowing a lyric from "Immigrant Song": "All the energy that had been smoldering inside us getting ready for a lot of gigs came out in the writing and later in the studio. What we have is an album that is so Zeppelin. It sounds like the hammer of the gods."

Years later, Plant remained very enthusiastic about *Presence*, telling Nigel Williamson, "*Presence* has got some of the hottest moments Led Zeppelin ever had—agitated, uncomfortable, druggy, pained." Some of the pain was obvious; Richard Cole, in his book, asserted that he, Page, and Bonham were messing with heroin at the time. The subject didn't come up when Page discussed *Presence* with *Guitar World*:

GW: *Presence* is one of your favorite albums. Why?

JP: I guess it was because we made it under almost impossible circumstances. Robert had a cast on his leg and no one knew whether he would walk again. It was hairy!

GW: So you remember it fondly because it was a triumph over adversity.

JP: That is exactly it. It was a reflection of the height of our emotions of the time. There are no acoustic songs, no keyboards, no mellowness. We were also under incredible deadline pressure to finish the record. We did the whole thing in 18 days. I was working an average of 18 to 20 hours a day. It was also grueling because nobody else really came up with

Earls Court, London, May 17, 1975. *Chris Walter/Getty Images*

"Really, Led Zeppelin was Jimmy. I was a great foil. He was very much . . . there's a word, not 'perpetrator,' but definitely he had a premeditated view of the whole thing. Even though with my lyrics and some of my melodies it took off in directions he might not have been ready for . . . a couple times later on, when I got more confident I might have turned his head around a little . . . but the big role was his. The *risks* were his. The *risks* made it memorable. Without Jimmy it would have been no good. When people talk about how good other guitarists are, they're talking about how they play within the accepted structures of contemporary guitar playing, which Pagey plays miles outside of. He plays from somewhere else. I like to think of it as . . . a little left of heaven."

—*Robert Plant, quoted in Cameron Crowe's "Led Zeppelin: Light And Shade"*

Earls Court, London, May 17, 1975. *Ian Dickson/Redferns*

song ideas. It was really up to me to come up with all the riffs, which is probably why *Presence* is so guitar-heavy. But I don't blame anybody. We were all kind of down. We had just finished a tour, we were non-resident and Robert was in a cast so I think everybody was a little homesick. Our attitude was summed up in the lyrics on "Tea For One."

GW: What is your strongest memory of that time?

JP: Fighting the deadline. We only had three weeks to work because the Rolling Stones had time booked after us. So after the band finished recording all its parts, me and the engineer, Keith Harwood, just started mixing until we would fall asleep. Then whoever would wake up first would call the other, and we would go back in and continue to work until we passed out again.

GW: Didn't you have the power at that time to demand more time from the record company to finish the album?

JP: Of course, but I did not want to. I did not want the record to drag on. Under the circumstances, I felt that if it had dragged on, a negative, destructive element might have entered the picture. The urgency helped us to create an interesting album.

The album cover featured a photo of a well-attired couple and their two nicely dressed young children, sitting at a table in a restaurant with a marina of sailboats visible out the window. (Could this have been a reference to Seattle's Edgewater Inn?) On the table is a small statue of a twisted obelisk, which is also pictured by itself on the inner sleeve. Page explained the symbolism of the object in a chat on AOL in 1999: "Well, the idea of it was a presence of something that could be viewed maybe from the future. It's like, let's see, maybe in 2050, and people look back and saw the equivalent of Bell Radio within the household, they wouldn't know what it was unless they were briefed on it. . . . In the future, somebody looking [at] that would see the object on the table, it would be like tube radios from the '50s. But it was a presence within the household. It was something so important that they liked . . . the radio would convey current music. The title was not a play upon words, but a play upon images." ●

Neil Young interview PAGE 14

J.J. Cale in the flesh PAGE 20

Amplification survey PAGE 34

LED ZEPPELIN STORM BACK

LED ZEPPELIN hit new, astronomical heights this week. The band are set to break sales records with the release of their seventh album, "Presence", tomorrow (Friday). Already, "Presence" is assured of gold disc status. It has become the fastest selling album — on advance sales to the record dealers — in the history of the WEA group, to which Zeppelin's own label, Swan Song, is affiliated.

Said Dave Dee, general manager of Atlantic Records: "This Zeppelin album is going to be a monster. It will be the biggest Zeppelin album in this country ever. We were prepared for this one. We'd heard the tapes of the album some time ago and knew demand would be enormous. Everyone here is very enthusiastic about it."

"Presence" was recorded over a three-week period before Christmas at the Musicland Studios in Munich. Three weeks ago, Page enthused to the MM about "Presence":

"There's a lot of urgency about it. There's a lot of attack to the music." And reviewing the album in this week's MM, Chris Welch writes:—

"The excitement Zeppelin generated with their relentless performances of 'Trampled Underfoot' at their last concerts was among the more memorable rock events of the last couple of years . . . now, a whole album of dynamic compositions, delivered with a fervour that shows how anxious the band were to get down their new ideas.

"This single album has certainly caught Zeppelin with their atomic particles flying."

"One track in particular, "Achilles Last Stand," captures the electric feeling prevalent on the entire album.

"'Achilles Last Stand' is Zeppelin at their most propulsive and its speed and pace, related by the locomotive drumming of John Bonham, have the knack of finding a fresh basis to work out on and provide the basis for the duelling role of Jimmy's guitar and Robert's vocals."

● Album review in depth: page 9.

Melody Maker reports the imminent release of *Presence*.

MIKE WATT ON THE MUSIC AND JONESY
"NOT UPTIGHT, NOT FREAKED OUT"

BY DENNIS PERNU

Since co-founding the seminal 1980s So-Cal punk band the Minutemen with middle-school pal D. Boon, Mike Watt has become one of the most respected bass players on the planet. Spend some time with him, *Bass Player* magazine has enthused, "and you're bound to learn lessons beyond most scholars' comprehension."

While it may seem anathema to Watt's close, historical association with indie rock and even avant garde jazz, his musical vocabulary has always been strewn with references to "classic rock." He recalls seeing Led Zeppelin at Long Beach in 1975, not long after he picked up the bass guitar. If he had hoped to learn anything about the four-string from those shows, the hockey-arena acoustics of the day left him disappointed.

"You gotta understand the gigs in those days," Watt says. "I mean, the PA was mainly for singing. When you see those old pictures, there are all kinds of amps up there. The bass was more of a droning instead of hearing, like, notes. Plant, especially with the sound situation, could cut right through. That's a really big thing that Zeppelin had that the other bands didn't, except maybe Humble Pie with Steve Marriott. There was nothing limiting that frequency. And then, Page . . . man, he had a vocabulary."

Back in their bedrooms, Watt and Boon, like countless other teenagers before and since, encamped next to their turntables and parsed riffs from the backlists of AOR bands, including Zeppelin. "*Led Zeppelin III* was kind of weird," Watt remembers. "Just kind of acoustic music, but Boon liked that. He learned all the chords and stuff on that third record, but I still couldn't hear the bass parts. We're listening through a little record player, but it's little plastic speakers, you know. I can't hear it.

"A little later," Watt continues, "we saw *The Song Remains The Same* and got into 'Black Dog,' and me literally just doubling the guitar parts. And, it turns out, on some of 'em, the bass is doubling the guitar so it was okay."

Eventually, Watt, Boon, and Minutemen drummer George Hurley realized the creative limitations of merely covering other bands. "The idea of music as a form of expression, that was completely lost," Watt explains. "Copying riffs and stuff was like building models. 'Well, it kind of looks like the real thing, but it's a little plastic.' Nobody thought maybe there's something inside of you to get out through the music. I didn't find out about that 'til seeing punk—people not even knowing how to play but trying to make songs. You're never gonna write as good as 'Black Dog,' you know?"

As the Minutemen drifted toward L.A.'s nascent punk scene, they felt the peer pressure to reject Zeppelin and the other acts whose records they had begun to hone their chops to. "With Zeppelin, it was weird," Watt explains. "It was kind of like the Beatles—they're these incredible musicians, a pretty excellent band . . . I just was hung up over everybody else liking 'em. We were more close-minded in those days than I think young people are nowadays."

After Boon's untimely death in 1985, Watt's musical future initially fell into a spiral of self-doubt, but since 1987 his prolific output has included seven releases with '90s indie-rock heroes fIREHOSE, as well as several experimental ensembles and solo albums. In 2003 he was enlisted to fill the bass slot with the reformed Stooges, and in 2006 he was recruited for recording sessions with American Idol Kelly Clarkson.

Twenty-five plus years as a (relentlessly) touring musician have given Watt a better appreciation of his forebears, not least of all John Paul Jones.

"I mean, Jesus, he's quite a bass player," Watt says. "I think he learned his role in Led Zeppelin. It seemed like he would submerge his persona, no problem, to serve the tune, serve the greater good, the band. He was secure in his own thing with a really relaxed sense of playing, too . . . not uptight, not freaked out. It seems like of all those big '70s bands, Zeppelin had the most relaxed, secure bass sounds."

Watt continues, "I read someplace where Jones said this great thing about being a session player before joining Zeppelin: no one knew how to write for bass so he was free. I went back and listened to [Donovan's] 'The Hurdy Gurdy Man,' which I remember hearing as a

Olympia Stadium, Detroit, MI, January 31, 1975. *Robert Matheu*

young man. You can hear him play this great, fuzz bass kind of trip. That's my favorite John Paul Jones bass.

"Also, a lot of stuff Jones did was mysterious. The idea of him coming off the bass and playing keyboards and acoustic guitar at the gig, you know, that was weird at the time."

Watt goes on to site Jones' production work with Texas psychedelic punk rockers the Butthole Surfers and avant garde composer and vocalist Diamanda Galas as specific proof of Jones' post-Zep street cred. Still, Jones' tasteful and always appropriate contributions to the Zeppelin catalog are what Watt admires most—what the latter refers to as being a tugboat rather than a ball hog.

"I hear [Jones'] parts now and, I mean—wow, yeah—Led Zeppelin makes a lot more sense, especially the way he worked [the bass] parts with the drums. John Bonham didn't use all the stuff like Keith Moon did and he had a weird way of syncopating, especially with the kick drum, which is the closest to the bass. But he kept real good time and I think John Paul Jones could play holes more because Bonham had the time already. It was kind of like a be-bop bassist—he's running the low end, pumping it out. In certain ways, he's running the rhythm really, really strong but not bogarting it, you know? Not 'Look at me! Look at me!'"

"IF I PLAYED GUITAR I'D BE JIMMY PAGE . . ."
BY TAD KUBLER, THE HOLD STEADY

It all started for me on the morning of December 25, 1980. I was a seven-year-old who'd just received his first record player. It came with two albums. The first was one my parents approved of: Marlo Thomas and Friends' *Free To Be . . . You And Me* was released in 1972 and became an immediate pop sensation . . . for parents. Its message was simple: Growing up is hard and you are, as the title stated, free to be whoever you want to be. The second album was one my parents did not approve of, but after I had listened closely to the older neighborhood kids and then spent weeks negotiating and outright begging with my father, it came wrapped in green tissue paper with a red bow: *Led Zeppelin* was released in 1969, and had a slightly different message than the one Marlo and her friends were attempting to dispatch. And though in 1980, at seven years of age, I couldn't possibly understand what it was, I would spend the next seven years trying to figure it out.

By fourteen, I finally managed to wrap my head around it, and then I spent the next twenty years trying to reenact that message. By the time I picked up my first guitar, I knew that "If I played guitar I'd be Jimmy Page . . ." was more than just a segue to explain the age of girls I was into. And although it sounds better when Mike D says it, he doesn't really play guitar.

I grew up in the Midwest. Kind of. I started racing BMX with my little brother when I was seven years old. By the time I was nine, my brother and I had both progressed through the ranks of awkward beginners at local tracks to expert-level brats competing nationally. Our dad had caught the bug as well and this led to weekend travel—which, despite my mother's dissent, became weekly travel. This also led to growing up in hotel rooms all over the country with, as it turned out, little to no adult supervision.

There was a network of BMX parents and their kids from Secaucus to San Diego that became a sort of social happening. After the races, the moms and dads converged on the hotel bar and restaurant while the BMX kids were left under the supervision of the slightly older BMX kids. I was basically raised by a pack of sixteen- to eighteen-year-old dudes from various areas of the Midwest—dudes that were technically adults, yet technically still teenagers. This was the transition that my mother now refers to as an "expedited adolescence."

Any given evening in any given city went down like this: Several rooms on a floor were overrun with BMX hooligans of all ages. The scene was not unlike the "Riot House," which was explained to me in exacting detail not long after I began perfecting my vandalism skills. We kids left room-service trays everywhere, knocked over vending machines, pillaged pinball machines, rode bikes down hallways and on beds, threw anything that wasn't nailed down into the hallway or off the balcony, expelled the fire extinguishers into elevators and in general, terrorized the hotel staff. (Years later I learned what Fast Eddie Semo meant when he called me "Lil' Bonham" as he watched me set fire to a Holiday Inn bathroom. Long before that, though, I would learn that his nickname as "Fast," given to him by an ex-girlfriend, was not nearly as complimentary as the one he was paying me.)

To reference the Beastie Boys yet again, we were trashing hotels like it was going out of style—all to the soundtrack of lots of loud boomboxes blaring classic rock. There was everything from AC/DC to ZZ Top, Boston to Yes. The older kids were explaining how to score with girls, teaching me to clean weed, roll joints, and shotgun Heinekens (the beer made popular with the teenagers of the time by none other than EVH). While blasting me through their record collections at a furious pace, they explained to my prepubescent self the import and influence of every rock group of the '60s and '70s. But there was one band that was always on, and I never had to ask them to explain who they were or why they were listening to them: it was one of the first records I ever owned. The singer's howl was unmistakable, the bass more deeply aligned with what I imagined drums would sound like being played in an enormous parking garage. And last but not least . . . There have been so many attempts to describe it. Pontifications and pedantry. Discussions and deliberations. Thousands of metaphors and comparisons that certainly don't bear repeating here. To describe the sound of the guitar was quite simple. It was Jimmy Page.

One thing I'll never forget about sitting in those hotel rooms was wishing I was one of the big kids that understood what rock 'n' roll meant. Even more importantly, what Led Zeppelin meant. I listened to the dialogue among the teenagers as each Zeppelin track ended and a new one began; I wanted so badly to have the wisdom they had accrued in all of their eighteen years to be able articulate my knowledge and admiration for this band that even today, all others are compared to. I watched them so closely. I noticed that as one Zeppelin song changed to the next, so did their moods and body language. Their speech and colloquy. It seemed to have control over not just mind, but spirit and soul. Looking back on it now, I realize that's just what Led Zeppelin does.

None of these guys would ever argue that Plant got all the chicks. That Jonesy was a musical genius. That Bonham was (and is) the greatest rock 'n' roll drummer ever to play. But one thing I'll never forget was as the evenings progressed, every few seconds someone would interrupt with:

"Wait! Listen! Listen! Check out what Jimmy does right here, man! Listen!"

"No, no! Wait! Check this one! Check this!"

"Oh, man! Jimmy! Did you hear that?!"

"Hold on! Hold on! Listen to how Jimmy goes into this! Listen! Listen to this!"

A couple years went by and BMX became outrageously popular. There were now girls hanging out at racetracks. It had become a spectators' sport, and the guys that were good racers and good looking reaped the benefits. The guys I wanted to hang out with started bringing their acoustic guitars with them. I was amazed at how poorly they played compared to what I was used to listening to at home. But I think what surprised me even more was that these girls didn't care that they played so shitty. Apparently, they just liked guys that played guitar. (Though at the time I thought this absurd, I filed it away. Years later, at a drunken bonfire party in high school, I saw an acoustic guitar on the ground. I walked over and picked it up. And as soon as I noticed Becky C. was paying attention, and before she had the chance to leave with Ryan R., I used the last ace I had that evening. She never left with Ryan.)

As jealous as I was that the girls started spending more time with the older guys back at their rooms after races, I took advantage of the situation. I had been paying close enough attention to know that these guys weren't planning on playing these girls their shitty version of "More Than A Feeling" on their crappy guitars. I knew they figured turning over one of their guitars to me for a few hours would keep me out of their hair.

The sheer fucking hilarity of eleven-year-old me pining away by myself on an acoustic guitar in a trashed hotel room is not at all lost. In fact, I bet it looks a lot like many of the current indie bands working out some relationship issues. But trying to play along to classic rock on a crappy acoustic guitar for a few hours every now and again was all it took.

As my teenage years progressed, BMX came and went. The combination of travel and time out of school pretty much alienated me from the kids in high school. Which, in turn, probably led to eventually replacing my Van Halen and Led Zeppelin records in rotation on my turntable with the Clash and Black Flag. Along with the '80s punk rock scene came the notion that you didn't have to be a good player to start a band. Sometimes this statement is met with immense rebuttal. But as I said, it was only a notion. Sometimes it rang true. For better or worse, the coolest thing it did was allow a lot of kids to meet other kids that were playing music, poorly or otherwise. And eventually, I had the confidence to get up in front of people. Walking the walk has always really been the name of the game. From there on out, I had dozens of bands with dozens of different names switching from dozens of different sounds and genres. A lot of them were various degrees of shitty. Tales of basements and run-down rehearsal spaces. Van trouble and small clubs. Cheap beer and four-track demos. War stories and name dropping. But one thing that always stayed constant was my love for rock 'n' roll, and my memories of my initial exposure to it. And the band that always defined that for me was Led Zeppelin.

At eleven years old, I don't think I had ever heard, nor would I have understood the expression, "Through the looking glass." But reflecting back to those times, it's pretty safe to say I always knew what I wanted to do. It may have only took the four minutes and fourteen seconds of "Heartbreaker" for me to decide. But to this day, I still feel the same way that little kid in the hotel room felt.

If I was ever going to get anybody to listen to me, I was going to have to play guitar.

And I was going to have to try and play like Jimmy. 🦅

Jimmy Page, 1975.

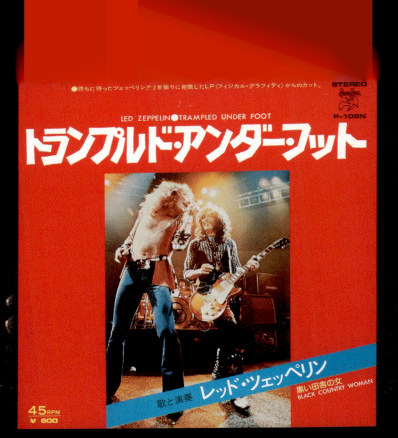

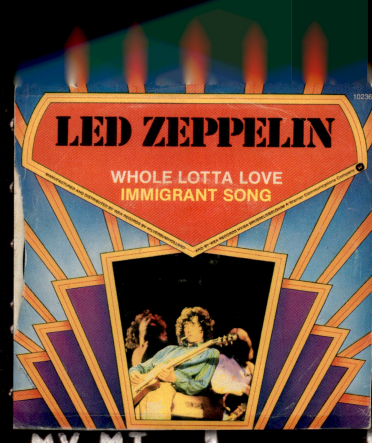

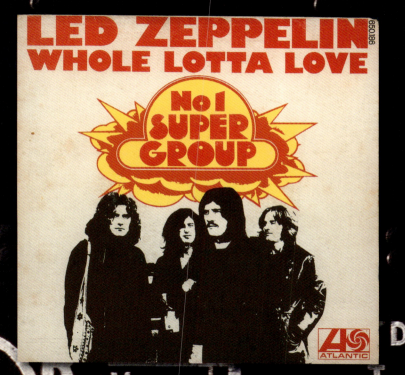

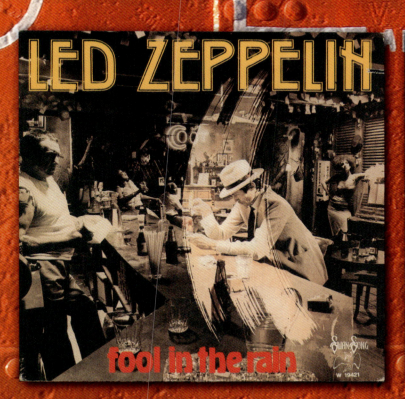

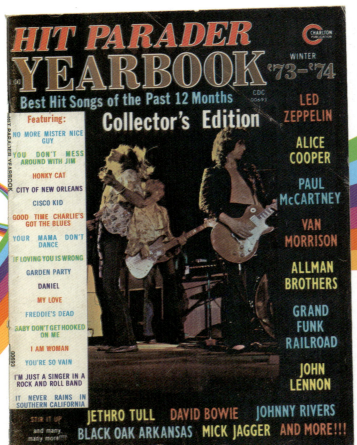

HIT PARADER YEARBOOK '73-'74
Best Hit Songs of the Past 12 Months
Collector's Edition

Featuring:
NO MORE MISTER NICE GUY
YOU DON'T MESS AROUND WITH JIM
HONKY CAT
CITY OF NEW ORLEANS
CISCO KID
GOOD TIME CHARLIE'S GOT THE BLUES
YOUR MAMA DON'T DANCE
IF LOVING YOU IS WRONG
GARDEN PARTY
DANIEL
MY LOVE
FREDDIE'S DEAD
BABY DON'T GET HOOKED ON ME
I AM WOMAN
YOU'RE SO VAIN
I'M JUST A SINGER IN A ROCK AND ROLL BAND
IT NEVER RAINS IN SOUTHERN CALIFORNIA
STIR IT UP
and many, many more!!!!

LED ZEPPELIN
ALICE COOPER
PAUL McCARTNEY
VAN MORRISON
ALLMAN BROTHERS
GRAND FUNK RAILROAD
JOHN LENNON

JETHRO TULL   DAVID BOWIE   JOHNNY RIVERS
BLACK OAK ARKANSAS   MICK JAGGER   AND MORE!!!

BOWIE • ZZ TOP • BEATLES • LYNYRD SKYNYRD • RUNAWAYS
$1.00
APRIL 1977
50p

America's Only Rock 'n' Roll Magazine
CREEM

LED ZEPPELIN
Page Gets The Led Out

BRUCE SPRINGSTEEN
Blinded By The Hype?

KINKS Interview
Ray Davies In Disgrace!

PARLIAMENT FUNKADELIC
Comin' To Getcha!

LEO SAYER
Dancing Fool

KISS
Dreem Date
Whips, Chains And Twinkies

SEX PISTOLS Last Shot?
MITCH RYDER Retread
ROLLERmania

• Marshall Tucker
• John Oates
• Blondie
• Abba

A PRE-TOUR TALK WITH JIMMY PAGE

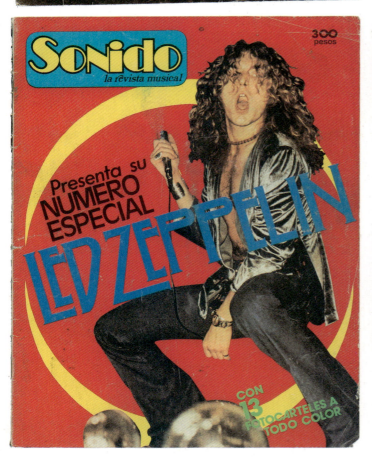

Sonido
la revista musical
300 pesos

Presenta su
NUMERO ESPECIAL
LED ZEPPELIN

CON 13 FOTOCARTELES A TODO COLOR

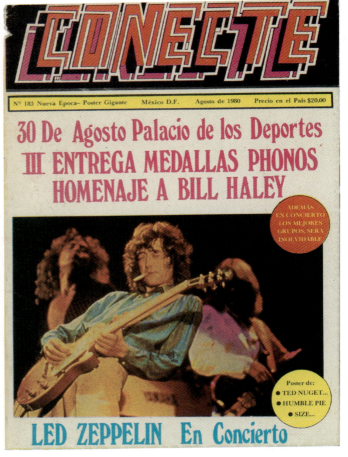

CONECTE
Nº 183 Nueva Epoca— Poster Gigante   México D.F.   Agosto de 1980   Precio en el País $20.00

30 De Agosto Palacio de los Deportes
III ENTREGA MEDALLAS PHONOS
HOMENAJE A BILL HALEY

ADEMÁS EN CONCIERTO LOS MEJORES GRUPOS, SERÁ INOLVIDABLE

Poster de:
• TED NUGET...
• HUMBLE PIE
• SIZE...

LED ZEPPELIN En Concierto

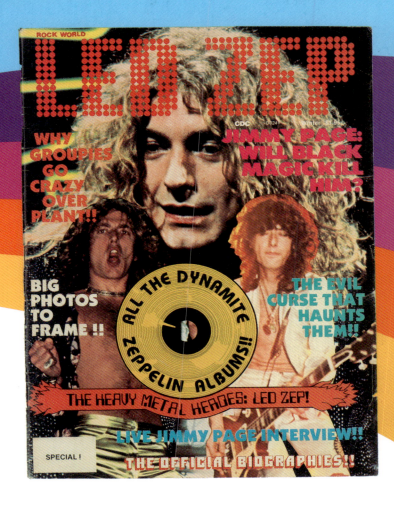

"They were Gods. Jimmy Page was my favorite guitarist. I wanted to look like him and play like him. And judging by our first record, you could see the influence there. I met Robert and Jimmy in '98 when they were playing in Toronto. They were just normal, everyday guys who wanted to talk about family and travel and cars and stuff like that. We sat on the stage, right by the monitor mixer, and watched them, and Jimmy kept looking over and winking and smiling and it was like 'Yes! My hero is a hero!'"

—Alex Lifeson, Rush

the LPs:
Presence
By Andrew Earles

Presence is the quintessential underdog within Led Zeppelin's proper studio discography. Released in March 1976, the band's seventh album alienated listeners hoping for a healthy serving of the softer pop, folk, psychedelic, and prog-rock concerns scattered about previous albums. *Presence*, however, is a visceral, minor masterpiece that effectively cleared out those cobwebs. Still, the only Led Zeppelin album that garners more critical causticity than *Presence* is the (unwitting) 1979 parting shot *In Through The Out Door*, an underdog in its own right courtesy of a band from which the wheels had totally fallen off.

In 1975, Led Zeppelin was the biggest band breathing. They had given world what is arguably the greatest classic rock double album of all time, *Physical Graffiti*, the eclectic tour de force that was the first Led Zeppelin title to carry their Swan Song imprint. When it appeared in February, the band was playing the early dates of a relatively large North American tour that established Zeppelin as the most profitable act in the business. Some vacation time, then a world tour—that's how the second half of 1975 was scheduled for Plant, Page, Jones, Bonham, and the notorious managerial tag team of Peter Grant and Richard Cole.

Things didn't work out that way. Zeppelin's infamous, autumnal dance with bad circumstances was initiated that August. A single car accident almost killed Plant, his immediate family (wife Maureen and both children), and Jimmy Page's daughter Scarlet as they were vacationing in Rhodes, Greece. Luckily, the children emerged relatively unscathed, but Maureen was seriously injured, saved only after a blood transfusion, and Plant's entire right leg and elbow were shattered. Excruciating physical therapy, a hip-to-toe cast, and a wheelchair—as well as painkillers and booze, it was reported—became Robert Plant's life for several months. Doctors told him that he might never again walk normally, much less prance about a stage. On the Bailiwick Island of Jersey, Plant brooded in a cocoon of convalescence. Not only was a world tour impossible, the jury was out on the band's future as a whole. As if Zeppelin and entourage needed the additional stress, they were tax exiles in their homeland. It has also been widely reported—and not just in Richard Cole's derided (by the band) biography *Stairway To Heaven: Led Zeppelin Uncensored*—that 1975 marked the year that heroin graduated from recreation to problematic ritual.

With spirits at an all-time low, Page and Plant sought refuge in the only feasible outlet: it was time to channel personal frustrations into a new album. Plant was still in a wheelchair when the band entered Musicland Studios in Munich, Germany, that November and December. They had a three-week window before the Rolling Stones were booked into the same studio for further work on what would become their *Black And Blue* LP. If heroin was indeed being used regularly by band members and management (Cole alleges that he, along with Page and Bonham, were becoming full-blown junkies by this point), it had no negative impact on Page's ability to focus. It took seventeen days to record and mix *Presence*, with Page enduring a couple of sleepless nights. Barring the approximately weeklong session that produced the band's self-titled debut, Zeppelin had never operated this efficiently in the studio.

Simply through the power of "Achilles Last Stand," *Presence* would be a classic even if the remainder was filled with recordings of John Bonham having drunken conversations with his vintage automobiles. Indeed, the song is Page's favorite Led Zeppelin track—a galloping, dour yet exhilarating onslaught of genuine heavy metal. Where other seventies hard rock bands utilized comparable song lengths to show off myriad time changes and stylistic aptitude, Led Zeppelin sticks to fewer tempo shifts. It's heavy enough to go up against what Judas Priest was creating at the time. To that end, "Achilles Last Stand" can be seen as a precursor to the new wave of British heavy metal that would soon explode all over Europe.

Does the rest of *Presence* deserve the claims of mediocrity leveled by so many critics? Not remotely. The second track, the loose, stripped-down "For Your Life" allows the listener a breath after the all-consuming (in the best possible sense) opening ride of "Achilles."

The undisputed star of *Presence* is Bonham, who pounds especially hard on "Nobody's Fault But Mine." A thinly veiled lyrical airing of drug-abuse dirty laundry, the song is classic rock aggression at its best. Ultimately, "Nobody's Fault But Mine" would be the closest that *Presence* would come to generating a sizeable hit. Striking a lethal blow against the instrument's common misuse in hard rock, it's a joy to hear Plant's cathartic harmonica tear through the speakers at a point when a guitar solo is expected.

The unforgettable hooks that anchor "Hots On For Nowhere" and "Royal Orleans" should have propelled these excellent rockers up the charts as well, yet they languish in the "album track" section of computer-controlled radio station air rooms.

That leaves the two songs actually worthy of the filler accusation. Even then, "Tea For One" qualifies only partially. The track lumbers forth on a doomy, hypnotic riff for a few seconds before morphing into Led Zeppelin's notoriously hit-or-miss card-up-the-sleeve: an interpretation of the blues. Meandering and whiny, "Tea For One" is nonetheless saved by Page's incendiary guitar solo.

"Candy Store Rock," however, is insufferable. The track's inoffensive boogie meets rockabilly nonsense is mercifully short at just under three minutes.

Because this is Led Zeppelin, a band that exists on a level that negates the term *contemporary*, even the misfires (every Zep album had them) trump the best that the majority of '70s hard rock had to give. The album was written and recorded when the band's future was threatened. Gross excess, general debauchery, and extreme adversity were barreling down them like a steamroller. (In fact, band misfortunes would continue with the death of Plant's oldest son, Karac, in 1977 from a stomach infection, and conclude in September 1980 with John Bonham's alcohol-related death.) That Led Zeppelin could knock off tracks that rocked like the band's early days is a minor miracle. An album born of necessity—an album that wasn't even supposed to happen—*Presence* is an important accomplishment that should be remembered as such. 🦅

PRESENCE
FROM
LED ZEPPELIN

Swan Song

DISTRIBUTED BY
ATLANTIC RECORDS

PRODUCED BY JIMMY PAGE

"THE OBJECT" ©1976 SWAN SONG INC.

© 1976 Atlantic Recording Corp. ⓦ A Warner Communications Co.

5

Print advertising for *Presence*, released in the U.S. on March 31, 1976.

5.17–18.75   Earls Court Arena, London, England
5.23–25.75   Earls Court Arena, London, England

"Being a hopeless Motown Funk Brothers addict, I naturally levitated toward the primal soul music of my black heroes from the very beginnings in the mid-1950s. As a guitar wrangler from the Joe Pedorsik Capitol School of Music on Grand River in Detroit, Led Zeppelin's music struck what I believe to be a much deeper chord in me, as I immediately identified the Howlin' Wolf, Muddy Waters, Robert Johnson, Mose Allison, *et al* touch in the licks and delivery. Though somewhat embarrassing that, instead of an American band, it took a combo of white limeys to accurately grasp, appreciate, and interpret the moving music of these black masters, I nonetheless worshipped the Bonham/Jones rhythm section as it propelled the thick, nasty-sex tones of Page's Les Paul and Plant's black-cat-moan vocals. This reintroduction of black American soul and blues music enflamed the American rock band explosion. God bless them."

—Ted Nugent

"Many people think of me as just a riff guitarist, but I think of myself in broader terms. As a musician I think my greatest achievement has been to create unexpected melodies and harmonies within a rock and roll framework. And as a producer I would like to be remembered as someone who was able to sustain a band of unquestionable individual talent, and push it to the forefront during its working career. I think I really captured the best of our output, growth, change and maturity on tape—the multifaceted gem that is Led Zeppelin."

—Jimmy Page, Guitar World *magazine, 1993*

TOUR DATES

Let Me Take You To The Movies
1976

Remember *The Song Remains The Same,* the documentary movie project? Well, neither the first nor the second director remained the same. Peter Grant canned second auteur Peter Clifton when he became paranoid that the Aussie filmmaker was living off the band (how dare he take a Zep limo to run another errand!) and had stolen the negatives to the film he was making (Clifton claimed he was making a "gift" short film of the outtakes for the guys). After the director delivered the film, Grant allegedly had Clifton's home searched (for extra footage) while he wasn't there, and then changed the closing credits on the film. (Clifton was still listed as the director, but his name was omitted from the posters and advertising campaign.) Meanwhile, Jimmy Page finished the soundtrack album to the film.

Zeppelin's ride experienced other turbulence. Without a tour and with little visibility in its homeland, rock's heaviest band no longer topped *Melody Maker*'s readers' poll in September 1976. Best band went to (oh no) Yes, with Zeppelin second. Similarly, Yes' Jon Anderson vanquished Robert Plant for best British singer, and Yes' Steve Howe bested Page for best guitarist. John Bonham was runner-up in the drummer derby to another prog-rock stalwart, Carl Palmer of Emerson, Lake, and Palmer. In addition, Page received a low blow in the press when filmmaker Kenneth Anger ripped him over *Lucifer Rising,* which had been in the works since 1967 and for which Page had been working on the soundtrack for more than three years. The devil-loving director declared, "I'm all ready to throw a Kenneth Anger curse" at Page. To add insult to injury, Anger eventually hired Bobby Beausoleil, a member of mass-murderer Charles Manson's cult, to compose the music—from prison.

On October 20, 1976, *The Songs Remains The Same* finally had its world premiere in New York City (the album

Japanese program, The Song Remains The Same, *1976.*

Pass to the world premiere of *The Song Remains The Same, October 19, 1976.*

A Warner Communications Company Presents "THE SONG REMAINS THE SAME"—THE LED ZEPPELIN Technicolor®

Stills from *The Song Remains The Same.*

Pages 202–209: bootleg album covers.

had dropped in the United States on September 28), with Clifton on hand to supervise the quadraphonic sound mix (imagine a proto–surround sound). The concert footage was culled from three 1973 shows at Madison Square Garden, plus from some try-to-fool-viewers rehearsals in 1974. On cue, the band's forever-nemesis, *Rolling Stone*, served up a scathing review penned by Dave Marsh. The movie "isn't the landmark in rock cinema Led Zeppelin would like it to be," Marsh wrote. "In fact, it's barely a movie at all, just some concert footage interspersed with trick photography (in a fantasy sequence devoted to each member). . . . It is hard to think of another major rock act making a film so guileless and revealing. Far from a monument to Zep's stardom, 'The Song Remains The Same' is a tribute to their rapaciousness and inconsideration. While Led Zeppelin's music remains worthy of respect (even if their best songs are behind them), their sense of themselves merits only contempt."

While hardly as bilious as Marsh, Robert Plant himself admitted to *Circus* magazine that he didn't enjoy working on the film. "Film people really puzzle me," he said. "I believe that music is the master; that is, it can bring you elation and sadness and satisfaction while the visual part of film is just the diversion. The attitude and antics of the people involved with film, the way they follow their own odd trips are really beyond my comprehension altogether. I could never imagine being involved in movies by myself. If I had to repeat the work on that film again, I would refuse to do it."

What *The Song Remains The Same* tried to assert was that Zeppelin was, above all, a great live band. The musicians relished playing together, giving performances that weren't the same every night. To be sure, set lists were similar but, unlike other big-time bands playing arena and stadium shows, the song never remained the same from night to night. Pagey, Percy, Jonesy, and Bonzo loved being on stage together, immersed in the chemistry that allowed Led Zeppelin to become more than the sum of its parts.

"The actual chemistry—or is it alchemy—of the group is that everything just always fits together," Page told *People* magazine in 1975. "I can go roaring off on a solo, then suddenly break off into staccato. I look up at Robert and somehow we're all there. It's like ESP."

"We brought these influences in, and Led Zeppelin was this place in between us all," Jones told the *San Diego*

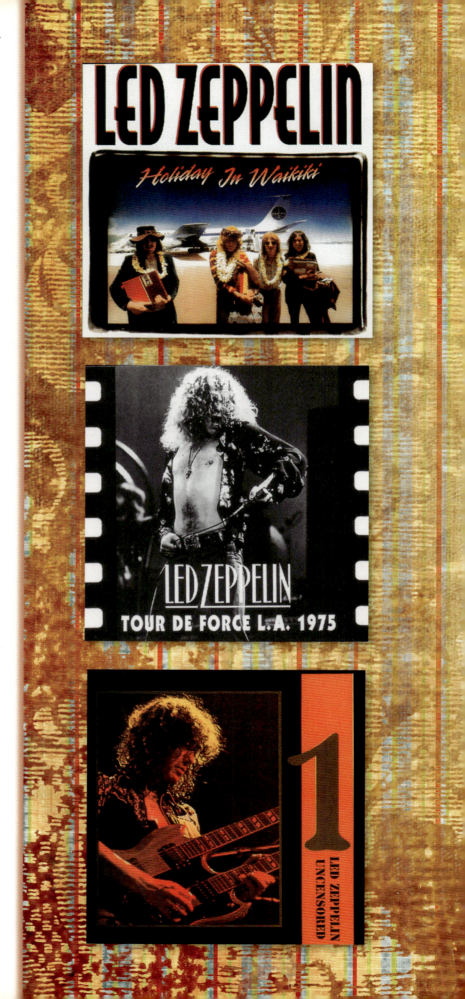

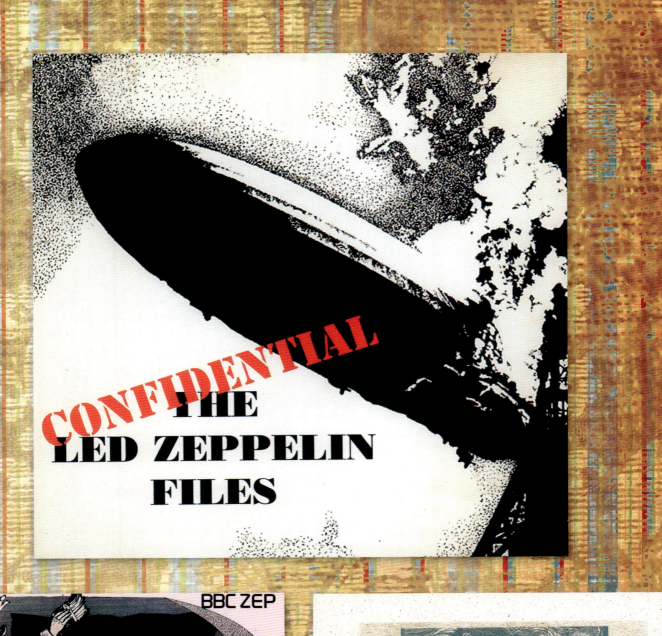

Union Tribune in 2003. "And it was so unique, all you can do is copy it off a stage show or record, but never create it the same way. To be like Zeppelin, you'd have to have that diversity of influences, which gave our music a timeless quality."

In 1973, Plant had rhapsodized about performing to journalist Lisa Robinson: "As long as there is a face looking up at me, as long as there's a face that knows what I'm doing, it could never be boring. It's the ability to make people smile or just to turn them on one way or another for that duration of time. And for it to have some effect later on. . . . I like them to go away feeling the same way you do at the end of a good chick, satisfied and exhausted."

Back to Jones in 2003: "Live shows were what Led Zeppelin was all about for me. The records were kind of starting points for the live shows. That's what I looked forward to most—the tours and playing with Robert, John and Jimmy."

Jones on Bonham: "Bonzo was known as the heaviest of the hard-hitting drummers, but when you watch the [2003] DVD, you can see all the other stuff that adds texture to his playing. And that's the same for the whole of the band."

Bonzo's son, Jason Bonham, weighed in on his dad's style in a 1989 interview with the *San Diego Union Tribune*: "My dad told me, 'Hold back, because then when you do something it will really sound exciting. Wait for the right moment, instead of being Mr. Busy.' My dad had the fastest right foot ever, and the most sampled. He got a huge sound without any padding, just two drum heads. It was amazing how he did it."

Let Jonesy have the last word: "I don't think we ever thought we were creating a legacy. We were just combining the influences of four good musicians and making something else—which was Led Zeppelin—and enjoying ourselves, keeping ourselves interested, alive and awake, and generally having a good time in life and maybe on stage. There was good and bad about it. Good, in that more and more people came to see and hear us. Good, in that we stopped touring in buses and ended up in a private plane, which is still the only way to tour. Less good, because we were playing bigger and bigger places, which for me was not so much fun. After a while, we were just turning up at big events, and they weren't so much fun. But there wasn't too much that was bad—world domination can be recommended!" ✒

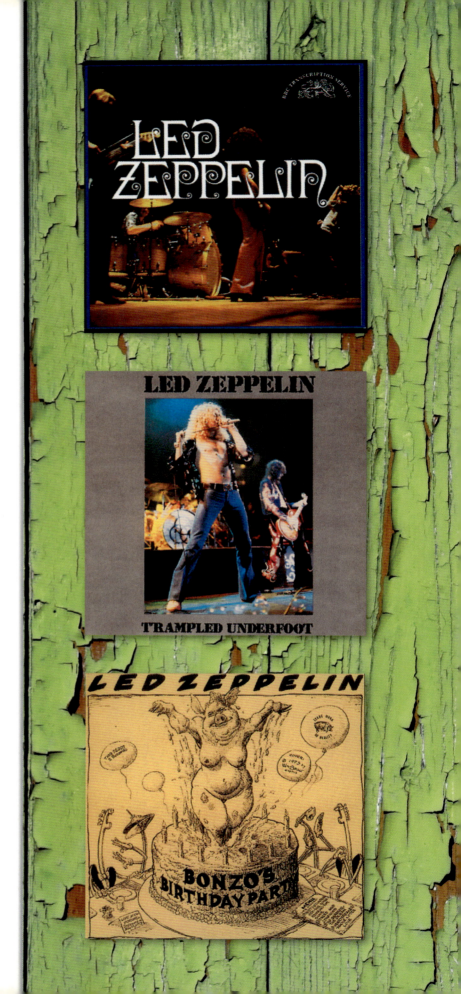

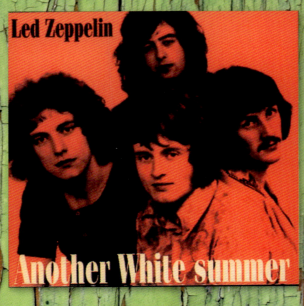

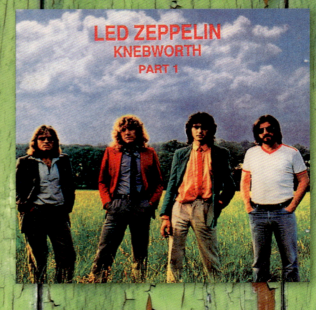

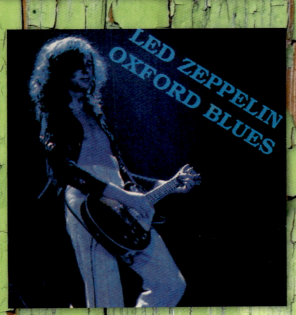

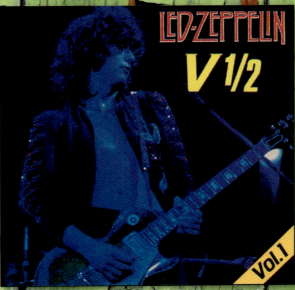

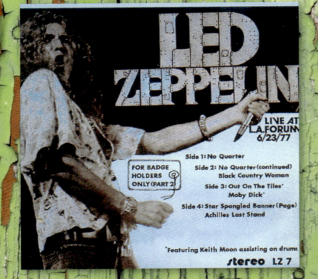

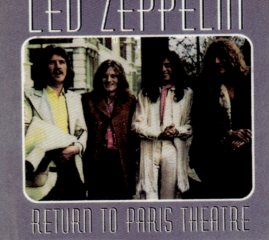

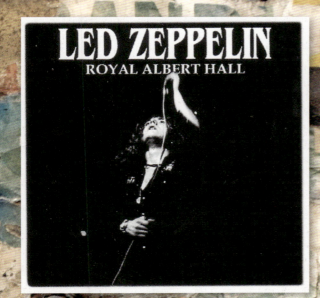

LED ZEPPELIN
ROYAL ALBERT HALL

LED ZEPPELIN

DESTROYER
FINAL EDITION

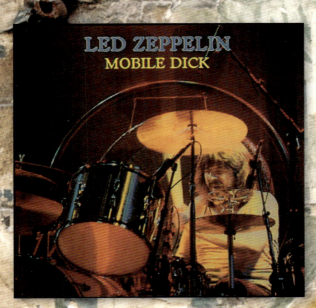

LED ZEPPELIN
MOBILE DICK

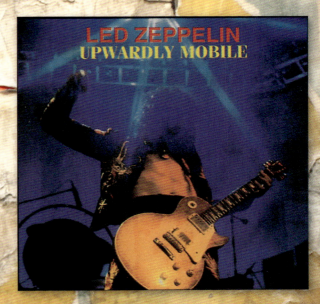

LED ZEPPELIN
UPWARDLY MOBILE

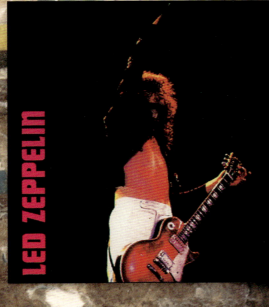

LED ZEPPELIN

WHO'S COUNTRY JOE?

LED·ZEPPELIN
TOUR OVER EUROPE 1980

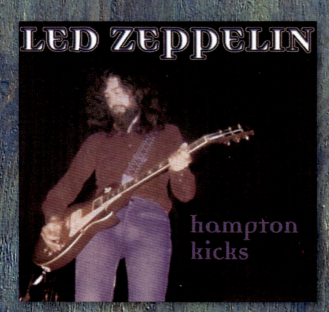

LED ZEPPELIN

hampton kicks

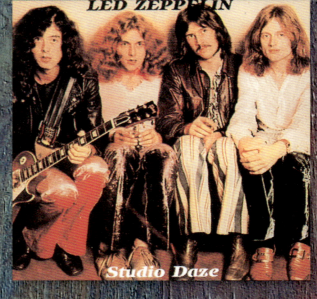

LED ZEPPELIN

Studio Daze

LED Z

DES

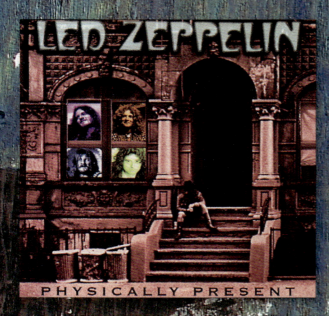

LED ZEPPELIN

PHYSICALLY PRESENT

Led Zeppelin

MUDSLIDE

LED Z
KILLIN

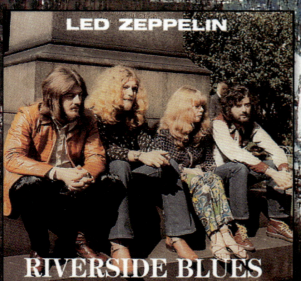

LED ZEPPELIN

RIVERSIDE BLUES

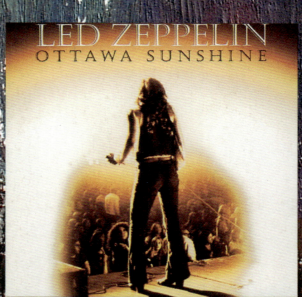

LED ZEPPELIN
OTTAWA SUNSHINE

plays

LED

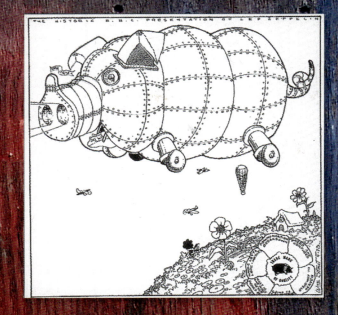

Led Zeppelin
Hot August Night

LED ZEPPELIN · BRUSSELS AFFAIR

LED ZEPPELIN
SOMETHING ELSE

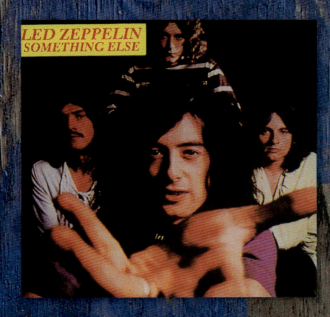

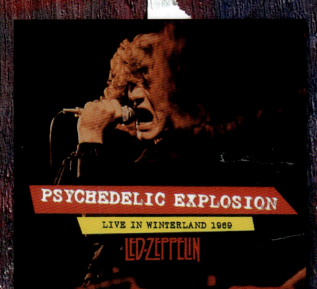

PSYCHEDELIC EXPLOSION

LIVE IN WINTERLAND 1969

LED·ZEPPELIN

MASTER
Silver
Rarities
SERIES

LED ZEPPELIN
LISTEN TO THIS EDDIE

the LPs:
The Song Remains The Same
By Chris Riemenschneider

Just how stoned do you have to be—Two trips to Taco Bell stoned? Darkest depths of Mordor stoned?—to feel dazzled by the scene of Jimmy Page swinging an Excaliburian sword into an ultra-hokey rainbow mirage during the movie version of *The Song Remains The Same*?

The moment that epitomizes the pomposity and prissy psychedelia of Led Zeppelin comes midway through the band's 1976 concert film, while Page is unfurling one of the lengthiest guitar masturbation sessions of all time, a twenty-seven-minute version of "Dazed And Confused." If you ever want to know why so many rock critics tried to deflate Zeppelin in its heyday, fast-forward to that part of the movie. And while you're at it, check out the clips of Zep manager Peter Grant working his own black magic backstage. It'll give you an idea of how the band got away with all that crap.

Thanks to its hopelessly overblown big-screen counterpart, the two-LP soundtrack to *The Song Remains The Same* never really stood a chance. Back in the day, it was also done in by the sheer inconvenience of two-sided vinyl. You'd flip over to Sides 3 and 4 and only get two songs. Side 2 ("Dazed") usually didn't get played at all. For stoners especially, that's simply an unacceptable work-to-music ratio.

Lo and behold, though, *The Song* hasn't remained the same. Its first pressing to CD opened the album up a little. Then the 2007 reissue blew it wide open, adding six bonus tracks that are among the best of the bunch, plus a noticeable remastering job by Kevin Shirley, the same guy who cleaned up the music for the excellent 2003 three-CD live collection *How The West Was Won*. Now, at least, you can feel John Bonham's drum solo in "Moby Dick" enough so it'll jolt you awake when it goes on too long.

Many Zep fans believe *How The West Was Won* made the previous live album obsolete. It's true, *The West* features better performances and a better overall song selection, but *The Song* is more definitive. Recorded over three nights at New York's Madison Square

Garden (perfect location!) during 1973's *Houses Of The Holy* tour, it's the snapshot versus the portrait—a bit out-of-focus and not well-framed, but realer and wilder.

Things are a tad awry from the get-go. It kicks off with a messy version of "Rock And Roll" that sounds like a rushed sound-check (or proof there wasn't a sound-check). But hey, that *is* rock and roll for ya.

"Rock And Roll" immediately hints at the ultimate shortcoming of *The Song Remains The Same*: its inadequate versions of some of Zeppelin's most cherished tunes, which even the reissue can't cover up. "Black Dog"—featured in the movie and the reissue but not the original album—never gets above a poodle-sized trot. The would-be climax, "Stairway To Heaven," comes off forced and uninspired, so much so that Robert Plant himself sounds like he's trying to wake up the crowd when he interjects, "Does anybody remember laughter?" But then he too sounds half-asleep by the time he gurgles out, "And she's buy-uy-uy-ing. . . ."

Worst of all, the fourteen-minute "Whole Lotta Love" ends the album on a tragicomic note as Page and Plant play musical footsy with each other, like an arena-rock version of the Bill Murray/Paul Shaffer lounge act from *Saturday Night Live*.

So where, exactly, are the good parts? Right after "Rock And Roll," for starters, as Page lights up on the wicked licks of "Celebration Song" and Bonham and John Paul Jones get into a pocket that's tighter than Plant's dangerously low-cut jeans. Disc 1 of the 2007 edition soon follows up with a duo of similarly straight-ahead bonus gems, "Over The Hills And Far Away" and "Misty Mountain Hop," and ends on a mighty note with one more, "The Ocean." Here, we finally have some of the energy and playfulness so missing in the movie and original LPs. There's an ebullient joy in "Misty Mountain" (which, by the way, you won't find on any other major Zeppelin live collection). Bonzo can be heard yelling out a goofy but emphatic countdown to "The Ocean," effectively sending his band mates off the deep end.

The Song Remains The Same is more about the ultra-serious and grandiose epics, though, and a few aren't bad. There's no escaping the bad Winds-of-Thor poetry in "No Quarter," but the icy version featured here is significantly more acidic and electric than the one on *Houses Of The Holy*. Wading through "The Rain Song" takes a little effort, but Plant winds up pouring himself into it like no other song on the soundtrack. And the reissue's

addition of "Since I've Been Loving You" features some of Page's most justified soloing.

And what about that twenty-seven-minute "Dazed And Confused"? Taken on its own, without the namby-pamby Mount Doom fantasy sequence or the walk to the record player, it's actually sort of fascinating. Even the part where Page pulls out the violin bow and wanks it across the strings merits a listen, albeit in a rubbernecking way. Except for maybe Yanni and Steve Vai, nobody in today's music world is this sure/full of themselves while playing their instruments anymore, or this willing to see where their egos can take them. The results are at least worth taking along on a trip to Taco Bell. ❧

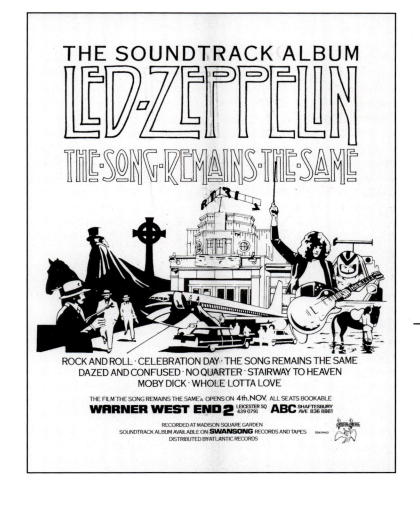

Alameda County Coliseum, Oakland, CA, July 23, 1977.
Ed Perlstein

Out Through The Out Door
1977-1980

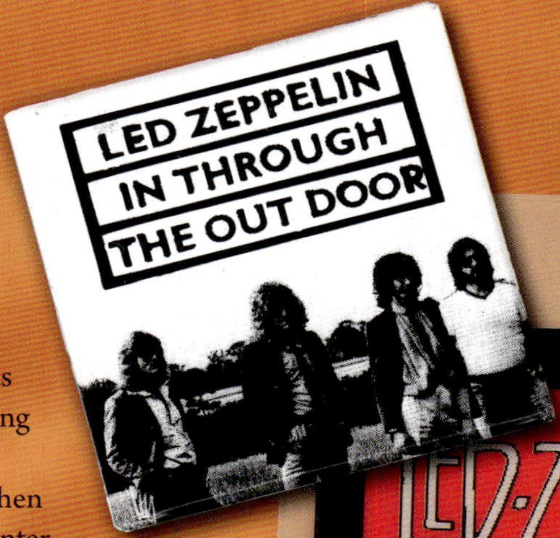

Had Led Zeppelin been grounded for good? Robert Plant was rehabbing his right leg, John Paul Jones was farming, and Jimmy Page and John Bonham were off recording in Montreux (see "Bonzo's Montreux" on 1982's leftovers collection, *Coda*). Rumors of Zep's demise were dispelled when a forty-nine-concert tour of the States was announced for winter 1977. The hype was that the band would draw more than 1.25 million fans and gross an incredible $10 million, more than twice their take in 1975.

But all that glitters doesn't necessarily turn to gold. After several weeks of rehearsal, old leather-throat Plant came down with tonsillitis, delaying the tour launch from February to April. Then Murphy's Law took over. *The Starship*, Zeppelin's usual ride, was being repaired, and the replacement jet, a Boeing 707 owned by Caesar's Palace of Las Vegas, couldn't accommodate the band's ever-growing entourage (each musician had at least one personal assistant). Page was actually nervous about the tour.

"We had to postpone a lot of dates and reshuffle them, and I didn't touch a guitar for about five weeks," he told *Guitar Player* in 1977. "I got a bit panicky about that—after two years off the road that's a lot to think about." Moreover, Plant's now permanently enlarged right foot still caused significant pain. He even thought about not being able to return to the band. "I wouldn't have compromised. I couldn't have gone on a stage and sat on a stool all night. I've got to be able to move around," he told the *Los Angeles Times* after the opening show of the tour. "I tried to keep a positive attitude in the months after the accident, but even after I was able to walk again, I didn't know how the foot would hold up on stage. Even the rehearsals didn't prove it to me. I was so nervous before we went on stage last night that I almost threw up. I could feel the tenseness in my throat for the first couple of songs. I kept telling myself to loosen up."

LED ZEPPELIN
IN THROUGH
THE OUT DOOR

LED·ZEPPELIN

UNITED STATES OF AMERICA 1977

Backstage pass, U.S. tour, 1977.

Access All Areas

From the 1977 U.S. tour program.

TONITE
8:00 PM
LED ZEPPELIN
SOLD OUT

During the fifth show of the tour in Chicago, Page became ill on stage—food poisoning was the official word but drug abuse was the speculation—and the show was canceled after a mere sixty-five minutes. But the fans kept coming, including 76,229—a Zeppelin U.S. record—to the Pontiac Silverdome outside Detroit.

During a tour break, the band headed home while Page, a traveler of time and space, wandered off to Egypt. Visiting other cultures was his way of recharging and growing, he told Cameron Crowe: "God, you know what you can gain when you sit down with the Moroccans? As a person and as a musician. That's how you grow. Not by living like this [on tour], ordering up room service in hotels. It's got to be the opposite end of the scale. The balance has got to swing exactly the opposite. To the point where I'll have an instrument and nothing else. . . . I like change and I like contrast. I don't like being stuck in one situation, day to day. Domesticity and all that isn't really for me. Sitting in this hotel for a week is no picnic. That's when the road fever starts and that's when the breakages start."

The dogs of doom howled more when Zeppelin resumed its eleventh U.S. trek. During a stadium show in Tampa, Florida, on June 30, a torrential storm pelted the seventy thousand fans, and the plug was pulled after only three songs. The enraged crowd revolted, and sixty concertgoers and several police ended up in the hospital. More bad karma ensued in Oakland, California, on July 23 and 24. On the first night, Peter Grant's son, Warren, was nabbed by a security guard while trying to remove a wooden sign (emblazoned with LED ZEPPELIN) from the band's dressing-room door. This brought Grant, John Bonham, and other crew backstage where a fracas ensued. We know who won this battle (the security guard was hospitalized), but who won the war? The morning after the second concert, Bill Graham, who had been presenting Zeppelin stateside since its first tour, filed charges, and police arrested Bonham, Grant, and two others at the band's hotel. All four were eventually found guilty, fined, and given suspended sentences. Later, three Graham employees filed a $2 million civil suit against the four, making headlines around the world. (The suit was settled out of court.) Graham, America's most powerful promoter, vowed never to book Led Zeppelin again. As it turned out, the band would never play another show in the United States.

(continued on page 220)

U.S. tour, 1977. *Adrian Boot/urbanimage.tv*

U.S. tour, 1977. *Richard E. Aaron/Rockpix.com*

U.S. tour, 1977. *Richard E. Aaron/Rockpix.com*

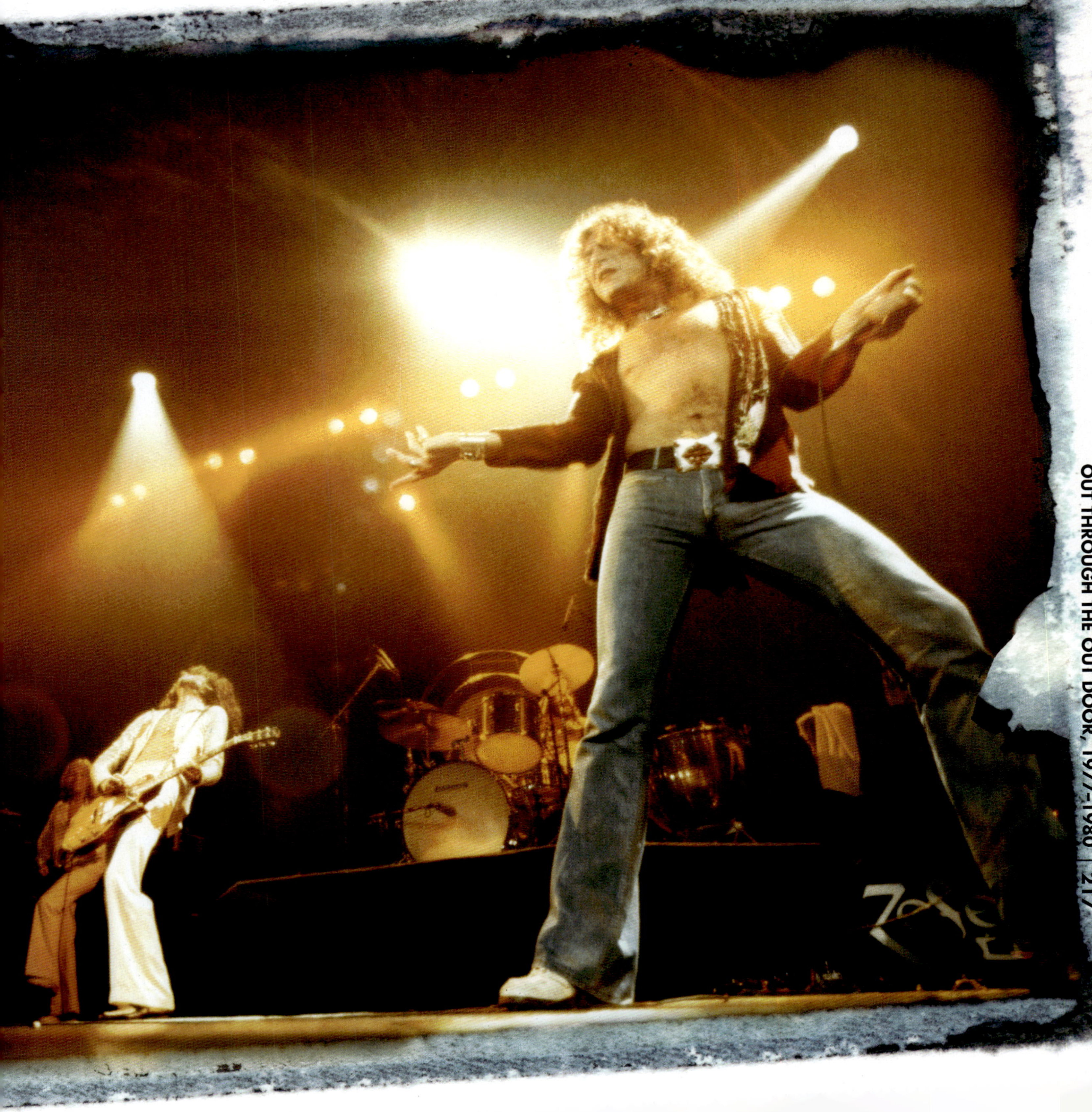

LED·ZEPPELIN

FRIDAY, APRIL 17, 1977   8:00 P.M.
MARKET SQUARE ARENA
All Seats Reserved: $7.00, $8.00 & $9.00
TICKETS AVAILABLE AT MARKET SQUARE ARENA BOX OFFICE; ROSS & BABCOCK, ALL IN TOWN. L.S. AYRES STORES, KARMA in BLOOMINGTON, THE STRAND in MUNCIE, SUN RECORDS in ANDERSON

"Led Zeppelin is a stag party that never ends.... There is no last tour. We're here and we'll always come back. It would be a criminal act to break up this band."

—Jimmy Page on the 1977 tour, quoted in Stephen Davis' Hammer Of The Gods

THIS SPREAD: Market Square Arena, Indianapolis, IN, April 17, 1977. *Robert Alford*

(continued from page 214)

Plant traveled on to New Orleans, where the band was set to play for eighty thousand at the Superdome. At his hotel, he received a startling call from his wife, Maureen, reporting that their five-year-old son, Karac, was gravely ill after not responding to medication for a sudden respiratory illness. A couple of hours later, she phoned to say that Karac had passed away. Plant, Bonham, and tour manager Richard Cole flew back to Britain while Grant stayed in the States to cancel the rest of the tour.

Already devastated, Plant fell into a deeper funk when Page, Jones, and Grant didn't make it to Karac's funeral. The singer went into mourning. Life—and Led Zeppelin—would never be the same for Plant. "I haven't taken a drug since that day," the singer told *Uncut* magazine in 2005. Nearly thirty years after Karac's death, Plant was still numbed by it all, he told British journalist Nigel Williamson. "The perspective of that, losing one's child, is the bitterest pill to take. I've got two more boys now who are gems—different kinds of guys, but really good friends of mine. But at that time, nothing was in my favor at all."

The hurt deepened with the sensational accusations that it was nobody's fault but Jimmy Page's, that the guitarist's interest in the occult had brought a curse on the band. "The comments about it at the time all connected it to Jimmy's dalliances and preoccupations with the dark side and whatever. I've never shared those with him and I don't really know anything about it," Plant told Williamson. "Fate is already written. I tried to pick myself up, and as I did so slowly, I realized my family was more important than the luxurious life I'd been living in Zeppelin."

The misfortune continued, with Bonham breaking two ribs when he crashed his car in September. Meanwhile, Page did what he always did—got lost in making music. He eventually relied on Bonzo as a go-between to see if and when Plant would return to Zeppelin. The singer kept vacillating. Finally, at a band meeting where the principals were talking about Bad Company, Maggie Bell, and other Swan Song artists, Plant agreed to try a little jamming with his mates.

In October 1978, fifteen months after Karac's death, Plant was ready to record ten new songs with the band. The sessions were held in ABBA's studio in Stockholm (ABBA was signed to Atlantic Records in the United States, and the tax exiles in Zeppelin couldn't record in the United Kingdom). For the first time, Jones asserted some leadership, starting songs by laying down his keyboard tracks with Plant's vocals. During the sessions, there seemed to be something

UPPER LEVEL
SEC. ROW SEAT 6
321A 9 1977
APR. 30, 1977
ADMIT ONE ON ABOVE DATE ONLY
S&L B.V. IN ASSO.
JERRY WEINTRAUB & CO.
LED ZE
PONTIAC SILVERDO
30
GOOD THIS
DAY ONLY
NO CANS BOTTLES OR
ALLOWED IN STAD

LED
ZEPPELIN
1977 North American Tour
Backstage
Access

SEC/BX ROW SEAT
60333
ADMIT ONE THIS DATE
JULY 30, 1977
S&L B.V. IN
ASSOCIATION
WITH CONCERTS
WEST / JERRY
WEINTRAUB
PRESENTS
LED ZEPPELIN
SATURDAY
JULY 30, 1977
$10.00
TAX INCL.
LOUISIANA
SUPERDOME
-NO REFUNDS-
NO REFUND NO EXCHANGE
SEC/BX ROW SEAT
60333

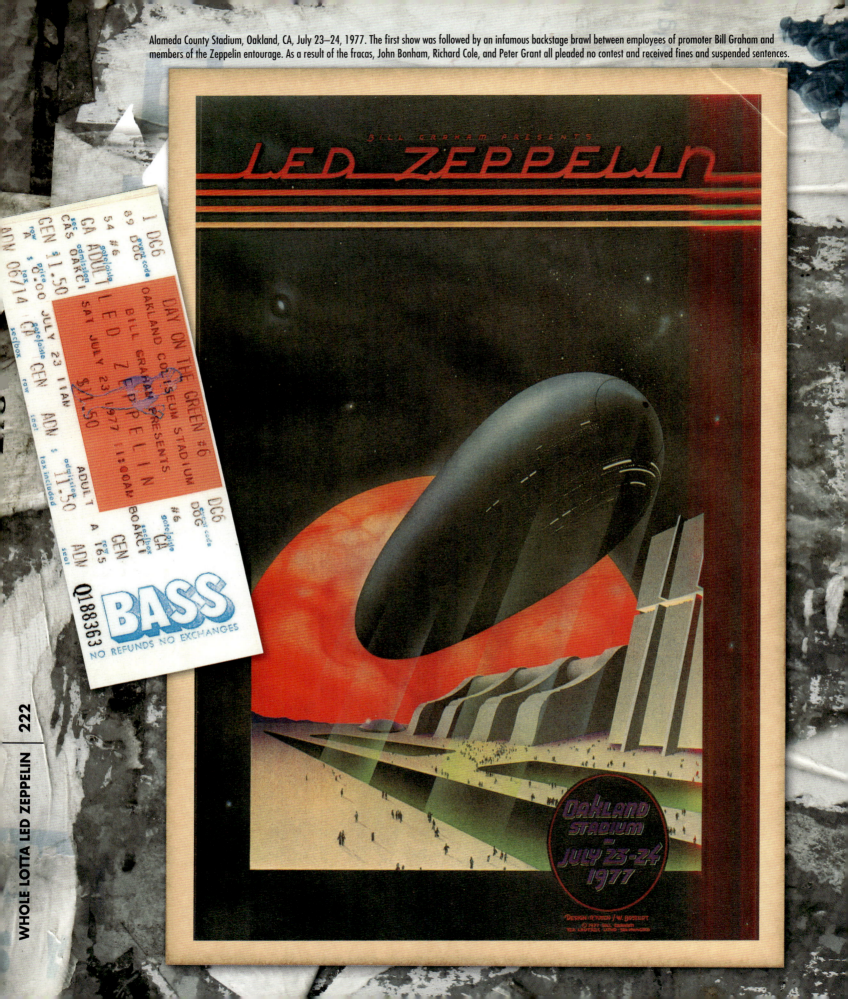

Alameda County Stadium, Oakland, CA, July 23–24, 1977. The first show was followed by an infamous backstage brawl between employees of promoter Bill Graham and members of the Zeppelin entourage. As a result of the fracas, John Bonham, Richard Cole, and Peter Grant all pleaded no contest and received fines and suspended sentences.

New York Times advertisement for the Madison Square Garden residency, June 1977.

of a communication breakdown, between the sober (Jones and Plant) and the reportedly not-so-much so (Page and Bonham). Still, the recordings were finished in three weeks (three leftovers would be heard on 1982's *Coda*).

In early 1979, Maureen Plant gave birth to another son, and her husband was determined to be a family man, not a touring musician. Ever-eager manager Peter Grant hatched the idea of Zeppelin making two appearances over consecutive weekends at a summer festival at Knebworth in the countryside, some forty-five miles north of London. After a theater warm-up gig in Copenhagen, Zeppelin hit the stage in front of one hundred thousand fans—their first U.K. show in nearly four years. But a much smaller crowd turned out for the second show. A week later, on August 15, 1979, *In Through The Out Door* was released, packaged in a brown paper bag with one of six different sleeves inside. The album zoomed to No. 1 in the States, where it was ensconced for seven weeks; it spent only two weeks at the top in the United Kingdom.

Page later discussed the album with *Guitar World*:

GW: That record seems to be dominated by John Paul Jones; at least his contribution seems to be more significant than on other albums. Did you feel that it might be more interesting for you to function as an accompanist rather than at center stage?

JP: See, you had a situation with *Presence* where Jonesy did not contribute anything, and that was a strain. I mean I would have preferred having some input at that point. But he had bought a new synthesizer [Yamaha GX-1], and it inspired him to come up with a bunch of things for *In Through The Outdoor*. He also started working closely with Robert, which was something that had not happened before.

GW: I thought maybe you were losing your enthusiasm for the band.

JP: Never. Never. In fact, Bonzo and I had already started discussing plans for a hard-driving rock album after that. We both felt that *In Through The Out Door* was a little soft. I was not really very keen on "All Of My Love." I was a little worried about the chorus. I could just imagine people doing the wave and all of that. And I thought: "That is not us. That is not us." In its place, it was fine, but I would not have wanted to pursue that direction in the future.

Alameda County Coliseum, Oakland, CA, July 23, 1977. *Ed Perlstein*

"I like to think that people go away knowing that we're pretty raunchy and we really do a lot of the things that people say we do . . . this is what we're getting over: it's the *goodness*. It's not the power, revolution, put your fists in the air. I like them to go away feeling the way you do after a good chick, satisfied and exhausted. . . . Some nights I just look out there and want to fuck the whole first row."

—*Robert Plant, quoted in Stephen Davis'* Hammer Of The Gods

Tragedy continued in the Zeppelin world. In October 1979, a nineteen-year-old man was found dead of a drug overdose in Page's house.

Grant, of course, wanted to get the band on tour again in the States but Plant resisted. Eventually, he relented to a brief European tour: fourteen concerts, dubbed "Over Europe 1980," in modest-sized venues, averaging four thousand per gig. Plant was in good form, according to all reports, but Page's performances were erratic and sometimes sloppy. At the final show in West Berlin on July 7, Plant, according to *The Rough Guide To Led Zeppelin*, bid the crowd *Auf Wiedersehen*: "Thank you very much everybody who's worked with us and put up with us and all those sort of things—and goodnight."

Grant was plotting a return to North America, starting October 17 in Montreal and winding up with four nights in Chicago, ending on November 15. On September 24, the band convened at Page's new manor (which he'd just purchased from actor Michael Caine) before rehearsing at a nearby studio. Bonham was in a dark mood. Plant recalled to *Uncut* magazine in 2005 driving with the drummer that morning. "He was saying: 'I don't want to do this. You play the drums and I'll sing.' We got to the studio and that's what happened. I played the drums and he sang a bit." Bonzo was drinking, and the rehearsal was far from satisfactory. Not surprisingly, he continued to drink into the night. A roadie carried the drummer to bed. Two roadies apparently checked on Bonzo in the morning. When he hadn't appeared by afternoon, Jones went to kick him out of bed. But he discovered Bonham dead, having choked on his own vomit. Later, a coroner concluded that John Henry Bonham, aged thirty-two, had consumed the equivalent of forty shots of vodka in the twenty-four hours before his death.

The three surviving members and Grant met several times to discuss Zeppelin's future. On December 4, Grant issued a statement that concluded: "We could not carry on as we were."

Years later, the survivors reflected on the decision." Well, Bonzo wasn't just our drummer, he was a quarter of Led Zeppelin, and we just couldn't see going on without him," Jones told the *San Diego Union Tribune* in 2004. "To be fair to some other bands, if a band is song-based, then it's not quite so important who is playing the song. But Led Zeppelin was performance-based, and it would have been a different band, completely, without Bonzo. The chemistry was so interlocked and dependent on the four members, that if you replaced anyone, it would have been another band entirely. And that's not what we wanted to do."

Plant told *Details* magazine: "I didn't say it should finish, you know. I didn't say it should be over. I didn't say it should end. It just ended."

Page, the band's founder, architect, and leader, told Cameron Crowe in 1993 for *The Complete Studio Recordings*: "It was impossible to continue, really. Especially in light of what we'd done live, stretching and moving songs this way and that. At that point in time especially, in the early eighties, there was no way one wanted to even consider taking on another drummer. For someone to 'learn' the things Bonham had done—it just wouldn't have been honest. We had a great respect for each other, and that needed to continue—in life or death." ◗

The August 4, 1979, *Melody Maker* previews Knebworth and interviews Page on the forthcoming *In Through The Out Door*, the Oakland donnybrook of the previous month, and punk rock. Of the LP, Page told writer Steve Gett, "There's a lot more keyboards and synthesizer employed by John Paul. He has one of those Yamaha monster electronic machines that practically sound like a one-man orchestra."

THE DRUMS WILL SHAKE THE CASTLE WALL
ON JOHN BONHAM

BY DON BREWER, GRAND FUNK RAILROAD

> "Bonham is the greatest rock drummer—he just *is*. When people say Buddy Rich is technically the greatest drummer ever, John Bonham is hands-down the greatest rock drummer ever. Just everything he did felt good. It's just incredible."
>
> —Chad Smith, Red Hot Chili Peppers

> "I've never tried consciously to be one of the best drummers and I don't want to be. A lot of kids come up to me and say, 'There's a lot better drummers than you,' or something. But I enjoy playing to the best of my ability and that's why I'm here doing it. I don't claim to be more exciting than Buddy Rich. But I don't play what I don't like. I'm a simple, straight-ahead drummer and I don't try to pretend to be anything better than I am."
>
> —John Bonham, quoted in Stephen Davis' Hammer Of The Gods

> "Bonzo sounded that way because he hit the drums harder than anyone I ever met. He had this bricklayer's ability to bang the drum immensely hard. Yet he had a very light touch. In many ways, he was the key to Led Zeppelin. You could work fast with him. The only reason Led Zeppelin ever did retakes was the extremely tricky time sequences of most of the songs. Once Bonzo mastered his part, everything else would fall into place."
>
> —Eddie Kramer, quoted in Stephen Davis' Hammer Of The Gods

> "People for years haves categorized Led Zeppelin with a lot of other groups called heavy metal. I think they were a loud, adventurous modernist blues group. Bonham played a certain kind of way where he hit the bass drum [and] it landed with a certain kind of impact that hit you in a way that no one ever hit you with a bass drum before—ever."
>
> —T-Bone Burnett, interviewed on CMT Crossroads

It was a very creative time period back then. I remember going to the Grande Ballroom in Detroit and seeing the Soft Machine from England, Terry Reid from England, all those drummers who came over doing things I'd never seen an American drummer do before. There was a lot of heavy foot stuff going on, foot-pedal stuff. That's where Bonham came up; he was hearing other drummers do stuff with the foot, thinking he could do it—and even cooler than that.

We all came up hearing big-band drummers, learning what they were doing, and hearing rock drummers with Jerry Lee Lewis and Chuck Berry and what they were doing. We all came up learning that kind of stuff, basic rock 'n' roll stuff. Then, as you get into the sixties, all this pop, Motown stuff, then R&B. That's where I think a lot of the foot syncopation came from, listening to Otis Redding and Wilson Pickett and drummers that were playing on those—that was a heavy influence for rock guys going with heavier stuff.

Bonham had a freedom about the way he played. He had his chops down, but he could also do all of these different things drummers would listen to and think, "What the hell is he doing?" We'd sit at the drums and try to figure it out. He . . . came up with incredible riffs and licks. It comes down to style; he just had this style between the foot and his left hand and his right hand and all these drum fills he would do.

He had a great sound, too. I don't know how much of his drum sound was him and how much was Page's production. From what I understand, they would put him in a concrete room and just mic the room and the drums. That's what made the drum sound so big—that combination of things.

I think he was a perfect complement to Jimmy Page's guitar playing. Page had a lot of really unusual kinds of rhythms and guitar feels—guitar grooves are what they are, really. They were different; that's what made Led Zeppelin so special, kind of like how Keith Richards makes the Rolling Stones sound unique. Page would put Bonham up against those guitar grooves and [he would] come up with these great drum licks to complete them. I don't know if any other drummer, including myself, would've heard those guitar lines Page was playing and come up with those grooves. He wasn't just sitting there playing 4/4 time to them; it was all the syncopation that he was doing along with those guitar licks that was so phenomenal. Like on "Rock And Roll," he's playing this right-handed open high-hat with this left-handed shuffle that's usually reserved for more of a boogie shuffle, but here it is in this rock thing, and it just sounds amazing.

All I can say is song after song with him is just an attitude. It all goes with the sound of Led Zeppelin—the sound of him, the sound of his drums, the syncopated thing. He's just playing great stuff. He was one of a kind, and without him Led Zeppelin would've sounded completely different. 🕊

—As told to Gary Graff

KNEBWORTH '79

£1.00

LED·ZEPPELIN

Knebworth Festival program, August 4, 1979.

KNEBWORTH PARK NEAR STEVENAGE HERTS

SAT. 4th & SAT. 11th AUGUST 1979 11AM to 11PM

FREDERICK BANNISTER IN ASSOCIATION WITH PETER GRANT PRESENTS

LED· ZEPPELIN

The NEW BARBARIANS 11th only.

featuring RONNIE WOOD KEITH RICHARD STANLEY CLARKE
BOBBY KEYES IAN McLAGEN and JOSEPH MODELISTE

TODD RUNDGREN AND UTOPIA
SOUTHSIDE JOHNNY AND THE ASBURY JUKES
MARSHALL TUCKER BAND
CHAS AND DAVE
FAIRPORT CONVENTION 4th only

Co-ordination And Fun From Nicky Horne   553/1,000 '99

TICKETS £7.50 IN ADVANCE £8.50 ON THE DAY (THE PRICE OF THE TICKET INCLUDES VAT & AGENTS COMMISSION **DO NOT PAY MORE** TICKETS AVAILABLE FROM ALL BRANCHES OF VIRGIN RECORDS & HARLEQUIN RECORDS, ALSO AVAILABLE BY POST (S.A.E. PLEASE) FROM: KNEBWORTH CONCERT, 201 OXFORD STREET, LONDON W1
The nearest station is Stevenage and a coach shuttle service has been arranged between the Station and the Park (Do not get out at Knebworth Station) For motorists, Knebworth Park is situated directly off the A1(M) at the A602 Southern Intersection. Pedestrians make for Stevenage and follow signs.

Poster advertising dates of the 1980 European tour, the band's last.

DO NOT TEAR PERFORATION AS THIS WILL INVALIDATE TICKET
KNEBWORTH PARK Nr STEVENAGE HERTS
SATURDAY 4th AUGUST 11.00 a.m.—11.00 p.m.
FREDERICK BANNISTER IN ASSOCIATION WITH PETER GRANT PRESENTS

LED ZEPPELIN
at Knebworth

ADV. BOOKING PRICE £7.50 inc. VAT.
TICKET No C   **06824**   TICKET No. C   **06824**
WARNING The cost of this ticket includes VAT and Ticket sellers commission **DO NOT PAY MORE**

Knebworth Festival ticket, August 4, 1979.

Knebworth Festival, August 11, 1979.

Knebworth backstage pass, August 4, 1979.

The iconic Knebworth publicity photo.

LED·ZEPPELIN

OVER EUROPE '80

6/17 DORTMUND
6/18 COLOGNE
6/20 BRUSSELS
6/21 ROTTERDAM
6/23 BREMEN
6/26 VIENNA
6/27 NUREMBERG
6/29 ZURICH
6/30 FRANKFURT
7/2 MANNHEIM
7/3 MANNHEIM
7/5 MUNICH
7/7 BERLIN

Posters advertising dates of the 1980 European tour, the band's last.

LED-ZEPPELIN
TOUR OVER EUROPE 1980

ROTTERDAM
AHOY
JUNE 21ST

BREMEN
STADTHALLE
JUNE 23RD

BERLIN
EISSPORTHALLE
JULY 7TH & 8TH

HANNOVER
MESSEHALLE
JUNE 24TH

BRUSSELS
FOREST NATIONAL
JUNE 20TH

DORTMUND
WESTFALENHALLE
JUNE 17TH

KÖLN
SPORTSHALLE
JUNE 18TH

FRANKFURT
FESTHALLE
JUNE 30TH

MANNHEIM
EISSTADIUM
JULY 2ND & 3RD

NÜRNBERG
MESSEZENTRUM HALLE
JUNE 27TH

MÜNCHEN
OLYMPICHALLE
JULY 5TH

VIENNA
STADTHALLE
JUNE 26TH

ZURICH
HALLENSTADION
JUNE 29TH

SWAN SONG

Backstage passes, 1980 European tour.

Ticket, Vorst Nationaal,
Brussels, Belgium, June 20, 1980.

LED·ZEPPELIN

Tour of Europe 1980

GUEST

FOREST - VORST NATIONA(A)L.

LED ZEPPELIN

Jeudi 5 Juin 1980 à 20 h 30.
Donderdag 5 Juni 1980 te 20.30 u.

All glass containers, cans, firecrackers, fire-
works, recorders and cameras excepting small
instamatic type cameras are strictly prohibited
in the hall and can be seized by artist
management and/or concert promotors.

350 Fr.   05185

TAXES ET TVA COMPRISES
A présenter s. demande - Non valable s. souche
TAKSEN EN BTW INBEGREPEN
Te tonen op aanvraag - Niet geldig zonder strook

Tickets VOET - 9800 DEINZE

LED·ZEPPELIN
TOUR OVER EUROPE 1980

STAFF

LED·ZEPPELIN

TOUR OF EUROPE 1980

STADIUM CREW

LED·ZEPPELIN

TOUR OF EUROPE 1980

LOCAL CREW

In Through The Out Door
By George Case

Led Zeppelin's final album as an active band was *In Through The Out Door*, released in the late summer of 1979. With a market starved for new Zeppelin material—their last release had been 1976's *Presence*—and which remained cool to critically embraced punk and new wave acts, the record was an immediate success and prodded a much-needed revival of the entire pop music industry. Yet, more than ten years after Zeppelin first hit the airwaves and turntables of the world, *In Through The Out Door* was recognized as a departure for the group, short on the fast and heavy blues guitar tunes with which they had made their name and long on a swirling eclecticism that was even more adventurous than the experiments of *Houses Of The Holy* or *Physical Graffiti*. This was not your big brother's Led Zeppelin.

The quartet itself was in transition. It was alleged that Jimmy Page and John Bonham had both become addicted to heroin—still capable of playing, certainly, but professionally unreliable. Bonham had barely escaped jail time after an assault committed backstage at a concert in Oakland during the band's last tour of America, in 1977. Robert Plant's young son, Karac, had suddenly died of a viral infection shortly thereafter and the singer took more than a year off to mourn his child and consider his future. For *In Through The Out Door* it was John Paul Jones, always the most pragmatic and dependable member of Led Zeppelin, who did the instrumental and compositional heavy lifting. The album, recorded during a three-week period in November and December 1978 at Polar Music Studios in Stockholm, Sweden, featured two out of seven tracks for which Page received no songwriting credit, and six for which Jones was cited as co-author. Jones and Plant, nightly left alone in the studio without their bandmates, had begun to work on songs together. "Robert and I spent much of the time drinking pints of Pimms and waiting around for it to happen," Jones said later. "So we made it happen." Dynamics within the band had changed.

In Through The Out Door still bears Page's stamp as producer, assisted by engineers Leif Mases and Lennart Östlund. Ten completed tracks were put on tape in Stockholm (three turned up on the posthumous *Coda*) and mixed at Page's home of Plumpton Place in Sussex. Polar Studios had an almost metallic natural echo that resounded through all the new songs; one of the disc's most noticeable qualities is the consistency of its crisp live ambience. Its opening number, "In The Evening," began with an eerie, abstract prelude by Page playing his Fender Stratocaster with a bow and a mechanical novelty called the Gizmotron ("I like drones and things like that," said the guitarist) before banging into its jagged chord progression. The intro was reminiscent of the other "ghost" noises with which Zeppelin's *II*, *III*, and *IV* were commenced.

"South Bound Suarez" was a tight little piano groove done up by Jones and Plant, hammered into place by Bonham and which featured a heavily compressed Page solo. Next was the samba-style "Fool In The Rain," featuring a lyrical plotline derived from the Diamonds' 1957 doo-wop hit "Silhouettes" and a convincing Latin rhythm, and highlighting Jones' new Yamaha GX-1 synthesizer, prominent throughout the LP. Catchy and innovative, "Fool In The Rain" was put out as a Led Zep single and reached number twenty-one on the U.S. charts. Another genre surprise came with "Hot Dog," a funny but plausible pastiche of country music (albeit with heavily distorted guitar) and in the simple chords of G, C, and D7, making it the only track on the album likely to be strummed around a campfire.

Side 2 launched the dense, disturbing "Carouselambra," Jones' keyboard as lead instrument and Page playing his iconic Gibson EDS-1275 double-neck, which he rarely used offstage. "All My Love," arguably the album's finest piece, was written by Jones and Plant and ventured about as far away from the blistering rock of "Immigrant Song" or "Black Dog" as the ensemble could go. A pretty and heartfelt ballad of affirmation and devotion, its easy-listening vibe made Page uncomfortable: "I was a little worried about the chorus," he commented. "I could just imagine people doing the wave and all that." Finally came the tortuous "I'm Gonna Crawl," a slow minor-key blues that compared well with older cuts like "Since I've Been Loving You" from *III* and "Tea For One" off of *Presence*, and featured a syrupy synthesizer fanfare that could have been conducted by Nelson Riddle, an anguished Plant vocal, and one of Page's most emotional solos.

In Through The Out Door came in a typically enigmatic sleeve designed by Zeppelin's preferred designers at Hipgnosis, with a plain brown wrapper outside—recalling the wordless cover of *IV*—and two of six possible scenes of closing-time desolation inside, depending on which edition was purchased. (On my vinyl copy, actually, one of the pictures is different from any reproductions I've seen elsewhere—the guy at the bar is *about* to burn the note but it hasn't caught fire yet.) Inside this were two-tone close shots of the tequila, cigarettes, ashtray, and the Dear John letter that set the bluesy mood of the whole package, the first issues of which could be dampened to reveal hidden dyes in the print, an idea that came to Jimmy Page from a coloring book belonging to by his daughter, Scarlet.

For its formal innovations and synthesized tones *In Through The Out Door* is rarely picked as a favorite among Zep fans, and Page reported that he and Bonham "both felt that [the album] was a little bit soft," the guitarist and drummer planning "a hard-driving rock album after that." Yet the record is an intriguing closer to the Led Zeppelin catalog, implying an ongoing evolution in the band's sound and style that had already gone beyond what anyone had expected ten years before.

The last Led Zeppelin record was my first. I'd already been exposed to the group through friends who'd lent me tapes or played sides from their own collection, but in about 1985, when I was eighteen, *In Through The Out Door* became my initial purchase from their repertoire. A strange choice? What made longstanding Zepheads skeptical was precisely what I liked about the album: the way it belied their wider reputation—as it then stood—as one-dimensional purveyors of heavy metal bombast or pretentious occult posturing. Playing "Hot Dog," "All My Love," or "I'm Gonna Crawl" for outsiders would always provoke a puzzled response. These were the guys who did that headbanging anthem "Whole Lotta Love"? The overblown epic "Stairway To Heaven"? Drawn-out stoner threnodies like "Dazed And Confused"? This was the same four people? Sure were. Just when Led Zeppelin had threatened to become passé, dinosaur rock before anyone had thought of classic rock, here came *In Through The Out Door*. I won't say the work is their greatest, but it's the one that best indicates Led Zeppelin's range and creative maturity. That it is also the concluding product of their twelve-year career makes it all the more poignant. 🦇

4.1.77	Memorial Auditorium, Dallas, TX
4.3.77	The Myriad, Oklahoma City, OK
4.6–7.77	Chicago Stadium, Chicago, IL
4.9–10.77	Chicago Stadium, Chicago, IL
4.12.77	Met Center, Bloomington, MN
4.13.77	Civic Center, St. Paul, MN
4.15.77	Blues Arena, St. Louis, MO
4.17.77	Market Square Arena, Indianapolis, IN
4.19–20.77	Riverfront Coliseum, Cincinnati, OH
4.23.77	The Omni, Atlanta, GA
4.25.77	Freedom Hall, Kentucky Fair & Expo Center, Louisville, KY
4.27–28.77	Richfield Coliseum, Cleveland, OH
4.30.77	Pontiac Silverdome, Pontiac, MI
5.18.77	Jefferson Memorial Coliseum, Birmingham, AL
5.19.77	Assembly Center, Louisiana State University, Baton Rouge, LA
5.21.77	The Summit, Houston, TX
5.22.77	Tarrant County Convention Center, Fort Worth, TX
5.25–26.77	Capital Centre, Landover, MD
5.28, 30.77	Capital Centre, Landover, MD
5.31.77	Coliseum, Greensboro, NC
6.3.77	Tampa Stadium, Tampa, FL
6.7–8.77	Madison Square Garden, New York, NY
6.10–11.77	Madison Square Garden, New York, NY
6.13–14.77	Madison Square Garden, New York, NY
6.19.77	Sports Arena, San Diego, CA
6.21–22.77	The Forum, Inglewood, CA
6.23.77	The Forum, Inglewood, CA
6.25–27.77	The Forum, Inglewood, CA
7.17.77	Kingdome, Seattle, WA
7.20.77	Activities Center Arena, Arizona State University , Tempe, AZ
7.23–24.77	Alameda County Coliseum, Oakland, CA

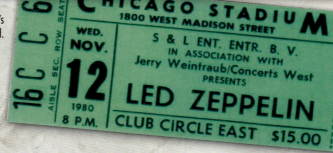

More tickets for shows that never were. After John Bonham's death, the 1980 U.S. tour was cancelled.

7.23–24.79	Falkoner Theatre, Copenhagen, Denmark
8.4.79	Knebworth Festival, Stevenage, England
8.11.79	Knebworth Festival, Stevenage, England
6.17.80	Westfalenhalle, Dortmund, Germany
6.18.80	Sporthalle, Cologne, Germany
6.20.80	Vorst Nationaal, Brussels, Belgium
6.21.80	Ahoy, Rotterdam, Netherlands
6.23.80	Stadthalle, Bremen, Germany
6.24.80	Messehalle, Hanover, Germany
6.26.80	Stadthalle, Vienna, Austria
6.27.80	Messenhalle, Nuremburg, Germany
6.29.80	Hallenstadion, Zurich, Switzerland
6.30.80	Festhalle, Frankfurt, Germany
7.2–3.80	Eisstadion, Mannheim, Germany
7.5.80	Münchner Olympiahalle, Munich, Germany
7.7.80	Eissporthalle, Berlin, Germany

TOUR DATES

Advertisement, Olympiahalle, Munich, July 5, 1980.

Samstag, 5. Juli 1980
LED ZEPPELIN
Sonntag, 6. Juli 1980
SANTANA
OLYMPIAHALLE 21 UHR

Led Zeppelin "Tour 77"

April 1	Memorial Auditorium, Dallas, Tex.
April 3	The Myriad, Oklahoma City, Okla.
April 6, 7, 9,10	Chicago Stadium, Chicago, Ill.
April 12	Metropolitan Sports Center, Minneapolis, Minn.
April 13	Civic Center, St. Paul, Minn.
April 15	Blues Arena, St. Louis, Mo.
April 17	Market Square Arena, Indianapolis, Ind.
April 19, 20	Riverfront Coliseum, Cincinnati, Ohio
April 23	The Omni, Atlanta, Ga.
April 25	Kentucky Fairgrounds & Exposition Center, Louisville, Ky.
April 27, 28	Coliseum, Richfield, Ohio
April 30	Silverdome, Pontiac, Mich.
May 18	Coliseum, Birmingham, Ala.
May 19	L.S.H. Assembly Hall, Baton Rouge, La.
May 21	The Summit, Houston, Tex.
May 22	Tarrant County, Convention Center, Ft. Worth, Tex.
May 31	Coliseum, Greensboro, N.C.
May 25, 26, 28, 30	Capital Center, Largo, Md.
June 3	Tampa Stadium, Tampa, Fla.
June 7, 8, 10, 11, 13, 14	Madison Square Garden, New York, N.Y.
June 19	Sports Arena, San Diego, Cal.
June 21, 22, 23, 25, 26, 27	Los Angeles Forum, Los Angeles, Cal.

THE SOUNDTRACK FROM THE FILM
LED ZEPPELIN
THE SONG REMAINS THE SAME

Led Zeppelin albums are available on Swan Song Records & Tapes.

Swan Song

Tour itinerary printed on the reverse of the 1977 "Led Zeppelin Ticket Stakes" scratch card.

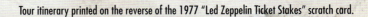

The Evermore

The post-Zeppelin work of Jimmy Page, Robert Plant, and John Paul Jones has been, frankly, diverse and, frankly, spotty, with unexpected and often intriguing turns—kind of like the post-Beatles work of John, Paul, George, and Ringo.

Dazed and confused by John Bonham's death, Jimmy Page "didn't touch a guitar for ages," he later remarked. He had a false start in 1981 with a new band featuring Chris Squire and Alan White of Yes, but the resulting album was never released. So the guitar hero reverted to his studio-musician instincts and accepted an invitation to provide the score for the Charles Bronson film *Death Wish 2*.

Page dutifully compiled *Coda*, a 1982 Zeppelin outtakes collection, and returned to the road briefly with a couple of other Yardbirds alums, Eric Clapton and Jeff Beck, for the Ronnie Lane–initiated A.R.M.S. (Action into Research for Multiple Sclerosis) tour. But he really wanted a new band. He fizzled with the Firm (featuring singer Paul Rodgers of Free and Bad Company fame) and then with Coverdale–Page (featuring Plant-evoking David Coverdale of hair-metal stalwarts Whitesnake). Among those projects, Page offered a guitar-heavy solo album, *Outrider*, which went over like, well, a lead balloon. Finally, after an MTV *Unplugged* performance (dubbed *Unledded*) with Moroccan, Egyptian, and classical musicians, Page and Plant teamed up for two ambitious albums, 1994's *No Quarter/Unledded* and 1997's *Walking Into Clarksdale*. But two recordings and a tour were enough for Plant. So Page, have guitar will travel, became a sideman in the Black Crowes for nearly two years.

Consistently trying to distance himself from the Led Zeppelin legacy, Robert Plant has relished his solo career. In early 1981, he explored his blues and R&B roots with the Honeydrippers before making a proper solo album, *Pictures At Eleven*, with a new sound (drum machines and synths) and a new look (trimmed hair and designer clothes).

Rehearsal on December 9, 2007, for the Ahmet Ertegun Tribute Concert, O2 Arena, London. Jimmy Page plays Chuck Berry's original Gibson ES-350. *Ross Halfin/Exclusive by Getty Images*

Robert Plant's blues, R&B, and rockabilly album, *The Honey Drippers, Volume One*, 1984, featuring guitarist Robbie Blunt and guest appearances by Jeff Beck, Nile Rodgers, and Jimmy Page.

Jimmy Page teamed up with Bad Company and Free vocalist Paul Rodgers as the Firm, releasing a eponymous debut in 1985, followed by *Mean Business* in 1986.

Backstage pass, Robert Plant solo tours.

Touring behind his second solo disc, *Principle Of Moments*, he did not play any Zeppelin songs in concert. Then he enlisted Page, Beck, and producer/R&B guitarist Nile Rodgers for *The Honeydrippers, Volume One*. In 1985 in Philadelphia, Led Zeppelin made a cameo reunion—with drummers Phil Collins and Power Station's Tony Thompson—at Live Aid, an all-star benefit to fight famine in Ethiopia.

Plant regretted the under-rehearsed reunion. In 1988, he told *Details* magazine:

> Live Aid was awful, I mean for us. We were awful, Live Aid was wonderful, let's get it right. I was hoarse, I'd rehearsed all afternoon, I'd sung three concerts in succession with my own band at the time, and when I came to sing that night I had nothing left at all. Nothing there. And the whole Led Zeppelin saga returned to me instantly on that stage. What I hated about Led Zeppelin came right back. It was like some kind of aimless dog trying to bite its tail, that was the actual vibe on stage. The road manager handed Page his guitar and it was out of tune, because he hadn't taken it out of the case even for about 10 years. And the guitar leads weren't long enough. He was staggering around. I was trying to get to the front of the stage. It was a joke.

> The project had no balls then. It had seemed like a good idea, but the whole thing ran away with itself, and it was almost too much of an emotional thing for me, to stand there absorbing this kind of congratulations, when really I was on my way to Cleveland to do a solo gig. It was quite strange, and it was also a kind of defeat for me as an individual, as a solo performer. The day being the day it was, and it being such a special day, for me to stand there and do probably one of the worst performances I've ever done in my life seemed to contradict my very being, my reason to be, as an entertainer, as a musician. It was a most peculiar sensation. The idea of doing that every night is probably one of the least attractive things I could think of. Being in Cleveland the day afterwards with my own band was much more fun. Part of everybody's past and present is what I was at Live Aid. Now I'm an artist competing alongside a lot of pretenders, and a lot of pretty decent musicians. And this is much more realistic.

At the very least, the reunion whetted Plant's appetite for Led Zeppelin because when he toured after his fifth solo album, 1990's *Manic Nirvana*, he played a handful of Zep numbers. From 1994 to 1998, he teamed up with Page before forming a new group, Priory of Brion, in 1999 to play

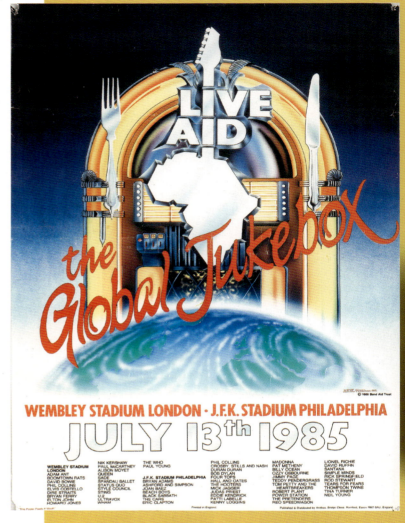

WEMBLEY STADIUM LONDON · J.F.K. STADIUM PHILADELPHIA

JULY 13th 1985

Backstage passes, *Outrider* tour, 1988.

Durban Laverde   Jason Bonham   Jimmy Page   John Miles

JIMMY PAGE

Jimmy Page released his first—and so far, only—solo album, *Outrider*, on June 19, 1988, featuring Jason Bonham on drums.

Live Aid, JFK Stadium, Philadelphia, PA, July 13, 1985. *Robert Matheu*

A.R.M.S. Benefit, The Forum, Inglewood, CA, December 6, 1983. *Robert Matheu*

covers of late-1960s psychedelic rock. In 2001, he established another combo, Strange Sensation, which pursued more of his world-music interests. In 2007, Plant made another surprising move, joining bluegrass queen Alison Krauss on a haunting collection of folk/country/blues called *Raising Sand*. The odd couple toured together in 2008.

After Zeppelin crashed, John Paul Jones retreated back to the studio world. In 1984, he did a film score, *Scream For Help*, with Page contributing on two tunes. He produced albums for R&B legend Ben E. King, hard-rocking Heart, and avant-garde singer Diamanda Galas; played on projects by Peter Gabriel and Brian Eno; and did arrangements for R.E.M.'s *Automatic For The People*. After building two recording studios, he finally released his first solo album, the all-instrumental *Zooma*, in 1998, and then on 2001's *The Thunderchief* he tried his hand at writing lyrics and singing for the first time. Jones was miffed that Page and Plant did not invite him to participate in their mid-1990s regrouping. In fact, when Led Zeppelin was inducted into the Rock and Roll Hall of Fame in 1995, Jones sarcastically commented, "Thank you, my friends, for finally remembering my phone number."

The three Led Zeppelin survivors, augmented by Bonham's son Jason on drums, gave a brief performance together at their Hall of Fame induction ceremony, just as they had at Jason's wedding in 1990 and at a fortieth anniversary concert for Atlantic Records in 1988. But the real reunion finally came on December 10, 2007, at a tribute to the late Ahmet Ertegun, founder of Atlantic Records. A staggering 16 million ticket requests were received for the eighteen thousand seats at London's new O2 arena. After short sets by Foreigner, Paul Rodgers, and Paolo Nutini—and a twenty-eight-year wait— this was a full-blown Led Zeppelin concert: sixteen songs in two hours.

Fans and critics raved. One of the most encouraging reviews came from Kitty Empire in England's *The Observer*: "Most enthralling of all, perhaps, is the way Plant and Page exchange happy, engaged glances, and egg each other on throughout."

Sounds like they might be ready for a whole lotta Zeppelin concerts. ⬤◗

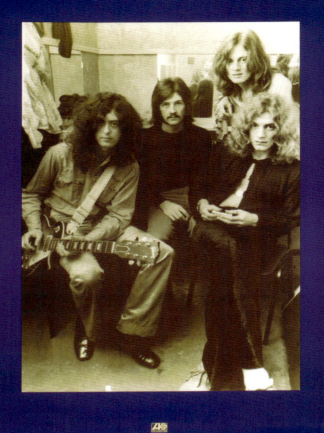

Posters announcing the release of *Led Zeppelin Remasters*, 1990.

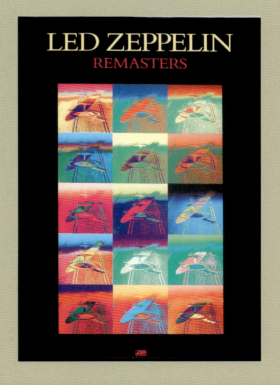

"The first thing I think of is being a freshman in high school and coming in straight off the hair bands and being introduced to them and blown away by this totally different tone they had. They didn't fit in any sort of genre. I heard Led Zeppelin and was like, 'What is *that*?!' I didn't know if it was new or old or what; it was just this timeless, unique sound."

—Dierks Bentley

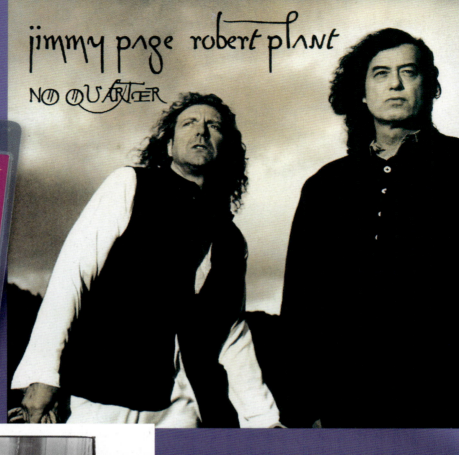

Backstage pass, *No Quarter* tour, 1995.

 jimmy page robert plant

Robert Plant and Jimmy Page reunited on *No Quarter*, released on October 14, 1994.

Program, *No Quarter* tour, 1995.

jimmy page robert plant

The Guitar and the Voice of

LED ZEPPELIN

Tour 1998

25.2.'98 od 20 hod
Sportovní hala
Výstaviště – Praha

What Is And What Shall Ever Be

Ann & Nancy Wilson On Zeppelin Today

By Gene Stout

Ann and Nancy Wilson's only chance to work with a member of Led Zeppelin came in 1995 when they recorded "The Road Home" with John Paul Jones, whom Nancy describes as "a really jovial, jokey cutie-pie."

"What I learned from Jonesy was, first of all, not to be a gushing fan around him," Nancy says. "But most of all, how to be more a consummate and dedicated musician. It made me want to take out my music theory books from college and just get more of the language under my belt—because it's really vast."

Ann's 2007 solo album, *Hope & Glory*, features another nod to Zep with a cover of "Immigrant Song." Producer Ben Mink suggested that Ann reinterpret the song in the style of Peruvian-born "exotica" singer Yma Sumac.

"We didn't want to go, 'OK, let's do another cover of a Led Zeppelin song.' We wanted it to sound really scary," Ann says.

Nancy—whose husband, rock journalist and movie director Cameron Crowe has written extensively about Led Zeppelin—missed the 2007 Zeppelin reunion concert at London's O2 Arena. But Ann text-messaged her a song-by-song account from the venue.

"She was texting me during the first four or five songs," Nancy remembers. "And I was like, 'You don't have to do this, you don't have to do this! Just enjoy the show!' And she was like, 'No, no, I really want to experience this with you.' But when the band got to 'No Quarter,' Ann was sucked into the vortex and she was gone. No more text messages."

"It was like I was eighteen again," Ann says. "It was like a dream. I couldn't believe that I had seen them when I was eighteen, and then there I was all these years later seeing them again—and the same animal magnetism was coming off the stage."

Jimmy Page and the Black Crowes tour, 1999.

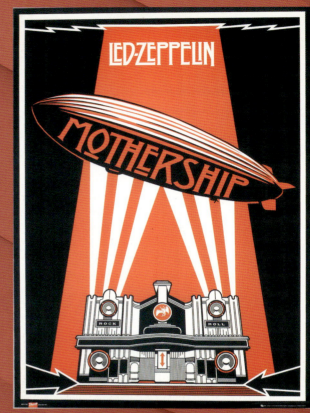

Promotional poster for *Mothership*.

Experience the new digitally remastered and remixed classic film!

Handbill promoting the release of the remixed and newly edited *The Song Remains The Same*, 2007.

Mothership, the remastered greatest hits collection released November 13, 2007.

"FRIENDS"
On Jimmy Page

By Joe Perry

*J*oe Perry isn't just *the ultimate Led Zeppelin fan. He is also friends with Jimmy Page. Their paths have crossed often through the years, sharing a dinner on the road or Jimmy sitting in with Aerosmith at the Marquee Club in London. Suffice it to say, Joe's world was turned upside down by Zeppelin and he loves talking about them—especially about Page. Perry and Aerosmith singer Steven Tyler also inducted Zep into the Rock and Roll Hall of Fame.*

Favorite Zeppelin Tunes

All of them! What can you say? Every one has so much to it. There's something about it that's unique and makes you want to hear it again, and that hadn't been done before. It's all about how they played it. It isn't about them reading off a chart. . . . They really took ownership of those songs. They're so talented and so skilled, and with Jimmy leading the way, it was just unbelievable.

The Albums

There's not one album above the others. There are so many, especially the early records. You just put them on at the beginning, and you listened to the end because that's how you listened to albums back then. . . . And they played their music with the sexual innuendo that it was meant to be played with. They played it for their audience, which is the positive thing. They didn't try to just copy songs. They put the Zeppelin thing on it and made it sound fresh and new. And with Jimmy's genius for producing, he knew what he wanted to hear and how he wanted to use that material. He turned the stuff into magic. So those first three or four records were just, "God, where did this stuff come from?"

Early Meetings With Jimmy

I first met him in about '74 or '75 when they were just starting to do multiple dates at Madison Square Garden and most places. They reconfigured the way that bands played arenas and how they got paid. They broke a lot of ground. Their management was brilliant and they made it so that bands could make more money. They made it profitable for bands to tour, which it wasn't up until then. So anyway, I met him around that time and over the years have bumped into him and we got to be friends and then close friends. We'd spend most of our time talking about family and stuff.

Learning From Zeppelin's Arena Sound

We learned a lot in terms of playing big places with the echo. . . . Rock 'n' roll, a lot of it, is all about sex and the tribal rhythms, and there are certain tempos that work better in a big, echoey hall. It

may sound great and exciting when you listen to it on a record in your living room, but live in a great big arena it doesn't sound the same. You lose it and it's just awash with the singer just screeching over the top of it. It loses all of the sex. And they knew how that kind of music, if you played it a certain way with certain rhythms, was going to work better . . . because it was played slower, and the sounds of certain instruments will work better in some places than others. So you sort of maneuver it. It's a style of playing that works best in bigger halls.

Interviewing Page For *Guitar World* Magazine

It gave me the opportunity to ask questions about his sound. Some of them he was really forthcoming about. Some of them he didn't remember. And he was cagey, which was typically English. His generation was before ours. It was really the start of bands being very competitive on stage. They would come up with some new trick or new way to get the guitar to sound a certain way. And he used a lot of tricks—the violin bow and using Fuzz-Tones in a certain way, and linking them together; or having his guitar tech— they called them roadies then—tweaking the amps to get certain sounds. And using certain guitar strings and tuning them a certain way. But they kept it close to the vest.

On Page's Planning For Zeppelin

He had spent so much time in the studio before Zeppelin, that that's where it must have come from. There's a boxed set somewhere that is a compilation of all of his studio work up until that point, and there's something like 1,400 bits of music on there—every commercial that he did and every soundtrack that he worked on, just everything. After school, he would get on the train with his guitar and go down to the studio, and they paid him ten pounds for three hours' work, and he never knew what he was going to play. It could be anything from movie soundtracks to commercials for bread. He just never knew. But that's how he learned to expand. He was already a great player, but that's how he became more versatile. He would go and figure it out right away, on the spot. . . . So when he started Zeppelin, he knew what he wanted. He really had a plan. That was the biggest thing that struck me when I got to ask him some of these questions. Just how canny and clever he was at what he was planning on doing. And he sure did it.

Friendship With Page

Over the years I've become really good friends with Jimmy. . . . If we have a chance, we'll have dinner together or just hang out. [Aerosmith] did some gigs where he came and sat in with us. He played some Yardbirds songs with us and some Zeppelin songs. We played at the Marquee Club. He played "I Ain't Got You" and "Train Kept A-Rollin,'" just a bunch of the classic Yardbirds stuff. And he played some classic Aerosmith stuff. We also had about a five-hour soundcheck that day—and that was the place to be. It was incredible.

—As told to Steve Morse

LED ZEPPELIN

PERFORMING AT

THE WALDORF ASTORIA
NEW YORK CITY

JANUARY 12 1995 • 301 PARK AVENUE

Rock and Roll Hall of Fame induction, January 12, 1995.

ROCK

AND

ROLL

The *Tenth* Annual Induction Dinner

HALL

of

FAME

THE ALLMAN BROTHERS BAND
AL GREEN
JANIS JOPLIN
LED ZEPPELIN
MARTHA AND THE VANDELLAS
NEIL YOUNG
FRANK ZAPPA
PAUL ACKERMAN
THE ORIOLES

Program, Rock and Roll Hall of Fame induction, January 12, 1995.

the LPs:
Coda
By Chuck Eddy

Coda, if you want to get merely factual, comprises eight odds and sods recorded in 1970, 1972, 1976, and 1978 (all even numbers!), almost none of which had shown up on any previous Led Zeppelin album. The only exception is a live 1970 soundcheck of Mississippi bluesman Willie Dixon's "I Can't Quit You Baby," which had appeared in a studio version on the band's debut LP. On *Coda*, it's the album's most leaden pile of elephant plod. But hey, nobody else could plod like Zeppelin, right? And its lyrics still concern Robert Plant asking his buttercup why she builds him up just to let him down.

Coda came out in 1982, a couple years after John Bonham died, and he kills on the thing.

Three songs, including the first two, involve trains. Sort of. In fact, the first line of the first song, "We're Gonna Groove," has Plant's baby "comin' down the track." As the long, black mystery train carries her home, Bonham and John Paul Jones concoct a rhythm almost as deliriously funky as Spencer Davis Group's "I'm A Man" or Deep Purple's "Hush," which is to say totally disco-worthy, though disco didn't exist yet (and it should be noted here that some early disco DJs, according to Tim Lawrence's 2003 disco history *Love Saves The Day*, were known to work Zeppelin into their sets). "We're Gonna Groove" (reportedly recorded by Zep in 1970, though nitpicky fans have been known to quibble about such details) was written by soul man Ben E. King, but good luck finding it on a compilation by the guy. Jimmy Page's guitar, allegedly overdubbed on a later date, builds to a monster howl. This band sure knew how to pack a lot of music into 2:37.

Track 2, also railroad oriented and also from 1970, is "Poor Tom," wherein Page strums nimble Celtic and/or Appalachian stuff over a big-shouldered, almost marching-band-like Bonham shuffle. Or maybe it's Delta blues as art-rock. Its words, though, clearly make it a murder ballad: Plant (who eventually also honks some harmonica) wails about Tom, who's been working on the railroad all the livelong day for decades while his spouse has been running around on him. So, as often happens in such numbers, he shoots her dead. At the end, Plant repeatedly instructs us to "keep a truckin'," harking not only forward to the Grateful Dead's 1971 "Truckin'" and Eddie Kendricks' 1973 disco prototype "Keep On Truckin'," but also back through R. Crumb's 1968 Zap Comix "Keep On Truckin'" cartoon to North Carolina hokum blues man Blind Boy Fuller's 1937 "Truckin' My Blues Away," which is frequently credited with inventing said slogan.

For the third train song, you have to jump ahead to track six, the 1978-recorded "Darlene," a blatant boogie-woogie from Jones' Moon Mullican–style piano all the way down to Plant explicitly *telling* us it's a boogie-woogie. (And, though I promise to drop the issue after this, readers should remember that, in 1978, the term *boogie*—as in "boogie oogie oogie"—was unarguably a *disco* term.) Anyway, the train part is, uh, how Plant consistently insists on pronouncing the name "Darlene" as "Double E," which was of course the species of train that lady's man Warren Zevon had laid down his head on in "Poor Poor Pitiful Me" in 1976. Toward the end of "Darlene," as the song evolves into more of a rockabilly hoedown, Plant also mentions his "pink carnation and pickup truck," blatantly referencing Don McLean's 1971 chart-topper "American Pie," which in turn was quite possibly referencing Marty Robbins' 1957 country crossover "A White Sport Coat (And A Pink Carnation)" (or "crustacean," as Jimmy Buffett would say).

Another blatant hillbilly reference on *Coda* is Plant repeatedly if incomprehensibly telling us he's "walking the floor over you" (directly quoting Ernest Tubb's 1941 honky-tonk progenitor of that title) in track four, "Walter's Walk," a reported 1972 *Houses Of The Holy* outtake that generally revolves around the idea that it had been a long time since Walter did the stroll. Also, Bonham's magnificent rumble sounds a lot like the theme from the late-sixties cartoon *George Of The Jungle* in some parts. Except louder.

In fact, "Walter's Walk" is probably the second *heaviest* track on the album, outdone only by *Coda's* actual coda, "Wearing And Tearing" from 1978, which bangs its Burundi-metaled head through a tempo-shifting 5:28 of monstrous Page riffs and crazily shrieked proto–Judas Priest lyrics about painkillers. Ed Christman, veteran retail columnist at *Billboard*, tells me the track was initially "intended as a single in 1979 and was positioned as Zeppelin's answer to punk rock, as if the band that recorded 'Communication Breakdown' needed to respond to punk criticism." Good point!

"Wearing And Tearing," interestingly, also has one weedy line ("just a-foolin' after school") where Plant sounds like the White Stripes' Jack White two decades early; likewise, in track five, "Ozone Baby," also recorded in 1978, he anticipates Billy Squier's squealy singing style in the line "tired of you doin' the things that you do." But the true highlight of "Ozone Baby" (which oddly has nothing to do with fluorocarbon emissions) is probably Page's lovely exploratory solo, two and a half minutes in. All in all, the three *In Through The Out Door* rejects on *Coda*, as many observers have pointed out, would have made that eccentric 1979 album punch much harder and kept its feet on the ground more. (They would not necessarily have made it *better*, but that should not be held against the songs.)

So, okay, that leaves the album's only chronologically mis-ordered cut: track seven, "Bonzo's Montreux," a fire set on the Lake Geneva shoreline in 1976, yet too often dismissed as a mere "drum solo." To my ears, Bonham's ultimate breaks and beats and Page's squelchy electronic effects forecast everything from the mid-eighties robot-jazz fusion of Herbie Hancock's *Sound-System* and Ronald Shannon Jackson's *Decode Yourself* to the late-nineties big-beat rock-techno of the Chemical Brothers and Prodigy.

Yet more proof, as if any were needed, that Led Zeppelin were as ahead of their time as they were behind it. 🦅

"Technique doesn't come into it. I deal in emotions."

—*Jimmy Page, quoted in Stephen Davis'*
Hammer Of The Gods

"They're one of my favorite bands. I've listened to them my whole life. I love Robert Plant's voice. He's got one of the best rock voices of all time. And they nailed it. I'd say their first five records were just spot-on, badass albums. . . . I would love to see Led Zeppelin play live or do something new and see what kind of magical things happened."

—*Chester Bennington, Linkin Park*

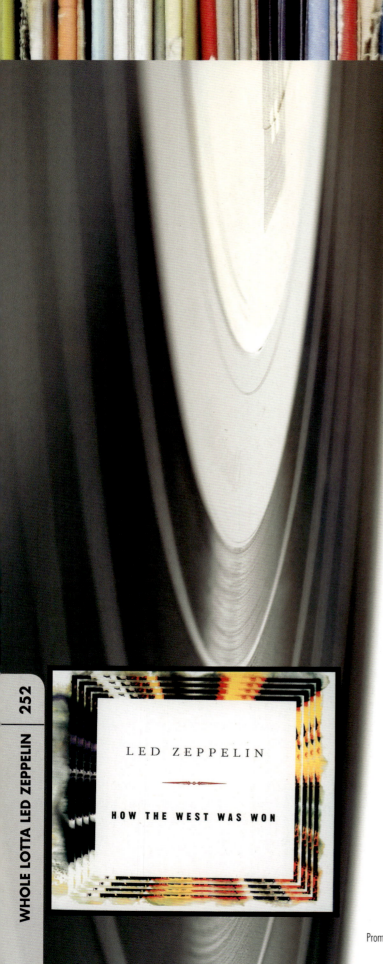

the **LPs:**
How The West Was Won
By Melissa Ruggieri

Without a proper live album to satiate them, for years, Zeppelin fans swapped bootlegs of two shows of reputed greatness: June 25, 1972, at the L.A. Forum and one two nights later at the Long Beach Arena.

It wasn't until 2003, under Jimmy Page's strict editing hand, that the soundboard recordings from those West Coast concerts were dissected to become *How The West Was Won*, a three-CD monster collection of songs taken from both nights, and whose geographic location bestowed the package its title.

Purists were slightly disappointed at Page's decision to interchange the tracks, rather than presenting one complete concert from start to finish. But most Zepheads were simply delighted to have a representation of one of rock 'n' roll's most muscular live acts beyond the middling soundtrack to *The Song Remains The Same*.

By cherry-picking the strongest performances from each night, Page guaranteed that *West* would be incomparable: this is Zeppelin at its most robust, filled with cheeky swagger and unleashing the type of musical virtuosity that still causes jaws to unhinge.

Seconds after the opening blast of "Immigrant Song," the sheer brawn of the band is felt through John Bonham's thundering drums, as he beats his high-hat and snare with sticks that sound like a caveman's clubs. His power is devastating—and almost overshadows Robert Plant's frantic shrieks.

Though Page's skittering blues riffs are always as much an anchor to these songs as John Paul Jones' concrete bass lines, the trio of "Immigrant," "Heartbreaker," and "Black Dog" makes a persuasive argument that it was Bonzo, not Page, who thrust the band into its deep, visceral song patterns.

Hearing Bonham hurl himself at his kit for the nearly-twenty-minute exercise that is "Moby Dick," his rapid-fire double-bass-drum paddling and nuanced trips around the tom-toms indicating that plenty of finesse lurked beneath his beefy exterior, it's impossible not to feel sadness knowing that less than a decade later he would be gone.

But as inspiring as "Moby" is technically, and as much as it showcases the legend of Bonham, it, along with the other epic on Disc 2, "Dazed And Confused," also epitomizes the infuriating side of Zeppelin.

Page's performance on "Dazed," after an introduction of reverberating gongs and Jones' ominous lumbering, is nothing short of staggering—even the famed bit with the violin bow,

Promotional four-song CD for *How The West Was Won*.

usually better appreciated when seen as well as heard—is mesmerizing as he woozily rakes the strings.

But at more than twenty-five minutes, "Dazed" slips into pockets of monotony that can't be saved by Page's grinding power chords or Plant's tense yelps because they're exactly the problem. Self-indulgence is a realistic tendency for bands that are this good because they know they're superior, and Zeppelin could often be charged with overextending their stay live. Their ability and desire to improvise is commendable, and perhaps in an actual live setting the jamming would resonate more deeply. But on record, that live exhilaration doesn't completely translate.

A more satisfying solution is their treatment of "Whole Lotta Love," a twenty-three-minute opus that kicks off Disc 3 with Page's guitar steamrolling through with a buzzy explosion. His masterful wizardry with effects and Plant's echoey cries are bookended by phenomenal segues into a medley of breathless, straight-up blues (John Lee Hooker's "Boogie Chillun") and fusion swing (Gene Pitney's "Hello Mary Lou"), among other classics that serve only to accentuate the swooping majesty of the song's chorus.

Among these eighteen tracks (some fans are still miffed that more, such as "Communication Breakdown" and an infrequently played version of "Louie Louie" didn't make the final cut), though, the strongest are those that are the most compact. And for Zeppelin, "Immigrant Song" aside, compact usually meant nothing less than five minutes.

Still, it was when forced to churn out a fireball of raw fury, with no time to meander aimlessly, that the band detonated. This "Rock And Roll," a boogie-infused gust of Bonham's loose high-hat and Plant's up-from-the-toes bellowing, is tight and punchy, with Plant's staccato spitting of the final words as fine as any punctuation mark. Likewise, his "Black Dog" drips with so much sexual energy that without even seeing the band, it's a cinch to visualize Plant's sensual preening because it's carried through his voice as much as his hips.

As critical as fans were likely to be after what felt like an interminable wait for West to finally arrive in official form, it's worth noting that the sound quality is impeccable. The clarity of Bonham's ride cymbal on "The Ocean," the octave drop in Plant's voice after his bluesy harmonica intro to "Bring It On Home," the textured squeals and skids from Page's fret board, and the bottomless thumps from Jones' bass throughout the more than two-and-a-half-hour collection, are clean and discernable, but not so perfect as to suggest a ton of studio tinkering.

Led Zeppelin thrived on its live reputation, and West was the band's opportunity to illuminate the masses that either never had the opportunity to see them in concert or wanted to live—or perhaps relive—the experience. Forget any bootlegs—this is the live Zeppelin that is immortalized. 🦅

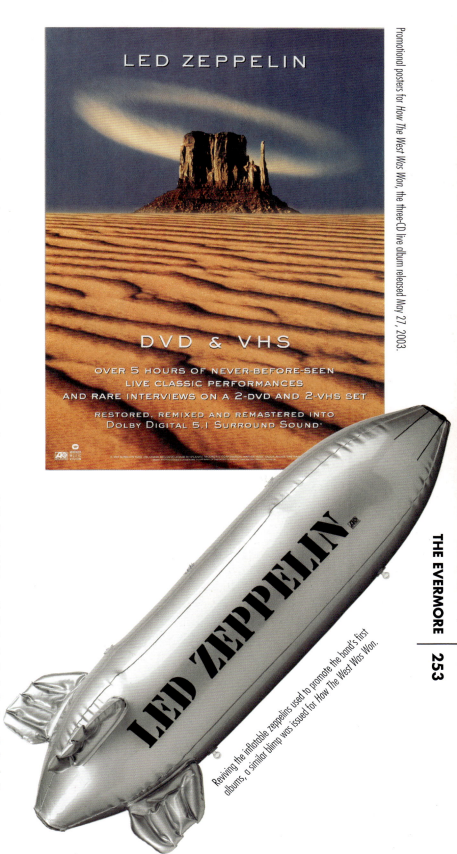

Promotional posters for *How The West Was Won*, the three-CD live album released May 27, 2003.

Reviving the inflatable zeppelins used to promote the band's first albums, a similar blimp was issued for *How The West Was Won*.

The Return of Led Zeppelin

The Story of How the Most Sought-After Reunion in Rock & Roll Came to Be, and What Happens Next

By David Fricke

Rolling Stone *senior editor David Fricke has reported on Led Zeppelin since 1988, conducting the "Rolling Stone Interview" with Robert Plant in RS 522. He wrote this article about the 2007 reunion plans as the cover story to RS 1041, published on December 13, 2007.*

On June 10th of 2007, at 2:30 in the afternoon, the surviving members of Led Zeppelin—guitarist Jimmy Page, singer Robert Plant and bassist John Paul Jones—met in a rehearsal space to play some songs. It was the first time they had been in the same room with instruments since their rough four-song set at Led Zeppelin's 1995 induction into the Rock & Roll Hall of Fame. This time, the stakes were higher: to see if they had the strength, empathy and appetite to truly perform as Led Zeppelin again, in their first full concert since the death of drummer John Bonham in 1980.

The location of the rehearsal, somewhere in England, is still a zealously guarded secret. In interviews a few weeks before Led Zeppelin's December 10th show at London's O2 arena—a benefit tribute to the late Ahmet Ertegun, the co-founder of Atlantic Records—Page, Plant and Jones claim they can't remember the date, what they played or even how the idea of reuniting in honor of Ertegun, a close friend and mentor during and after the band's years on the label, came up. They all agree that playing together again, after so long, was a momentous, emotional occasion.

"It was immediate," Page says brightly, sporting a small splint on his left pinkie, the result of a fracture suffered in a fall at home that forced a pause in rehearsals and the rescheduling of the concert, originally set for November 26th. "Everybody went in with a will to work and to enjoy it. It was a delight."

Plant recalls "a lot of big smiles," wearing one himself. The day was "cathartic and therapeutic. No pressure, no weight." Jones claims he "didn't have any doubts. Someone picked a song. We got through it. And it rocked."

But Bonham's son, Jason, can tell you the exact date and hour Led Zeppelin became a band again, because he was there, taking over for his dad. "They might not know what time it was," he says of the other three, "but I know." For him, it was "a real lump in the throat.

"I didn't think there would be an instant sound," says Jason, 41, currently a member of Foreigner and now a father of two himself. "I thought, 'It's going to take some time.'" He was wrong. The band went right into the slow, dark fury of "No Quarter," from 1973's *Houses Of The Holy*. "When the riff came in, there was this look that went around. It was brilliant." Next, the four hit the desert-caravan march of "Kashmir," from 1975's *Physical Graffiti*. "Then we stopped. Jimmy said, 'Can you give me a hug?' And Robert shouted, 'Yeah, sons of thunder!'"

Finally, at the end of that day, Jason says, "They said, 'When we get together next . . .'" He laughs. "I thought, 'You mean I get another chance at this?'"

The hardest thing was getting the four of us in that rehearsal room without anyone knowing about it," Page reflects between sips of coffee in a London hotel suite with a panoramic view of Hyde Park. "We could have fallen at the first hurdle. It would have been too intimidating, having everybody around us going mental."

That, of course, was the original plan. Page was twenty-four, an ex-Yardbird and already a certified guitar hero when he formed Led Zeppelin in the summer of 1968. He wanted not just a band but "a powerhouse—four virtuoso musicians," he says, "that made this fifth element." Within a year, Led Zeppelin were the biggest new band in the world and about to rule the Seventies with a vengeance, crushing audiences and selling out stadiums. Six of the band's eight studio albums, all produced by Page, went to Number One. The group's sudden end, after John Bonham's fatal drinking binge on the eve of a North American tour, created continual, overheated demands for a reunion.

Technically, the London show is much more than that. Proceeds go to the Ahmet Ertegun Education Fund, and the other acts on the bill—ex-Free and Bad Company singer Paul Rodgers, Pete Townshend, Foreigner, former Rolling Stones bassist Bill Wyman and singer-songwriter Paolo Nutini—were, like Led Zeppelin, Atlantic artists who enjoyed long relationships with Ertegun.

Still, for the estimated 20 million people who applied for the 16,000 available tickets in an online lottery, December 10th is basically an impossible dream come true: a Led Zeppelin gig. And that one show has set off raging speculation about a subsequent tour. "I'm not saying it's gonna happen—I just don't know," says veteran New York promoter Ron Delsener.

"But if they do fifty stadiums, 60,000 people a show, an average ticket price of $100, that's $300 million gross, up there with the Stones or U2."

Page, 63, his once-jet-black hair now a white shoulder-length blizzard, professes shock at the hysteria ignited by Zeppelin's surprising resurrection: "The way tickets went—that was totally unexpected." But from the start, he has been an astute, determined guardian of his band and its legacy, personally attending to all catalog matters and reissues. He produced the new two-CD anthology, *Mothership* (disclosure: I wrote an essay included in the package), and has overseen new DVD and soundtrack editions of Zeppelin's 1976 film, *The Song Remains The Same*. And when he speaks of Zeppelin, in the past or present tense, it is with a steely gleam in his eyes and a straight, sharp edge in his surprisingly soft voice. In rehearsals, Jason says, "Jimmy is very thorough. I can see him thinking, concentrating on what he wants to do, what he wants to achieve."

"What are my expectations for the show?" Page asks, repeating the question thoughtfully. "There was only one: that if we did it, we did it really well, because of the shambolic appearances in the past"—a reference to half-baked reunions at Live Aid in 1985 and a 1988 miniset, with Jason, at an Atlantic fortieth-anniversary concert. Jones complains that at Live Aid, "We had drummers who didn't know the songs"—Phil Collins and Chic's Tony Thompson. Jason accepts some of the blame for '88. "I took it for granted," he says. "I expected it and didn't do my homework."

This time, Page says firmly, "We had to be prepared and committed." Zeppelin were told by the Ertegun-benefit organizers that they only had to do an hour. But Page says it was clear, after the first rehearsals in June and further practices in July, that an hour wasn't enough. The set list is now "100 minutes-plus, and it's not just the usual numbers—'Whole Lotta Love,' 'Dazed and Confused' and 'No Quarter.'"

According to Plant, Zeppelin spent their second and third days together working on "For Your Life," a never-played-live track from their 1976 album, *Presence*. "Then we jettisoned it—but that was the mood of the thing," he says, nursing a cold in his manager's North London office. At fifty-nine, with a trimmed gray beard and a mix of silver and lingering blond in his long mane, he looks like an elder-chieftain version of the twenty-year-old Viking who first came to America with Zeppelin in December 1968. Even sitting on a sofa, his booming voice and confident body language radiate a conqueror's poise.

"There was almost too much mutual respect at first," he continues, "but that soon went. John Paul's eyebrows kept going up and down, and there was that ironic smile. I knew we were back at where we left off with [1979's] *In Through The Out Door*." Plant quickly corrects himself. "No, we'd progressed even further back."

"There was one song—I couldn't remember what I played on it," Jones, 61, says one afternoon over tea, speaking in a lilting near-whisper spiked with jolts of extra-dry humor (he calls his twelve years in Zeppelin "the longest steady job I ever had"). "I said, 'Jim, do you remember what you played on this?' He went, 'No, why is that?' Then we realized it was because we haven't played it onstage before." Fortunately, Jason has an encyclopedic recall of every live bootleg and studio outtake. "When you think, 'How should we segue into this part?'" Jones says, "Jason will go, 'In 1971, you did it this way, and in 1973, at so-and-so auditorium, you did it this way into that.'"

"Jason knows the numbers," Page says. "But not only that, he understands them. That makes a lot of difference."

"That's the second main reason for doing this, for me," Plant explains. "When Jason was younger and more juvenile, he thought [playing in Zeppelin] was a hereditary situation." Jason concedes that he and Plant "had our ups and downs—before my sobriety, when I was still drinking and partying."

"But now," Plant contends, "Jason knows that not only is he the right guy for this—with his enthusiasm and prowess, he's changing it."

Jones and Plant are changed men in their own right. In 2004, on a whim, Jones attended a bluegrass festival in North Carolina. "I met this great community of musicians, all Zeppelin fans," he says, still slightly shocked, "and ended up playing this old-time music." He recently produced an album for the female bluegrass quartet Uncle Earl; the night before this interview, he played mandolin with them at a club in London.

Plant has been making solo records since 1982, plays his own Indian and North African redesigns of Zeppelin songs in concert and has a new hit album in *Raising Sand*, a sublime Delta-blues and gothic-country collaboration with singer-fiddler Alison Krauss. Last year, right after the Nashville sessions for that record, I asked Plant the usual Zeppelin-reunion question. "I would love to work with him again," he said of Page, "so long as it's not a big deal—so long as it's real."

Reminded of that quote, Plant shrugs at the suggestion that the reunion is, in fact, a very big deal. "No," he says. The first rehearsals "were no big deal. They were just really good." And the part that's real now? "What happens in that room when there's nobody about has been, at times, as good as it ever was.

"I never wanted to do it," he confesses. "Now I want to do nothing else. How about that?"

"I had a blueprint," Page says, going back to the summer of 1968. "There was a vocal character I was going for, the kind you found in early Steve Winwood and Steve Marriott—someone who's not afraid to project. That's why I wanted Terry Reid"—the young, precociously soulful British singer who famously turned down Page's offer. Instead, Reid suggested Plant, then making his bones in heavy psychedelic-rock bands in the English

Midlands. (Plant, in turn, would recommend a drummer to Page—Plant's friend John Bonham.)

Jones, who knew Page from the London session-man grind and was eager to join the guitarist's new group, remembers speaking to Page on the phone shortly before the latter went to see Plant at a college gig in Birmingham: "Jim said, 'I'm going up to see this bloke. I'll tell you what he's like when I get back.' He got back and said, 'He's unbelievable. He's got this huge voice.'"

Plant was also fluid, intuitive—like Page, interested in the dramatic possibilities both in and beyond blues progressions. "The whole thing was expansion," Page says, citing "Babe I'm Gonna Leave You," on 1969's *Led Zeppelin*, as an early defining Zeppelin performance. "It came from folk roots"—a ballad Page knew from a 1962 Joan Baez album—"but it's got all these colors in it, the hypnotic, rippling guitar in the verses, the flamenco breaks in between. There was pedal steel, acoustic guitar—things that were hard, as well as extreme sensitivity."

"I've been listening to the songs for the first time in a long time," Plant says, "from an analytical angle, to see how many bars there are between particular parts. There was a canny, chemical thing that made some songs go in different directions, at different times. 'Nobody's Fault But Mine' [on *Presence*] was very spiky—a lot of clenched teeth. But 'In My Time of Dying' [on *Physical Graffiti*] was spectacular and monstrous. It sped up, slowed down, went sideways, careened and spiraled—and I'm in the middle of it all.

"I had an idea initially," Plant says of the reunion show, "that we should do our entire Royal Albert Hall set [from January 9th, 1970], starting with 'We're Gonna Groove.'" He belts the first verse of the Ben E. King song, Zeppelin's opening number on most nights in 1970, originally cut by King for Atlantic live at New York's Apollo Theater in 1963. "Just do that! I was there at the Albert Hall, but I don't know what the fuck happened," he claims, grinning. "I was flying in the middle of that great storm."

Zeppelin's Seventies aura of invincibility—immortalized in classic photographs of the band lounging on its tour jet, *The Starship*, and Plant royally preening on an L.A. hotel ba1cony—took its first hit in August 1975, when Plant was seriously injured in a car crash in Greece. In the summer of 1977, Zeppelin canceled the final weeks of a sold-out U.S. tour after Plant's son, Karac, died of a sudden virus in Britain. The group never played in America again. There were two massive outdoor shows in Knebworth, England, in 1979, to promote the unusually polished *In Through The Out Door*, a short European tour in the summer of 1980—then nothing.

Page claims there was no way forward after Bonham's death. "There had been discussions about the next album," Page says. "I'd been talking about it with John, of something more riff-based, hard-hitting. It wasn't a creed, but every album had to be a move on from what had been done before." The music Zeppelin would have made in the Eighties, Page declares,

"wasn't going to get softer." Ironically, the December 10th reunion falls almost exactly on the anniversary of the press release, issued December 4th, 1980, in which Page, Plant and Jones announced they were breaking up.

They have all since played Zeppelin songs on their own, in a variety of settings. Page and Plant collaborated on the 1994 MTV special *Unledded*, then spent most of the late Nineties touring together. "It was not Led Zeppelin," Page insists. "It was two members of Led Zeppelin." Jones was not invited to *Unledded* and only found out about it when he saw the show on TV while touring in Germany. He says he's long over the hurt: "It's a long time ago." In fact, he points out, "Next year, it will be forty years since we got together. That's unbelievable."

"It doesn't surprise me that we can get together like this now," says Page. "That's how we always were. You have nothing one minute. The next, *boom*, you have that. The great tragedy for me would be if I didn't have that ability in me anymore. To be able to get to this place, to work with the others—it's a gift, and I respect and cherish it."

In one important way, the return of Led Zeppelin is not a true reunion: There is no Bonzo.

Jason speaks frankly about the emotional complications of succeeding his father, whose nicknames—Bonzo, the Beast—referred equally to his drumming, extreme drinking and legendary raging-animal behavior offstage. Jason says that after his first practice with Page, Plant and Jones last June, his mother, Pat, asked him how it went. "I didn't want to say it was too good. I didn't want to take anything away from Dad. 'It's great,' I said, 'but it's not as great as Dad.' I was trying to be politically correct."

"John had this amazing technique," Page says, "but he also had the imagination to go with it. You hear the pattern he comes up with in 'Good Times Bad Times,' from the first album"—an opening combination of thunder-stick beats, cutting, staccato accents and stampeding rolls—"that still perplexes drummers. Nobody else can do that. Nobody else had that imagination."

"I recognized it in Bonzo immediately," Jones claims. At Led Zeppelin's first-ever rehearsal, in 1968, they started with an old Yardbirds cover, "Train Kept A Rollin'." "As a bass player, my first concern was 'What's the drummer like?' If we don't gel, it's useless. And right away, it was like we were on our twentieth tour. We felt and moved in the same place."

The DVD release of *The Song Remains The Same*, a peculiar blend of prime-Zeppelin live footage from Madison Square Garden in 1973 and overearnest fantasy vignettes filmed later, shows a John Bonham unlike the one unleashed each night during his quarter-hour "Moby Dick" solo. In their respective sequences, Jones gallops through the night like an eighteenth-century highwayman, Plant plays a heavy-metal King Arthur and Page is a mysterious guru swinging a light saber. Bonham rides a tractor on his farm, plays snooker and kisses Pat as they walk down a country path. A prophetic shot features Jason, not yet a teenager, playing drums while John watches proudly, jamming with his son on bongos.

"That was his real character," Jones says. "He was a homebody. He was portrayed very badly in a couple of books. But one of the things that was difficult for him was being away from home."

"The finale—he didn't plan it," Plant says soberly. "Intervention, the idea of confronting people, saying, 'This has got to stop now'—it's part of our hip, baby-boomer society now. But it didn't happen then. Everybody would go, 'Oh, he'll be all right.'

"There were negatives all the way through," he says of Bonham's excesses, "but not half as many as people thought. It was John who looked after me after I lost Karac. He used to drive over with Pat. He was very tender, with a humility and understanding that was fantastic. It was he who got me back to writing 'Carouselambra' and all that stuff with the guys."

"He might have been Bonzo the god on the road, but at home he was Dad," Jason says proudly, nursing an espresso late one night in a London hotel. "I did motorcycle racing on weekends. But if my grades weren't good, he would go, 'No, you broke the rule. The bike goes.'"

Jason saw his father perform with Zeppelin only three times. But Jason is the only drummer other than his dad to have played with Zeppelin in the Seventies—at the soundcheck for Knebworth, while his father was listening to the PA mix out in the field. "We played 'Trampled Underfoot,'" recalls Jason, then thirteen. "Dad made me rehearse all week. I asked, 'Will it be the same as it is on the record?' 'No, the solo will be longer. Wait for Jimmy to give you the nod when he's done—the hand going up.'"

In a way, Jason knows and loves his father's work a little too much. He can point out John's rare mistakes on record: "He goes to the ride cymbal at the end of 'Trampled Underfoot' by accident." And in one rehearsal, Jason asked the others about doing some kind of tribute to John during the London show. "They said, 'You're doing the work. Don't you feel he'd want you to stand tall, rather than go, "Here you are, have it back"'?

"That was hard to accept," Jason admits. "I want to be respectful to where it comes from. He couldn't give me the last twenty-seven years of his life. Let me give it back to him for that one night."

But is Jason prepared for it to be only one night?

"To give a truthful answer, probably not. To walk away afterwards and go, 'Thanks, keep in touch. . . .' I try not to think about it. If I thought about it going any further, it would take away from what we set out to do. My mum's worried for me on that aspect. She says, 'Take it for what it is.'"

Page, Plant and Jones all respond to the hopes and rumors of additional shows with genial evasion. "I've got to go through it, see how I feel," Jones says with an added dash of hesitation. "I'm not sure how I feel. But I'm not concerned that I'm not sure. I've lived my life like this. Something comes along, and if it's interesting, I do it."

"It's a collective, isn't it?" Page says, acknowledging that the band he started was never merely an instrument of his will. "What I know is that we've had so much genuine fun just getting together. It's good to be able to do this gig and show what we're about—still. Our target is the O2. That's it." And if it sounds too good to stop? "It's just one day at a time."

Plant is already filling up his 2008 calendar: a tour with Alison Krauss; a new album with T Bone Burnett, who produced *Raising Sand*. "The conveyor belt of expectation is bullshit," he says impatiently. "If people don't talk about a tour, anything is likely. The more people talk, the more pressure it puts on everybody."

And if there is no more Zeppelin after December 10th, "That's fine," Plant says, "because we will do it with a good heart. Ahmet will look down and go, 'Hey, guys!' Bonzo will smile. Pat will feel really good. Jason will stand up and go, 'Yeah!' Jimmy will take a bow. Jonesy will shrug. And"—Plant briefly turns on the old rock-god wail— "I'll be going, 'Baby, baby, baby!'"

"I never wanted to do it [a Led Zeppelin reunion]. Now I want to do nothing else. How about that?"

—*Jimmy Page*

"Jimmy will take a bow. Jonesy will shrug. And I'll be going, 'Baby, baby, baby!'"

—*Robert Plant*

Poster, Ahmet Ertegun Tribute Concert, O2 Arena, London, December 10, 2007.

Ticket and wristband, Ahmet Ertegun Tribute Concert, O2 Arena, London, December 10, 2007.

Rehearsal on December 9, 2007, for the Ahmet Ertegun Tribute Concert, O2 Arena, London.

Ross Halfin/Exclusive by Getty Images

Ahmet Ertegun Tribute Concert, O2 Arena, London, December 10, 2007. *Kevin Westenberg/Exclusive by Getty Images*

Led Zeppelin Snapshots

By Charles Shaar Murray

Led Zeppelin—the last group of the 1960s and the first group of the 1970s.

When they formed in 1968, the Beatles were still working on what was to become "The White Album," Brian Jones was still—in theory, anyway—a functioning member of the Rolling Stones, Jimi Hendrix was at the height of his powers and about to release *Electric Ladyland*, the Who were a year away from *Tommy*, Rod Stewart and Ron Wood were still members of the Jeff Beck Group, and the Woodstock Festival was yet to take place. Jimmy Page was twenty-five years old.

When they disintegrated in 1980 in the wake of John Bonham's ugly and unnecessary death, David Bowie's "Ziggy Stardust" persona, the Bee Gees's surfing of the disco boom, Peter Frampton's brief moment in the spotlight, and the carnage and chaos of the Sex Pistols had all come and gone; the Clash were touring their triumphant *London Calling*, America's new rockin' love objects were Van Halen and the Police. Jimmy Page was thirty-seven years old.

During the dozen years of Led Zeppelin's existence they were effectively the biggest band in rock, comfortably outselling the Rolling Stones by a margin often quoted as five to one. But more to the point they were the band that defined what rock actually was, contriving both to encapsulate much of what had gone before and to foreshadow much of what was to follow. If anything, Led Zeppelin's afterlife—the extent to which their influence continued to dominate the aesthetic of hard rock and, later, heavy metal—was as extraordinary as that of any disbanded group other than the Beatles.

Led Zeppelin simultaneously encapsulating so much of what preceded them—the classic musical dynamic of the great three-instrument bands like the Who, Cream, the Jimi Hendrix Experience, and the Jeff Beck Group; the rich and checkered history of the Yardbirds, from whose ashes they arose so

phoenix-like; the visual and creative dynamic of great singer/guitarist pairings like Mick Jagger and Keith Richards, Roger Daltrey and Pete Townshend, and Rod Stewart and Jeff Beck. Led Zeppelin also laid the groundwork for so much that was to follow in the eras of Aerosmith, Van Halen, and Guns N' Roses. Ultimately, they became as much one of rock's Grand Archetypes as the Beatles and the Rolling Stones. And if they found it as hard to emerge from their own shadow as did any of their imitators, that was almost the point. They seem to have been there, in one form or another, for most of my life.

In fact, they have.

SNAPSHOT: IT'S 1969. I am seventeen years old. I am staring, fascinated, at my brand-new vinyl copy of the very first Led Zeppelin album, which I have just bought but have not yet played. Even though the album contains only a little more than forty-two minutes of music, the grooves run almost all the way up to the label. I have other albums where this phenomenon occurs, but they tend to be jazz or blues compilations with around fifty minutes of music. Most albums the length of Led Zeppelin's debut leave a substantial run-off groove between the music track and the label. Looking closer at those grooves, I can see that certain areas of some of the tracks seem much deeper and wider than others, and much deeper and wider than I'm accustomed to seeing on other artists' records.

When I play the album, I find out why. Every sound seems louder, wider, deeper, and punchier than any comparable record I can find. At the time, I have absolutely no idea of what "mastering" a record means, but I subsequently realize that an awful lot of care and attention has gone into making this record sound as powerful as is humanly possible. Led Zeppelin started as they intended to continue.

And even the label itself is significant. Led Zeppelin appear on Atlantic Records, just as do soul greats like Aretha Franklin, Wilson Pickett, and Ray Charles, not to mention jazz giants of the caliber of John Coltrane, Ornette Coleman, and Roland Kirk. Atlantic's pop and rock roster—the likes of Cream, Buffalo Springfield, Vanilla Fudge, and even the pride of Memphis himself, Otis Redding—are relegated to the company's Atco subsidiary. Not Led Zep, though. They're right in there with the Big Boys.

SNAPSHOT: IT'S 1970. I'm nineteen by exactly one day. Among the performers at the Bath Festival Of Blues & Progressive Music (actually held near the town of Shepton Mallet) are Pink Floyd, Frank Zappa, Jefferson Airplane, the Byrds, Johnny Winter . . . and Led Zeppelin. Just as the sun begins to redden and sinks, a set by the Flock terminates somewhat abruptly (years later, it is revealed that this is because Zeppelin manager Peter Grant led the band's road crew onto the stage and unceremoniously evicted the Flock mid-song). Shortly thereafter, Led Zeppelin hits the stage and slams straight into "Immigrant Song," the lead-off track from their as-yet-unreleased third album, still three months away. An entire field full of tired, muddy hippies go completely and utterly monkeyshit. Among the freaking thousands is one single exception: me.

Despite being an Early Adopter of the Zep cause by purchasing their first album, I had skipped *Led Zeppelin II*. This was partly because it was one of those albums that was played so prevalently everywhere you went that actual ownership seemed superfluous (not unlike *The Dark Side Of The Moon* a few years later), and partly because, despite its manifold merits and extraordinary musical and sonic power, there was something rather off-putting about it. *Led Zeppelin II* was *too* powerful. Even in its more sentimental, pastoral, and exotic moments, it seemed armor-plated, invulnerable. It was a battering ram of an album, and Led Zeppelin had become a battering ram of a group.

True enough, other bands I'd loved—like Cream, the Who, Jimi Hendrix Experience, Jeff Beck's original group with Rod Stewart—had demonstrated power to spare. But in each case, there had been

a countervailing fragility, a vulnerability to offset their brute strength and skill. Whether it was Hendrix's shy, self-deprecating singing, or the Who's quirky eccentricity and Pete Townshend's manifest insecurities, or Cream's sweet, wavering vocals, there was a three-dimensional humanity to their music that appealed to me as much as the hard-rock thunder and Marshall-fuelled monumentalism. That was what I wasn't hearing in Led Zeppelin's performance.

Was anybody else in that field missing it? Were they fark? They were getting expertly beaten up, and they were loving every second of it. Meanwhile, I was going through as wide a range of emotional experiences as I've ever had watching a rock band. I was thrilled and repulsed. I was exhilarated and depressed. I was enraptured and—particularly during some of the lengthier instrumental excursions, primarily by Page and Bonham—I was bored. Most perplexing of all, whenever I realized that I was enjoying myself, I instinctively mistrusted whatever element of myself was having a good time. It was the first, and by no means the last, time that I found myself seriously questioning rock's relationship to power, and its abuses, and the capacity of the rock audience to collaborate with the abuse of power.

As I stood there, unmoved, watching the distant, capering figures on the stage—Jimmy Page no bestained pre-Raphaelite rock god, but a heavily bearded figure in an absurdly oversized farmer's tweed hat and matching overcoat—my relationship with Led Zeppelin thus became my first rock 'n' roll fusion of inextricably entangled love and hate.

SNAPSHOT: IT'S 1973. It is a few weeks before my twenty-second birthday, and I am now a music business professional. As a prominent

"Led Zeppelin was the band that defined what rock actually was, contriving both to encapsulate much of what had gone before and to foreshadow much of what was to follow."

—*Charles Shaar Murray*

feature writer for the London-based *New Musical Express*, I am dispatched to California to report on two performances by Led Zeppelin: one at the Forum in Los Angeles, a city which the band now unquestionably owns, and another at Kezar Stadium, San Francisco. The touring party is ensconced at the legendary "Riot House"—the Continental Hyatt House on Sunset Boulevard where, famously, a motorcycle was ridden up and down the hallway of one of the floors set aside for the band's use. In somebody's room, Iggy Pop sits crosslegged, seraphically smiling like a wiry Buddha, endlessly rolling joints. In a luxurious home in the Hollywood Hills, Led Zeppelin and their entourage, in which I am temporarily included, attend George Harrison's birthday party. For the first time, I see a domestic VCR machine and, for the only time, the movie it is showing and reshowing: *Deep Throat*. Everybody, including the guest of honor, seems to be getting thrown into the pool under the direction of John Bonham and Peter Grant. Even though, I have passed out overcome by jetlag, I somehow escape this fate.

A real, as opposed to metaphorical, snapshot exists to document this occasion: I have it framed on the wall above my desk. Taken at Kezar Stadium the following day by photographer Ross Halfin, it shows Robert Plant and John Paul Jones taking sidestage refuge at Kezar Stadium whilst John Bonham performs his flailing, thunderous drum solo. I am seated behind and between them, roundfaced, beshaded, and coiffed with a 'fro that wouldn't have disgraced a roadie for Sly and The Family Stone.

SNAPSHOT: IT'S 1975. I am twenty-four years old. The Zep album du jour is *Physical Graffiti* and, on a Monday night, the band are playing the first date of a season at London's massive Earls Court arena. I attend to review the show, which boasts some thrilling moments and some decidedly lengthy quarter-hours, in a state of suitable chemical augmentation. During a manically funkt "Trampled Under Foot," I become convinced that the entire stage is going to roll forward like a huge tank, crushing the audience to

pulp, and that they will enjoy it. In the era predating email, the *New Musical Express*'s print deadlines require me to stay up all night writing the review in order to catch a printer's messenger first thing the following morning. Somewhat the worse for wear, I have to interview Paul and Linda McCartney that afternoon, on the occasion of the release of their album *Venus And Mars*, one song, "Rock Show," that actually mentions Jimmy Page. The album not being one of the highpoints in McCartney's career, the interview does not go well, and the resultant article generates a lifelong dislike of my poor self in McCartney and everybody close to him.

SNAPSHOT: IT'S 1978. I am twenty-seven years old. I find myself standing next to Robert Plant at a gig at Dingwall's Dancehall in Camden Town. Much to my surprise, he buys me a pint.

SNAPSHOT: IT'S 1979. I am twenty-eight years old. Led Zeppelin perform a huge open-air show at Knebworth. Having reviewed their *Presence* album and singled out "Nobody's Fault But Mine" for especial praise, I am surprised to be told that Plant, possibly to endear himself to any punk rockers who might have accidentally attended the show, introduced the song in performance by saying, "Charles Shaar Murray likes this one."

SNAPSHOT: IT'S 1980. I am twenty-nine years old. John Bonham dies in his sleep. Ever since the decline and death of Keith Moon, Bonham had been the greatest living hard rock drummer. Now, Led Zeppelin, in a display of collective sensitivity and dignity that impresses me to this very day, refuse to place him, and formally disband.

It should not come as a surprise that, even as a defunct band, they seem to become bigger and bigger. And for every tawdry bunch of Zep copyists xeroxing what was undeniably a unique style and sound, they seem—in retrospect—better and better, richer and grander. The more they are imitated, they more they grow.

SNAPSHOT: IT'S 2004. I am fifty-three years old. I am sitting in an English garden waiting for the sun (but the sun don't come) behind the house of the same photographer who caught that earlier image three decades earlier, conducting a joint interview with Jimmy Page and Jeff Beck for *MOJO* magazine concerning Page and Beck's shared history and occasionally intersecting career trajectories. At one point in the conversation, the subject of a Led Zeppelin reunion is mooted.

"The thing about Led Zeppelin," Page says, "was that every concert was different. You never quite knew what was going to be happening. Every time you walked onstage all manner of different departures were going to go on. There was a telepathic quality there, and when we lost John, what were we gonna do? Get someone in and play them a tape of what we played? At which concert? Because we were mutating all the time, there was no way it would have been honest if we'd brought in another drummer. The reality is that we knew what we had within that framework. If it had been Jonesy gone or me or Robert? Whoever was left would've closed it down."

"For my ten cents' worth, sitting here now, " Beck chipped in, "you probably would have been one of the few bands ever to make a successful go of it if you *had* got another drummer. It would have been amazing, because people want to see you. They want to see Led Zeppelin. If you got a suitable drummer—not necessarily someone who goes up the John Bonham path, but some nasty funk drummer that could enable you to stay together and create the songs you wanna play—then you'd sell twenty million tickets, because people could say, 'I'M GONNA SEE LED ZEPPELIN TONIGHT!'"

That interview's principal enigma centered around the question of what might 21st-Century Jimmy Page music sound like. The man himself wasn't terribly helpful. "I moved house, and during the process of moving house I found all of the past cassettes and rehearsal things I'd done with various musicians, so I put them all into a box. And the next project is to sift through all of that and see whether there's anything there. . . . I'm just curious, to be honest with you. That'll be a good impetus to get into writing and formulating, leaning on a few of the riffs I never actually worked with. Riffs and rhythm and melody is what it is. Syncopation and percussion have changed over the years, but riffs can still be the same. I don't know what I'm going to create next. One day you've got the guitar and you're playing, and the next minute you've got a riff and it's coming out of thin air. I've got about four avenues I could use to make whatever it is manifest but until such time as I'm really confident in the material that I've got together, I don't know which of those direction to go in. It's time to do something which is entirely new and radical. As far as Jimmy Page goes, it's time to do something new and unexpected."

Once again, there is a real, tangible snapshot associated with this occasion. Taken after the interview in the road outside the photographer's house, it depicts me flanked by Page and Beck. My hair is cropped and white. Theirs is long and black.

FINAL SNAPSHOT: IT'S 2007. I am fifty-six years old. Jimmy Page is sixty-three. With John Bonham's son, Jason, in the drum chair, they finally reunite for a charity concert after decades of teases—like the fumbled Live Aid appearance with *two* drummers filling in for the departed giant—and a couple of minor but intriguing collaborations between Page and Plant. It is, by all accounts a triumph, and Page, paradoxically, seems far more youthful with his hair at last reverting to its natural silver. Of "21st-Century Jimmy Page music" there, is, alas, still no sign. 🦅

"Led Zeppelin's afterlife—the extent to which their influence continued to dominate the aesthetic of hard rock and, later, heavy metal—was as extraordinary as that of any disbanded group other than the Beatles."

—*Charles Shaar Murray*

Acknowledgments

Thanks to Dennis Pernu and Michael Dregni for their vision, enthusiasm, and resourcefulness; Gary (Mr. Phoner) Graff, Steve Morse, and Gene Stout for stepping up to the plate; Robert Alford, Charlie Auringer, Robert Matheu, Ed Perlstein, Paul Quigley, and Tom Sweeney for preserving the past in photos; George Case, Barry Cleveland, Jim DeRogatis, Andrew Earles, Chuck Eddy, Barney Hoskyns, Greg Kot, William McKeen, Chris Riemenschneider, Melissa Ruggieri, and Jaan Uhelszki (who gave me my first national byline in 1974 at *CREEM*) for reexamining the music; Charles Shaar Murray for revisiting his past; Garth Cartwright for the band member bios; Scott Pearson for the discography; Don Brewer, Peter Frampton, Joe Perry, Mike Watt, Ann and Nancy Wilson, James Burton, and all the other stars for talking Zeppelin; Terry Manning and Danny Goldberg for the interviews; Howard Wuelf at Howlin' Wuelf Media; David Fricke and Richard Boehmke at *Rolling Stone*; Peter Knobler and Jocelyn Hoppa at *Crawdaddy!*, then and now; Vaughn Shinall at The Wylie Agency, Inc., representing the estate of William S. Burroughs; Danny Goldberg and Brady Brock at Gold Village Entertainment; James Bailey at Yep Roc Records; Ashley King at Getty Images; Jon Wilton at Redferns; Larry Andrew at Scope Features; poster artist Kenvin Lyman and Bob Driscoll for permission to reprint their works; collectors The Wyzyrd, Commander Chi, Joe Rockwell, Perry Pfeffer, and Peter Maxfield; Voyageur Press art director Becky Pagel and design manager Katie Sonmor; designer John Barnett/4 Eyes Design; my colleagues at the *Star Tribune*—especially Tim Campbell, Sandy Date, Peter Koeleman, Chris Ledbetter, Chris Riemenschneider, Bob Schaefer, and Tom Sweeney—for their support; Ken Abdo for the counsel; Geoff Boucher for the clips; Bill Crum for the poster; Q for the lyrics; B3 for the jokes; M for the marketing; GV for the effort; Andrew and Jan for their love, understanding, and tolerance; and, most of all, Jimmy, Robert, Jonesy, and Bonzo for the music.

—*Jon Bream*

Discography

by Scott Pearson

The following list of recordings is not intended to be exhaustive; it focuses on the band as a group, leaving out projects the individual artists were involved in both before and after Led Zeppelin. It comprises primarily the original records and the transition to the world of CDs and DVDs, without cataloging the various tape formats—reel to reel, eight track, and cassette—that formed "that confounded bridge" between vinyl and disc. It includes only official releases that are (or were) commercially available, not the occasional promotional release. And it includes only American and British releases, not foreign releases or imports. It ignores entirely the specter of endless bootlegs, which could fill a book on their own.

LPs

For a band as influential and legendary as Led Zeppelin, it is easy to forget—and perhaps hard to believe—that their original album releases on vinyl were limited to eight studio recordings and one live soundtrack, all of which appeared between 1969 and 1979. After John Bonham's death in 1980 brought an end to the band, bootleg live recordings were the fans' only source for "new" Zeppelin music. In response to this continuing interest, and because the band had an outstanding contractual obligation to Atlantic Records for one album, a collection of outtakes was issued in 1982 under the name *Coda*. For fifteen years after the release of *Coda*, the following ten albums would constitute Led Zeppelin's complete catalog.

Led Zeppelin

Atlantic SD 8216 (U.S.); 588 171 (U.K.)
Recorded October 1968, Olympic Studios, London
Released January 12, 1969 (U.S.); March 28, 1969 (U.K.)

SIDE 1

"Good Times Bad Times"
"Babe I'm Gonna Leave You" *
"You Shook Me"
"Dazed And Confused"

SIDE 2

"Your Time Is Gonna Come"
"Black Mountain Side"
"Communication Breakdown"
"I Can't Quit You Baby"
"How Many More Times"

* "Babe I'm Gonna Leave You" was originally listed as a traditional song arranged by Page; Anne Bredon informed the band in the mid-1980s that she had in fact written the song. The credits were corrected on future releases.

Led Zeppelin II

Atlantic SD 8236 (U.S.); 588 198 (U.K.)
Released October 22, 1969 (U.S.); October 31, 1969 (U.K.)

SIDE 1

"Whole Lotta Love" *
"What Is And Should Never Be"
    Recorded 1969, Olympic Studios, London
"The Lemon Song" * *
    Recorded 1969, Mirror Sound, Los Angeles
"Thank You"
    Recorded 1969, Morgan Studios, London

SIDE 2

"Heartbreaker"
    Recorded 1969, A&R Studios, New York
"Living Loving Maid (She's Just A Woman)"
    Recorded 1969, Morgan Studios, London
"Ramble On"
    Recorded 1969, Juggy Sound Studio, New York
"Moby Dick"
    Recorded 1969, Mirror Sound, Los Angeles
"Bring It On Home" * * *
    Recorded 1969, Atlantic Studios, New York

* "Whole Lotta Love," credited to all four band member, features lyrics similar to Willie Dixon's "You Need Love"; Dixon sued the band in 1985 and reached an out-of-court settlement. Later releases added Dixon's name to the credits.
** "The Lemon Song," credited to the band, borrows liberally from Howlin' Wolf's "Killing Floor" and, to a lesser extent, from Robert Johnson's "Traveling Riverside

Blues." ARC Music, the publishing company of Chess Records, sued the band in 1972, reaching an out-of-court settlement. Chester "Howlin' Wolf" Burnett received his credit on later pressings.

*** "Bring It On Home," credited to Page and Plant, has lyrics from the Willie Dixon–penned song of the same name, although the extended instrumental jam at the center of the song is an original Led Zeppelin creation. ARC Music sued in 1972 and, once again, reached an out-of-court settlement with the band. Ironically, Dixon still didn't receive any royalties and had to sue his own label to do so. How The West Was Won makes a medley of the tune, crediting Dixon for his song and all four members of the band for the jam, now titled "Bring It On Back."

Led Zeppelin III

Atlantic SD 7201 (U.S.); 2401 002 (U.K.)
Released October 5, 1970 (U.S.); October 23, 1970 (U.K.)

SIDE 1

"Immigrant Song"
"Friends"
"Celebration Day"
  Recorded 1970, Headley Grange, Hampshire
"Since I've Been Loving You"
  Recorded 1970, Island Studios, London
"Out On The Tiles"
  Recorded 1970, Olympic Studios, London

SIDE 2

"Gallows Pole"
"Tangerine"
  Recorded 1970, Headley Grange, Hampshire
"That's The Way"
  Recorded 1970, Island Studios, London
"Bron-Y-Aur Stomp"*
  Recorded 1970, Headley Grange, Hampshire
"Hats Off To (Roy) Harper"**
  Recorded 1970, Olympic Studios, London

* "Bron-Y-Aur Stomp" was named for the same Welsh cottage as was "Bron-Yr-Aur" on Physical Grafitti; the later album uses the correct spelling of the name. Some rereleases of the earlier song have corrected the misspelling.

** English folksinger legend Roy Harper was a friend of the band and opened some of their later concerts. He has an uncredited cameo in Peter Grant's fantasy sequence in the film The Song Remains The Same. Page guested on a number of Harper's early albums and also recorded an entire album with Harper, 1985's Whatever Happened To Jugula? Harper's most heard performance in the United States is, arguably, the guest lead vocal on Pink Floyd's "Have A Cigar" from Wish You Were Here.

Untitled Fourth Album

[known as Led Zeppelin IV, the Fourth Album, the Runes Album, Four Symbols, Zoso *
Atlantic SD 7208 (U.S.); 2401 012 (U.K.)
Released November 8, 1971 (U.S.); November 12, 1971 (U.K.)

SIDE 1

"Black Dog"
"Rock And Roll"
"The Battle Of Evermore"
  Recorded 1971, Headley Grange, Hampshire
"Stairway To Heaven"
  Recorded 1971, Island Studios, London

SIDE 2

"Misty Mountain Hop"
  Recorded 1971, Headley Grange, Hampshire
"Four Sticks"
  Recorded 1971, Island Studios, London
"Going To California"
"When The Levee Breaks"
  Recorded 1971, Headley Grange, Hampshire

* The album cover had no writing on it, not even the band's name. The gatefold was a painting of the Hermit, a tarot-inspired figure appearing as a robed old man carrying a lantern (the same character would make an appearance in Jimmy Page's fantasy sequence in The Song Remains The Same). The inner sleeve featured the lyrics of "Stairway To Heaven" on one side and the song list and credits on the other; above the song list there appeared four symbols, one for each band member. Page's symbol, which appeared first of the four, looked like the word Zoso.

Houses Of The Holy

Atlantic SD 7255 (U.S.); K 50014 (U.K.)
Released March 18, 1973 (U.S.); March 26, 1973 (U.K.)

SIDE 1

"The Song Remains The Same"
"The Rain Song"
"Over The Hills And Far Away"
  Recorded 1972, Stargroves, England
"The Crunge"
  Recorded 1972, Headley Grange, Hampshire

SIDE 2

"Dancing Days"
"D'Yer Mak'er"
  Recorded 1972, Stargroves, England
"No Quarter"
  Recorded 1972, Island Studios, London
"The Ocean"
  Recorded 1972, Stargroves, England

Physical Graffiti

Swan Song SS-2-200 (U.S.); SSK 89400 (U.K.)
Released February 24, 1975 (U.S. and U.K.)

SIDE 1

"Custard Pie"

Recorded 1974, Headley Grange, Hampshire

"The Rover"
    Recorded 1974, Stargroves, England

"In My Time Of Dying"
    Recorded 1974, Headley Grange, Hampshire

SIDE 2

"Houses of The Holy"*
    Recorded 1972, Olympic Studios, London

"Trampled Under Foot"

"Kashmir"
    Recorded 1974, Headley Grange, Hampshire, and
    Olympic Studios, London

SIDE 3

"In The Light"
    Recorded 1974, Headley Grange, Hampshire, and
    Olympic Studios, London

"Bron-Yr-Aur"

"Down By The Seaside"
    Recorded 1974, Island Studios, London

"Ten Years Gone"
    Recorded 1974, Headley Grange, Hampshire, and
    Olympic Studios, London

SIDE 4

"Night Flight"
    Recorded 1974, Headley Grange, Hampshire, and
    Island Studios, London

"The Wanton Song"
    Recorded 1974, Headley Grange, Hampshire, and
    Olympic Studios, London

"Boogie With Stu"
    Recorded 1974, Headley Grange, Hampshire

"Black Country Woman"
    Recorded 1974, Stargroves, London

"Sick Again"
    Recorded 1974, Headley Grange, Hampshire, and
    Olympic Studios, London

*"Houses of the Holy" was intended as the title track for the earlier album of that name, but the band felt it didn't fit in with the other tracks and left it off. It resurfaced on Physical Grafitti without any additional mixing or recording.

Presence

Swan Song SS-8416 (U.S.); SSK 59402 (U.K.)
Recorded November and December 1975, Musicland Studios, Munich, Germany
Released March 31, 1976 (U.S.); April 5, 1976 (U.K.)

SIDE 1

"Achille's Last Stand"

"For Your Life"

"Royal Orleans"

SIDE 2

"Nobody's Fault But Mine"

"Candy Store Rock"

"Hots On For Nowhere"

"Tea For One"

The Song Remains The Same*

Swan Song SS-2-201 (U.S.); SSK 89402 (U.K.)
Recorded live July 27–29, 1973, Madison Square Garden, New York
Released September 28, 1976 (U.S. and U.K.)

SIDE 1

"Rock And Roll"

"Celebration Day"

"The Song Remains The Same"

"Rain Song"

SIDE 2

"Dazed And Confused"

SIDE 3

"No Quarter"

"Stairway To Heaven"

SIDE 4

"Moby Dick"

"Whole Lotta Love"

* The best audio takes didn't necessarily coincide with the best film footage, so sometimes this double album live soundtrack doesn't match the movie; the troubled film's release was held up for more than three years.

In Through The Out Door

Swan Song SS-16002 (U.S.); SSK 59410 (U.K.)
Recorded November and December 1978, Polar Studios, Stockholm, Sweden
Released August 15, 1979 (U.S.); August 20, 1979 (U.K.)

SIDE 1

"In The Evening"

"South Bound Saurez"

"Fool In The Rain"

"Hot Dog"

SIDE 2

"Carouselambra"

"All My Love"

"I'm Gonna Crawl"

Coda

Swan Song SS-90051-1 (U.S.); A 0051 (U.K.)
Released November 19, 1982 (U.S.); November 22, 1982 (U.K.)

SIDE 1

"We're Gonna Groove"
> *Recorded live January 9, 1970, Royal Albert Hall, London**

"Poor Tom"
> *Recorded May 6, 1970, Olympic Studios, London*

"I Can't Quit You Baby"
> *Recorded live January 9, 1970, Royal Albert Hall, London***

"Walter's Walk"
> *Recorded May 15, 1972, Stargroves, England*

SIDE 2

"Ozone Baby"
> *Recorded November 14, 1978, Polar Studios, Stockholm, Sweden*

"Darlene"
> *Recorded November 16, 1978, Polar Studios, Stockholm, Sweden*

"Bonzo's Montreux"
> *Recorded December 9, 1976, Mountain Studios, Montreux, Switzerland*

"Wearing And Tearing"
> *Recorded November 21, 1978, Polar Studios, Stockholm, Sweden*

* and ** This Royal Albert Hall concert was filmed and eventually released on the Led Zeppelin DVD in 2003. These are the first two songs on that DVD.

45s

The band was committed to concerts and albums as their form of artistic expression and resisted the commercial compromises necessitated by the release of singles, which generally had to run less than three minutes for AM radio. Eventually, fewer than a dozen singles were released in the United States; no singles were released in the United Kingdom on vinyl.

"Good Times Bad Times"/"Communication Breakdown"
> *Atlantic 45-2613*
> *Released March 10, 1969*

"Whole Lotta Love"/"Living Loving Maid (She's Just A Woman)"
> *Atlantic 45-2690*
> *Released November 7, 1969*

"Immigrant Song"/"Hey Hey What Can I Do"*
> *Atlantic 45-2777*
> *Released November 5, 1970*

"Black Dog"/"Misty Mountain Hop"
> *Atlantic 45-2849*
> *Released December 2, 1971*

"Rock And Roll"/"Four Sticks"
> *Atlantic 45-2865*
> *Released February 2, 1972*

"Over The Hills And Far Away"/"Dancing Days"
> *Atlantic 45-2790*
> *Released May 24, 1973*

"D'Yer Mak'er"/"The Crunge"
> *Atlantic 45-2986*
> *Released September 17, 1973*

"Trampled Under Foot"/"Black Country Woman"
> *Atlantic SS 70102*
> *Released April 2, 1975*

"Candy Store Rock"/"Royal Orleans"
> *Atlantic SS 70110*
> *Released June 18, 1976*

"Fool In The Rain"/"Hot Dog"
> *Atlantic SS 71003*
> *Released December 7, 1979*

* Recorded in 1970, "Hey Hey What Can I Do" was originally released only as this B side, never on a Led Zeppelin LP (although it was included on a compilation album of various Atlantic recording artists, The New Age Of Atlantic, in 1972). For an officially released song, it remained difficult to find for nearly twenty years until it was included in the Led Zeppelin box set of 1990.

CDs

All ten Led Zeppelin albums were released in the mid-1980s on compact disc with their original track listings; these are not repeated following. Things got interesting when Jimmy Page started remastering the studio recordings, and then moved into the vaults of live recordings the band had stockpiled during years of touring. Digital technology allowed Page to achieve the near perfection he always strived for and that the live recordings rarely met. Because of this, official live releases from Led Zeppelin are somewhere between live and studio takes. From *The Song Remains The Same* on, most live Zeppelin has been heavily tinkered with by Page, including mixing together different performances of individual songs as well as adding studio overdubs. Beginning in 1994, after the release of *The Complete Studio Recordings* box set, the remastered albums were released separately with their original track listings; these also are not repeated following. Only full-length discs are listed, not various CD singles, promos, and samplers.

Led Zeppelin (Box Set, Vol. 1)

Four-CD box set, remastered; resequenced collection of two-thirds of the Zeppelin catalog with a few unreleased tunes thrown in.
  Atlantic 7567-8214-4
  Released September 7, 1990 (U.S.)

DISC 1

"Whole Lotta Love," "Heartbreaker," "Communication Breakdown," "Babe I'm Gonna Leave You," "What Is And What Should Never Be," "Thank You," "I Can't Quit You Baby," "Dazed And Confused," "Your Time Is Gonna Come," "Ramble On," "Travelling Riverside Blues,"* "Friends," "Celebration Day," Hey Hey What Can I Do,"** "White Summer"/"Black Mountain Side"***

DISC 2

"Black Dog," "Over The Hills And Far Away," "Immigrant Song," "The Battle Of Evermore," "Bron-Y-Aur Stomp," "Tangerine," "Going To California," "Since I've Been Loving You," "D'yer Maker," "Gallows Pole," "Custard Pie," "Misty Mountain Hop," "Rock And Roll," "The Rain Song," "Stairway To Heaven"

DISC 3

"Kashmir," "Trampled Under Foot," "For Your Life," "No Quarter," "Dancing Days," "When The Levee Breaks," "Achilles Last Stand," "The Song Remains The Same," "Ten Years Gone," "In My Time Of Dying"

DISC 4

"In The Evening," "Candy Store Rock," "The Ocean," "Ozone Baby," "Houses Of The Holy," "Wearing And Tearing," "Poor Tom," "Nobody's Fault But Mine," "Fool In The Rain," "In The Light," "The Wanton Song," "Moby Dick"/"Bonzo's Montreux,"**** "I'm Gonna Crawl," "All My Love"

* *Previously unreleased; recorded live, June 23, 1969, John Peel's Top Gear radio show.*
** *First time on compact disc.*
*** *Previously unreleased; recorded live, June 27, 1969, Playhouse Theatre Over Radio One show.*
**** *Combines the two previously released songs into one new version.*

Led Zeppelin Remasters

Two-CD box set; scaled-down collection from Box Set, Vol. 1
  Atlantic 7567-80415-2
  Released September 9, 1990 (U.S.); October 15, 1990 (U.K. and Japan); special edition released January 2, 1992, with a third CD, Profiled, *featuring interviews with Page, Plant, and Jones (previously released as a promotional disc at the time of the* Box Set, Vol. 1)

DISC 1

"Communication Breakdown," "Babe," "I'm Gonna Leave You," "Good Times Bad Times," "Dazed And Confused," "Whole Lotta Love," "Heartbreaker," "Ramble On," "Immigrant Song," "Celebration Day," "Since I've Been Loving You," "Black Dog," "Rock And Roll," "The Battle Of Evermore," "Misty Mountain Hop," "Stairway To Heaven"

DISC 2

"The Song Remains The Same," "The Rain Song," "D'yer Mak'er," "No Quarter," "Houses Of The Holy," "Kashmir," "Trampled Under Foot," "Nobody's Fault But Mine," "Achilles Last Stand," "All My Love," "In The Evening"

Led Zeppelin (Box Set, Vol. 2)

Two-CD box set, remastered; the remaining one-third of the Zeppelin studio catalog, plus one unreleased song.
  Atlantic 7567-82477-2
  Released September 21, 1993 (U.S.)

DISC 1

"Good Times Bad Times," "We're Gonna Groove," "Night Flight," "That's The Way," "Baby Come On Home,"* "The Lemon Song," "You Shook Me," "Boogie With Stu," "Bron-Yr-Aur," "Down By The Seaside," "Out On The Tiles," "Black Mountain Side," "Moby Dick," "Sick Again," "Hot Dog," "Carouselambra"

DISC 2

"South Bound Suarez," "Walter's Walk," "Darlene," "Black Country Woman," "How Many More Times," "The Rover," "Four Sticks," "Hats Off To (Roy) Harper," "I Can't Quit You Baby," "Hots On For Nowhere," "Living Loving Maid (She's Just a Woman)," "Royal Orleans," "Bonzo's Montreux," "The Crunge," "Bring It On Home," "Tea For One"

* *Previously unreleased; recorded October 10, 1968, Olympic Studios, London*

The Complete Studio Recordings

Ten-CD box set; the remastered tracks previously released in the Box Set, Vol. 1 *and* Vol. 2 *finally presented as the original albums, with "Baby Come On Home," "Travelling Riverside Blues," "White Summer"/"Black Mountain Side,"*

and "Hey Hey What Can I Do" added as bonus tracks to Coda; *the combined version of "Moby Dick" and "Bonzo's Montreux" from* Vol. 1 *is not included.*
Atlantic 7 82526-2
Released September 24, 1993 (U.K.); September 28, 1993 (U.S.)

Disc 1: *Led Zeppelin;* Disc 2: *Led Zeppelin II;* Disc 3: *Led Zeppelin III;* Disc 4: *Untitled Fourth Album;* Disc 5: *Houses Of The Holy;* Disc 6: *Presence;** Disc 7: *Physical Graffiti,* Disc One; Disc 8: *Physical Graffiti,* Disc Two; Disc 9: *In Through The Out Door;* Disc 10: *Coda*

* Presence and Physical Graffiti were transposed from their original release order so that the Physical Graffiti double album could be packaged together in one of the set's five two-disc booklets.

BBC Sessions
Two CDs, live.
Atlantic 7567-83061-2
Released November 17, 1997 (U.K.); November 18, 1997 (U.S.)

DISC 1
"You Shook Me"
"I Can't Quit You Baby"
　　Recorded March 3, 1969, Top Gear
"Communication Breakdown"
　　Recorded June 16, 1969, Chris Grant's Tasty Pop Sundae
"Dazed And Confused"
　　Recorded March 3, 1969, Top Gear
"The Girl I Love (She Got Long Black Wavy Hair)"
　　Recorded June 16, 1969, Chris Grant's Tasty Pop Sundae
"What Is And What Should Never Be"
"Communication Breakdown"
"Travelling Riverside Blues"
"Whole Lotta Love"
　　Recorded June 24, 1969, Top Gear
"Somethin' Else"
　　Recorded June 16, 1969, Chris Grant's Tasty Pop Sundae
"Communication Breakdown"
"I Can't Quit You Baby"
"You Shook Me"
"How Many More Times"
　　Recorded June 27, 1969, One Night Stand, *Playhouse Theatre, London*

DISC 2
"Immigrant Song"

"Heartbreaker"
"Since I've Been Loving You"
"Black Dog"
"Dazed And Confused"
"Stairway To Heaven"
"Going To California"
"That's The Way"
"Whole Lotta Love" (medley with "Boogie Chillun'"/"Fixin' To Die"/"That's Alright Mama"/"A Mess Of Blues")
"Thank You"
　　Recorded April 1, 1971, In Concert, *Paris Theatre, London*

Early Days: The Best of Led Zeppelin Volume One
Enhanced CD; compilation featuring thirteen tracks from the first four studio albums plus a 1969 promo video featuring a lip-synched performance of "Communication Breakdown."
Atlantic 7567-83268-20
Released November 23, 1999

"Good Times Bad Times"
"Babe I'm Gonna Leave You"
"Dazed And Confused"
"Communication Breakdown"
"Whole Lotta Love"
"What Is And What Should Never Be"
"Immigrant Song"
"Since I've Been Loving You"
"Black Dog"
"Rock And Roll"
"The Battle Of Evermore"
"When The Levee Breaks"
"Stairway To Heaven"

Latter Days: The Best of Led Zeppelin Volume Two
Enhanced CD; compilation featuring ten tracks from the last four studio albums plus footage of a 1975 live performance of "Kashmir" at Earls Court.
Atlantic 7567-83278-27
Released March 21, 2001

"The Song Remains The Same"
"No Quarter"
"Houses Of The Holy"
"Trampled Under Foot"
"Kashmir"
"Ten Years Gone"
"Achilles Last Stand"
"Nobody's Fault But Mine"
"All My Love"
"In The Evening"

How The West Was Won

Three CDs, live.
Atlantic 7567-83587-2
Released May 27, 2003

DISC 1
"LA Drone"
"Immigrant Song"
"Heartbreaker"
    Recorded June 27, 1972, Long Beach Arena
"Black Dog"
"Over The Hills And Far Away"
    Recorded June 25, 1972, Los Angeles Forum
"Since I've Been Loving You"
"Stairway To Heaven"
"Going To California"
    Recorded June 27, 1972, Long Beach Arena
"That's The Way"
    Recorded June 25, 1972, Los Angeles Forum
"Bron-Yr-Aur Stomp"
    Recorded June 27, 1972, Long Beach Arena

DISC 2
"Dazed And Confused" (medley with "Walter's Walk"/"The Crunge")
    Recorded June 25, 1972, Los Angeles Forum
"What Is And What Should Never Be"
"Dancing Days"
    Recorded June 27, 1972, Long Beach Arena
"Moby Dick"
    Recorded June 25, 1972, Los Angeles Forum

DISC 3
"Whole Lotta Love" (medley with "Boogie Chillun'"/"Let's Have A Party"/"Hello Mary Lou"/"Going Down Slow")
    Recorded June 25, 1972, Los Angeles Forum
"Rock And Roll"
    Recorded June 27, 1972, Long Beach Arena
"The Ocean"
"Bring It On Home" (medley with "Bring It On Back"*)
    Recorded June 25, 1972, Los Angeles Forum

* "Bring It On Back" is the renamed Zeppelin-penned music played in the middle of their cover of this Willie Dixon song.

Mothership

Two CDs, remastered; a twenty-four-track retrospective featuring songs from all eight studio albums, selected by Jimmy Page, Robert Plant, and John Paul Jones, and, yes, further remastered under the supervision of the band; deluxe edition includes a DVD with a selection of tracks from the Led Zeppelin DVD (see Video listings below).

Atlantic 8122-79961-5 (Standard); 8122-79961-3 (Deluxe)
Released November 13, 2007

DISC 1
"Good Times Bad Times"
"Communication Breakdown"
"Dazed And Confused"
"Babe I'm Gonna Leave You"
"Whole Lotta Love"
"Ramble On"
"Heartbreaker"
"Immigrant Song"
"Since I've Been Loving You"
"Rock And Roll"
"Black Dog"
"When The Levee Breaks"
"Stairway To Heaven"

DISC 2
"Song Remains The Same"
"Over The Hills And Far Away"
"D'Yer Mak'er"
"No Quarter"
"Trampled Under Foot"
"Houses Of The Holy"
"Kashmir"
"Nobody's Fault But Mine"
"Achilles Last Stand"
"In The Evening"
"All My Love"

The Song Remains The Same

Expanded two-CD live soundtrack, remixed and remastered. Previously all but disowned by the band, these live performances are finally rescued from their infamously muddy original sound through modern digital technology—but with some debatable editing choices due to the decision to have the new soundtrack match the existing film footage as closely as possible; contractual issues kept the film footage from being reedited in any way.
Rhino Records 328252
Recorded live July 27–29, 1973, Madison Square Garden, New York
Released December 11, 2007

DISC 1
"Rock And Roll"
"Celebration Day"
"Black Dog"*
"Over The Hills And Far Away"*
"Misty Mountain Hop"*
"Since I've Been Loving You"*
"No Quarter"

"The Song Remains The Same"
"The Rain Song"
"The Ocean"*

DISC 2
"Dazed And Confused"
"Stairway To Heaven"
"Moby Dick"
"Heartbreaker"*
"Whole Lotta Love"

Not included on original soundtrack release.

DVDs
Only featured songs are given following, not complete DVD scene listings.

The Song Remains The Same
Live performances plus additional sequences; shot in 1973, technical, artistic, and legal problems kept the film from being released in theaters until October 20, 1976; released on VHS by Warner Home Video on July 1, 1991; also released on laser disc in the 1990s before debuting on DVD.
Warner Home Video 7321900 113892
Performances shot live July 27–29, 1973, Madison Square Garden, New York
Released December 21, 1999 (U.S.); June 5, 2000 (U.K.)

"Rock And Roll"
"Black Dog"
"Since I've Been Loving You"
"No Quarter"
"The Song Remains The Same"
"The Rain Song"
"Dazed And Confused"
"Stairway To Heaven"
"Moby Dick"
"Heartbreaker"
"Whole Lotta Love"

Led Zeppelin DVD
Two DVDs, live.
Warner 0349 70198-2
Released May 26, 2003 (U.K.); May 27, 2003 (U.S.)

DISC 1
"We're Gonna Groove"
"I Can't Quit You Baby"
"Dazed And Confused"
"White Summer"
"What Is And What Should Never Be"

"How Many More Times"
"Moby Dick"
"Whole Lotta Love"
"Communication Breakdown"
"C'mon Everybody"
"Something Else"
"Bring It On Home"
  Shot January 9, 1970, Royal Albert Hall
"Communication Breakdown"
  Shot February 1969, Atlantic Records promotional clip
"Communication Breakdown"
"Dazed And Confused"
"Babe I'm Gonna Leave You"
"How Many More Times"
  Shot March 17, 1969, Danmarks Radio, Denmark
"Dazed And Confused"
  Shot March 25, 1969, Supershow, Staines Studio, London
"Communication Breakdown"
"Dazed And Confused"
  Shot June 19, 1969, Tous En Scène, Theatre Olympia, Paris

DISC 2
"Immigrant Song"
  Film shot February 27, 1972, Sydney Showground, Australia; studio audio track
"Black Dog"
"Misty Mountain Hop"*
"Since I've Been Loving You"
"The Ocean"*
  Shot July 27–29, 1973, Madison Square Garden, New York
"Going To California"
"That's The Way"
"Bron-Yr-Aur Stomp"
"In My Time Of Dying"
"Trampled Under Foot"
"Stairway To Heaven"
  Shot May 24 and 25, 1975, Earls Court, London
"Rock And Roll"
"Nobody's Fault But Mine"
"Sick Again"
"Achilles Last Stand"
"In The Evening"
"Kashmir"
"Whole Lotta Love"
  Shot August 4, 1979, Knebworth, Hertfordshire, England
"Rock And Roll"
  Shot February 27, 1972, Sydney Showground, Australia
"Over The Hills And Far Away"

"Travelling Riverside Blues"
Various live video clips with studio audio tracks,
Remasters *promo video, October 1990*

* *Previously unreleased footage shot during the filming of* The Song Remains The Same.

Mothership
DVD included with the deluxe edition of the Mothership *CD; selections from the Led Zeppelin DVD.*
Atlantic 8122-79961-3
Released November 13, 2007

"We're Gonna Groove"
"I Can't Quit You Babe"
"Dazed And Confused"
"White Summer"
"What Is And What Should Never Be"
"Moby Dick"
"Whole Lotta Love"
"Communication Breakdown"
"Bring It On Home"
Shot January 9, 1970, Royal Albert Hall
"Immigrant Song"
Film shot February 27, 1972, Sydney Showground, Australia; studio audio track
"Black Dog"
"Misty Mountain Hop"
Shot July 27–29, 1973, Madison Square Garden, New York
"Going To California"
"In My Time Of Dying"
"Stairway To Heaven "
May 24 and 25, 1975, Earls Court, London
"Rock And Roll"
"Nobody's Fault But Mine"
"Kashmir"
"Whole Lotta Love"
Shot August 4, 1979, Knebworth, Hertfordshire, England

The Song Remains The Same
Two-DVD special edition.
Warner Home Video DO72654
Performances shot live July 27–29, 1973, Madison Square Garden, New York
Released November 19, 2007 (U.K.); November 20, 2007 (U.S.)
HD-DVD (HDY15712) and Blu-Ray (BDY15711) released November 26, 2007

DISC 1
"Rock And Roll"

"Black Dog"
"Since I've Been Loving You"
"No Quarter"
"The Song Remains The Same"
"The Rain Song"
"Dazed And Confused"
"Stairway To Heaven"
"Moby Dick"
"Heartbreaker"
"Whole Lotta Love"

DISC 2
"Over The Hills And Far Away"*
"Celebration Day"*
"Misty Mountain Hop"
"The Ocean"

* *Previously unreleased footage.*

Miscellaneous
Although this discography is meant to include only Led Zeppelin recordings, there are a couple of releases that arguably deserve to be exceptions to the rule.

No Quarter: Jimmy Page & Robert Plant Unledded
CD of primarily Zeppelin material from live performances for the MTV Unplugged series; John Paul Jones was not invited to this reunion.
Atlantic 82706-2
Recorded live August 25 and 26, 1994, in London, and in Morocco and Wales
Released October 14, 1994

"Nobody's Fault But Mine"
Recorded in Wales
"Thank You"
Recorded in London
"No Quarter"
Recorded in Wales
"Friends"
"Yallah"
"City Don't Cry"
Recorded in Morocco
"Since I've Been Loving You"
"The Battle Of Evermore"
"Wonderful One"
"That's the Way"
"Gallows Pole"
"Four Sticks"
"Kashmir"
Recorded in London

"Down By The Seaside": Robert Plant and Tori Amos

Track featured on the Led Zeppelin tribute CD Encomium; Amos has said in interviews that it was recorded in a single take.

Atlantic 82731-2
Recorded 1995, RAK Studios, London
Released March 14, 1995

Live at the Greek: Jimmy Page & The Black Crowes

Two CDs, live performances of primarily Zeppelin material; enhanced with live video and photographs; a Japanese version included two bonus tracks, "In The Light" and "Misty Mountain Hop," recorded in 2000.

TVT Records 2140
Recorded October 18 and 19, 1999, Greek Theatre, Los Angeles
Released June 29, 2000

DISC 1

"Celebration Day"
"Custard Pie"
"Sick Again"
"What Is And What Should Never Be"
"Woke Up This Morning"
"Shape Of Things To Come"
"Sloppy Drunk"
"Ten Years Gone"
"In My Time Of Dying"
"Your Time Is Gonna Come"

DISC 2

"The Lemon Song"
"Nobody's Fault But Mine"
"Heartbreaker"
"Hey Hey What Can I Do"
"Mellow Down Easy"
"Oh Well"
"Shake Your Moneymaker"
"You Shook Me"
"Out On The Tiles"
"Whole Lotta Love"

No Quarter: Jimmy Page & Robert Plant Unledded

Remastered tenth-anniversary CD reissue with altered track list.

Atlantic 75695
Recorded August 1994
Released October 26, 2004

"Nobody's Fault But Mine"
"No Quarter"

Recorded in Wales
"Friends"
Recorded in London
"The Truth Explodes" (formerly "Yallah")
Recorded in Morocco
"The Rain Song"
Recorded in London
"City Don't Cry"
Recorded in Morocco
"Since I've Been Loving You"
"The Battle Of Evermore"
"Wonderful One"
"That's The Way"
Recorded in London
"Wah Wah"
Recorded in Morocco
"Gallows Pole"
"Four Sticks"
"Kashmir"
Recorded in London

No Quarter: Jimmy Page & Robert Plant Unledded

DVD featuring all the songs from the Unplugged sessions plus bonus track "Black Dog" performed live by Page and Plant at the 1995 American Music Awards.

Warner 970324
Recorded August 1994
Released October 26, 2004

"No Quarter"
Recorded in Wales
"Thank You"
"What is And What Should Never Be"
"The Battle Of Evermore"
"Gallows Pole"
Recorded in London
"Nobody's Fault But Mine"
Recorded in Wales
"City Don't Cry"
"The Truth Explodes" (formerly "Yallah")
"Wah Wah"
Recorded in Morocco
"When The Levee Breaks"
Recorded in Wales
"Wonderful One"
"Since I've Been Loving You"
"The Rain Song"
"That's The Way"
"Four Sticks"
"Friends"
"Kashmir"
Recorded in London

Bibliography

Books

Buell, Bebe. *Rebel Heart: An American Rock 'N' Roll Journey.* New York: St. Martin's Griffin, 2001.

Cole, Richard. *Stairway To Heaven: Led Zeppelin Uncensored.* New York: HarperCollins, 1992.

Davis, Stephen. *Hammer Of The Gods: The Led Zeppelin Saga.* New York: William Morrow & Company, 1985.

Des Barres, Pamela. *I'm With The Band: Confessions Of A Groupie.* New York: Beech Tree Books, 1987.

Graham, Bill. *My Life Inside Rock And Out.* New York: Doubleday, 1992.

Lewis, Dave with Simon Pallett. *Led Zeppelin: The Concert File.* London: Omnibus, 2005.

Matheu, Robert. *CREEM: America's Only Rock 'N' Roll Magazine.* New York: Collins, 2007.

Sander, Ellen. *Trips: Rock Life In The Sixties.* New York: Scribner, 1973.

Shadwick, Keith. *Led Zeppelin: The Story Of A Band And Their Music 1968–1980.* San Francisco: Backbeat Books, 2005.

Williamson, Nigel. *The Rough Guide To Led Zeppelin.* London: Rough Guides, 2007.

Welch, Chris. *Led Zeppelin: Dazed And Confused: The Stories Behind Every Song.* New York: Thunder's Mouth Press, 1998.

Welch, Chris. *Peter Grant: The Man Who Led Zeppelin.* London: Omnibus, 2002.

York, Ritchie. *Led Zeppelin: From Early Days To Page and Plant, 2nd Ed.* London: Virgin Books, 1999.

Magazines

Guitar World, 1995 and 1999
CREEM, 1974
Rolling Stone
Details
Melody Maker
New Musical Express
Circus
Disc & Music Echo
Uncut

Websites

www.led-zeppelin.org
www.ledzeppelin.com
www.jimmypage.co.uk
www.johnpauljones.com
www.robertplant.com
www.trublukris.tripod.com/cristopolo/lz.html
www.turnmeondeadman.net/Zep/Originals.php

Liner Notes

Crowe, Cameron. "Led Zeppelin: Light And Shade," *The Complete Studio Recordings.* New York: Atlantic Recording Corporation, 1993.

Palmer, Robert. "Led Zeppelin: The Music," *Box Set, Vol 1.* New York: Atlantic Recording Corporation, 1990.

Contributor Biographies

JON BREAM has been pop music critic at the Minneapolis *Star Tribune* since 1975. His reviews and features also have been published in the *Los Angeles Times, Boston Globe,* and numerous other newspapers, as well as in *Rolling Stone, CREEM, Billboard, Entertainment Weekly, TV Guide,* and many other magazines. He is the author of the best-selling biography, *Prince: Inside the Purple Reign.*

As noted in the June 1975 issue of *Crawdaddy!,* "WILLIAMS S. BURROUGHS is the author of *Naked Lunch* and a dozen other novels, and is generally conceded to be one of the most significant American writers of this century. When Samuel Beckett was asked about Burroughs, he replied, 'Well, he's a writer.' Mr. Burroughs considers this a great complement."

New Zealand–born, South London–based, and oft' wandering GARTH CARTWRIGHT is an award-winning journalist and critic who regularly contributes to *The Guardian, The Sunday Times, fRoots,* and the BBC's website. He is the author of *Princes Amongst Men: Journeys With Gypsy Musicians* and the forthcoming *More Miles Than Money: Journeys In Wild America.*

GEORGE CASE is a writer on popular culture and a long-time guitarist and Led Zeppelin fan. He is the author of the Jimmy Page biography *Magus, Musician, Man,* as well as a future history, *Silence Descends: The End Of The Information Age 2000–2500,* and a memoir, *Arcadia Borealis: Childhood And Youth In Northern Ontario.* He lives in Sault Ste. Marie, Ontario. He never saw Led Zeppelin live but has witnessed more Zeppelin tribute acts than he can count.

BARRY CLEVELAND is an associate editor at *Guitar Player* magazine and worked previously with *Mix* and *Electronic Musician* magazines. He is also a guitarist and recording artist, and author of *Creative Music Production: Joe Meek's Bold Techniques.*

JIM DEROGATIS (www.jimdero.com) is the pop music critic at *The Chicago Sun-Times,* the author of several books about music (including *Let It Blurt: The Life And Times Of Lester Bangs, America's Greatest Rock Critic*), and the co-host of *Sound Opinions* (www.soundopinions.org), "the world's only rock 'n' roll talk show," syndicated nationally on public radio.

ANDREW EARLES (www.failedpilot.com) is a writer and humorist based in Memphis, Tennessee. His work has appeared in several media outlets, including *SPIN*, *The Onion*, *Pitchfork*, *McSweeney's*, *Harp*, *Paste*, *Magnet*, *Alternative Press*, *The Washington City Paper*, and *The Memphis Flyer*. His comedy release, *Earles And Jensen Present Just Farr A Laugh Vol. 1 & 2*, was released on Matador Records in 2008.

CHUCK EDDY is the author of the books *Stairway To Hell: The 500 Best Heavy Metal Albums In The Universe* and *The Accidental Evolution Of Rock 'n' Roll: A Misguided Tour Through Popular Music*, and has served as music editor at *The Village Voice* and as a senior editor at *Billboard*. He has written thousands of pieces over the years for *CREEM*, *Rolling Stone*, *SPIN*, and other publications. He lives in Queens, New York.

DAVID FRICKE is a senior editor at *Rolling Stone*.

GARY GRAFF is an award-winning music journalist based in Detroit who has written extensively about Led Zeppelin since the late seventies. He is a regular contributor to the *New York Times* Features Syndicate, *Billboard*, UPI, the *Cleveland Plain Dealer*, the *Oakland Press* and *Journal Register* Company Newswire, *Revolver*, Red Flag Media, and other publications, as well as United Stations Radio Networks and radio stations in Detroit and Milwaukee. He is the editor of *The Ties That Bind: Bruce Springsteen A To E To Z* and the series editor of the "MusicHound Essential Album Guide" series.

BARNEY HOSKYNS is editorial director of the online library Rock's Backpages (www.rocksbackpages.com) and the author of several books including *Hotel California: The True-Life Adventures of Crosby, Stills, Nash, Young, Mitchell, Taylor, Browne, Ronstadt, Geffen, The Eagles, And Their Many Friends* and *Across The Great Divide: The Band And America*. His study of the fourth Led Zeppelin album is included in Rodale's new "Rock of Ages" series. A former U.S. correspondent for *MOJO*, Hoskyns writes for *Uncut*, *The Observer Music Monthly*, and other U.K. publications, and has contributed to *Rolling Stone*, *GQ*, *SPIN*, and *Harper's Bazaar*. His biography of Tom Waits, *Take It with Me*, will be published in 2009 by Doubleday.

GREG KOT has been the *Chicago Tribune*'s rock music critic since 1990. He co-hosts the nationally syndicated rock 'n' roll talk show *Sound Opinions* (www.soundopinions.org) on public radio and is the author of *Wilco: Learning How To Die* and *Ripped: The Digital Music Revolution*.

WILLIAM MCKEEN (www.williammckeen.com) is author of eight books, including *Outlaw Journalist: The Life And Times Of Hunter S. Thompson*; *Highway 61: A Father-And-Son Journey Through The Middle of America*; and the anthology *Rock And Roll Is Here To Stay*. He teaches a class called "Rock 'n' Roll and American Society" at the University of Florida, where he chairs the Department of Journalism. His writing has appeared in *American History*, *Maxim*, *Gourmet*, *Holiday*, *The Saturday Evening Post*, and other publications. He is married, has seven children, and lives on a farm near Wacahoota, Florida.

STEVE MORSE was a staff rock critic for the *Boston Globe* for nearly thirty years, during which he interviewed the likes of Aerosmith, Bob Marley, Jerry Garcia, Stevie Nicks, Muddy Waters, and Bruce Springsteen. Morse still freelances for the *Globe* and has contributed to *Billboard*, *Rolling Stone*, and *Musician* magazines. For seven years he was on the nominating committee for the Rock and Roll Hall of Fame and has been critic at large for Boston radio station WBOS-FM. His favorite memories include seeing Led Zeppelin twice in England in 1969.

CHARLES SHAAR MURRAY was a founding contributor to *Q* and *MOJO* magazines as well as a long-time rock writer for *New Musical Express*. His work has also appeared in *CREEM*, *Vogue*, *Guitarist*, *The Guardian*, *The Observer*, *The Daily Telegraph*, and *The Independent* as well as on Radio 3, BBC World Service Radio, Channel 4 News, and *Newsnight*. Among his several books are *Crosstown Traffic: Jimi Hendrix & The Post-War Rock 'N' Roll Revolution* and *Boogie Man: The Adventures of John Lee Hooker in the American Twentieth Century*.

SCOTT PEARSON is a writer and an editor at Zenith Press, a military history publisher. As a writer he has published literary fiction, humor, *Star Trek* short stories, poetry, a mystery story, and a nonfiction book about mosquitoes. Scott has purchased Zep on LP, unremastered CD, and remastered CD, and back in the day he went to see the Firm in concert just so he'd get to see Jimmy Page; the only thing he remembers is when Jimmy got out the violin bow for a guitar solo—but that's all he really wanted to see anyway. Scott lives in St. Paul, Minnesota, with his wife, Sandra, and daughter, Ella.

CHRIS RIEMENSCHNEIDER has been a music critic at the Minneapolis *Star Tribune* since 2001. He covered the Austin, Texas, music scene at the *Austin American-Statesman* for five years and has written for the *Los Angeles Times*, *Dallas Morning News*, *Billboard*, and *RollingStone*.com. A St. Paul, Minnesota, native, he took his paper-route money to the original Cheapo Records to amass the Zeppelin catalog at age thirteen, mostly from cutout bins. He still prefers *Physical Graffiti* with the hisses. He never saw Zeppelin live, but he did see Nirvana (his first date with his wife).

GENE STOUT began his journey in music when Little Richard knocked him out of the cradle; he's been a sucker for a great hook ever since. A Seattle native, Stout's been pop music critic for the *Seattle Post-Intelligencer* for more than two decades. Over the years, he has interviewed hundreds of musicians and celebrities from Eddie Vedder to Bob Hope.

JAAN UHELSZKI was one of the founding editors at Detroit's legendary *CREEM* magazine. Since that time, her work has appeared in leading publications, including *USA Today*, *MOJO*, *Uncut*, *Rolling Stone*, *Paste*, *Relix*, *SPIN*, *NME*, *Guitar World*, and the *Village Voice*. She accompanied Led Zeppelin on two tours of the United States and managed to leave without any beer in her face.

Index

"I think that Led Zeppelin was bold and brave and chaotic and honest—in a very loose framework, it was honest—and it took risks and chances which are no longer possible if you start a band from scratch today. Musically, it captured all the elements of the kind of wondrous music that we'd all been exposed to. What we did was, we were able to translate and kick on. It's like we were a filter for all the good things, we filtered it, and begged, borrowed and stole, and we made something that was particularly original, by which a lot of other music has been measured."

—Robert Plant on how he wants Zeppelin to be remembered,
High Times, *1991*